The Mysteries of Free Masonry • Morgan, William

Publisher's Note

Purchase of this book entitles you to a free trial membership in the publisher's book club at www.rarebooksclub.com. (Time limited offer.) Simply enter the barcode number from the back cover onto the membership form on our home page. The book club entitles you to select from millions of books at no additional charge. You can also download a digital copy of this and related books to read on the go. Simply enter the title or subject onto the search form to find them.

Note: This is an historic book. Pages numbers, where present in the text, refer to the first edition of the book and may also be in indexes.

If you have any questions, could you please be so kind as to consult our Frequently Asked Questions page at www.rarebooksclub.com/faqs.cfm? You are also welcome to contact us there.

Publisher: Books LLC™, Memphis, TN, USA, 2012. ISBN: 9781153714389.

Proofreading: pgdp.net

⁂ ⁂ ⁂ ⁂ ⁂ ⁂ ⁂ ⁂

Transcriber's Note:

While there are many cases of inconsistent spelling, there are a number of obvious typographical errors that have been corrected in this text. For a complete list, please see the bottom of this document 109

As the original is not divided into chapters, end of page footnotes have been converted into endnotes.

.... 0

THE

Mysteries of

Freemasonry

CONTAINING

ALL THE DEGREES OF THE ORDER CONFERRED IN A MASTER'S LODGE,

AS WRITTEN BY

CAPTAIN WILLIAM MORGAN.

All the Degrees Conferred in the Royal Arch Chapter and Grand Encampment of Knights Templars—Knights of the Red Cross—of the Christian Mark—and of the Holy Sepulchre.

ALSO

The Eleven Ineffable Degrees Conferred in the Lodge of Perfection—and the still higher degrees of Prince of Jerusalem—Knights of the East and West—Venerable Grand Masters of Symbolic Lodges—Knights and Adepts of the Eagle or Sun—Princes of the Royal Secret—Sovereign Inspector General, etc.

Revised and Corrected to Correspond with the Most Approved Forms and Ceremonies in the Various Lodges of Free-Masons Throughout the United States.

By GEORGE R. CRAFTS,

Formerly Thrice Puissant Grand Master of Manitou Council, N.Y.

[Pg 3]

MORGAN'S EXPOSE OF FREEMASONRY.

Ceremonies of Opening a Lodge of Entered Apprentice Masons.

One rap calls the Lodge to order; one calls up the Junior and Senior Deacons; two raps call up the subordinate officers; and three, all the members of the Lodge.

The Master having called the Lodge to order, and the officers all seated, the Master says to the Junior Warden, "Brother Junior, are they all Entered Apprentice Masons in the South?" He answers, "They are, Worshipful." Master to the Senior Warden, "Brother Senior, are they all Entered Apprentice Masons in the West?" He answers, "They are, Worshipful." The Master then says, "They are in the East;" at the same time he gives a rap with the common gavel, or mallet, which calls up both Deacons. Master to Junior Deacon, "Attend to that part of your duty, and inform the Tyler that we are about to open a Lodge of Entered Apprentice Masons; and direct him to tyle accordingly." The Tyler then steps to the door and gives three raps, which are answered by three from without; the Junior Deacon then gives one, which is also answered by the Tyler with one; the door is then partly opened, and the Junior Deacon delivers his message and resumes his situation, and says, "The door is tyled, Worshipful" (at the same time giving the due-guard, which is never omitted when the Master is addressed). The Master to the Junior Deacon, "By whom?" He answers, "By a Master Mason without the door, armed with the proper implements of his office." Master to the Junior Deacon, "His duty there?" He answers, "To keep off all cowans and eave-droppers, see that none pass or repass without permission from the Master." [Some say without permission from the chair.] Master to Junior Deacon, "Brother Junior, your place in the Lodge?" He answers, "At the right hand of the Senior Warden in the West." Master to Junior Deacon, "Your business there, Brother Junior?" He answers, "To wait on the Worshipful Master and Wardens, act as their proxy in the active duties of the Lodge, and take charge of the door." Master to Junior Deacon, "The Senior Deacon's place in the Lodge?" He answers, "At the right hand of the Worshipful Master in the East." [The Master, while asking the last question, gives two raps, which call up all the subordinate officers.] Master to Senior Deacon, "Your duty there, Brother Senior?" He answers, "To wait on the Worshipful Master and Wardens, act as their proxy in the active duties of the Lodge, attend to the preparation and introduction of candidates—and welcome and clothe all visiting brethren." [i.e., furnish them with an apron.] Master to Senior Deacon, "The Secretary's place in the Lodge, Brother Senior?" He answers, "At the left hand of the Worshipful Master in the East." Master to the Secretary, "Your duty [Pg 4] there, Brother Secretary?" He answers, "The better to observe the Worshipful Master's will and pleasure, record the proceedings of the Lodge; transmit a copy of the same to the Grand Lodge, if required; receive all moneys and money-bills from the hands of the brethren, pay them over to the Treasurer, and take his receipt for the same." The Master to the Secretary, "The Treasurer's place in the Lodge?" He answers, "At the right hand of the Worshipful Master." Master to the Treasurer, "Your duty there, Brother Treasurer?" He answers, "Duly to observe the Worshipful Master's will and pleasure; receive all moneys and money-bills from the hands of the Secretary; keep a just and true account of the same; pay them out by order of the Worshipful Master and consent of the brethren." The Master to the Treasurer, "The Junior Warden's place in the Lodge, Brother Treasurer?" He answers, "In the South, Worshipful." Master to Junior Warden, "Your business there, Brother Junior?" He answers, "As the sun in the South at high meridian, is the beauty and glory of the day, so stands the Junior Warden in the South the better to observe the time; call the crafts from labor to refreshment; superintend them during the hours thereof; see that none convert the hours of refreshment into that of intemperance or excess; and call them on again in due season, that the Worshipful Master may have honor, and they pleasure and profit thereby." Master to the Junior Warden, "The Senior Warden's place in the Lodge?" He answers, "In the West, Worshipful." Master to the Senior Warden, "Your duty there, Brother Senior?" He answers, "As the sun sets in the West, to close the day, so stands the Senior Warden in the West, to assist the Worshipful Master in opening his Lodge; take care of the jewels and implements; see that none be lost; pay the craft their wages, if any be due; and see that none go away dissatisfied." Master to the Senior Warden, "The Master's place in the Lodge?" He answers, "In the East, Worshipful." Master to the Senior Warden, "His duty there?" He answers, "As the sun rises in the East to open and adorn the day, so presides the Worshipful Master in the East to open and adorn his Lodge; set his crafts to work with good and wholesome laws, or cause the same to be done." The Master now gives three raps, when all the brethren rise, and the Master, taking off his hat, proceeds as follows: "In like manner so do I, strictly forbidding all profane language, private committees, or any other disorderly conduct whereby the peace and harmony of this Lodge may be interrupted while engaged in its lawful pursuits, under no less penalty than the by-laws, or such penalty as a majority of the brethren present may see fit to inflict. Brethren, attend to giving the signs." [Here Lodges differ very much. In some they declare the Lodge open, as follows, before they give the sign.] The Master (all the brethren imitating him) extends his left arm from his body, so as to form an angle of about forty-five degrees, and holds his right hand traversely across his left, the palms thereof one inch apart. This is called the first sign of a Mason—is the sign of distress in this degree, and alludes to the position a candidate's hands are placed in when he takes the obligation of an Entered Apprentice Mason. The Master then draws his right hand across his throat, the hand open, with the thumb [Pg 5] next to the throat, and drops it down by his side. This is called the due-guard of an Entered Apprentice Mason (many call it the sign), and alludes to the penalty of an obligation. The Master then declares the Lodge opened in the following manner:—"I now declare the Lodge of Entered Apprentice Masons duly opened for the dispatch of business." The Senior Warden declares it to the Junior Warden, and he to the brethren. "Come, brethren, let us pray."

Prayer. —Most holy and glorious God! the great Architect of the Universe: the giver of all good gifts and graces. Thou hast promised that "Where two or three are gathered together in Thy name, Thou wilt be in the midst of them, and bless them." In Thy name we assemble, most humbly beseeching Thee to bless us in all our undertakings, that we may know and serve Thee aright, and that all our actions may tend to Thy glory, and our advancement in knowledge and virtue. And we beseech Thee, O Lord God, to bless our present assembling; and to illumine our minds through the influence of the Son of Righteousness, that we may walk in the Light of Thy countenance; and when the trials of our probationary state are over, be admitted into the temple not made with hands, eternal in the heavens. Amen. So mote it be.

Another Prayer. —Behold how good and how pleasant it is for brethren to dwell together in unity! It is like the precious ointment upon the head that ran down upon the beard, even Aaron's beard, that went down to the skirts of his garments; as the dew of Hermon, and as the dew that descended upon the mountain of Zion, for there the Lord commanded the blessing, evermore. Amen. So mote it be. [This prayer is likewise used on closing the Lodge.]

The Lodge being now open and ready to proceed to business, the Master directs the Secretary to read the minutes of the last meeting, which naturally brings to view the business of the present. If there are any candidates to be brought forward, that is the first business attended to.
[1] 108

Ceremonies of the Admission and Initiation of a Candidate in the First Degree of Freemasonry.

At the first regular communication after the candidate has petitioned for admission, if no objection has been urged against him, the Lodge proceeds to a ballot. One black ball will reject a candidate. The boxes [Pg 6] may be passed three times. The Deacons are the proper persons to pass them; one of the boxes has black and white beans or balls in it, the other empty; the one with the balls in it goes before and furnishes each member with a black and white ball; the empty box follows and receives them. There are two holes in the top of this box, with a small tube in each, one of which is black, and the other white, with a partition in the box. The members put both their balls into this box as their feelings dictate; when the balls are received, the box is presented to the Master, Senior, and Junior Wardens, who pronounce clear or not clear, as the case may be. The ballot proving clear, the candidate (if present) is conducted into a small preparation room adjoining the Lodge; he is asked the following questions, and gives the following answers. Senior Deacon to candidate, "Do you sincerely declare, upon your honor before these gentlemen, that, unbiassed by friends, uninfluenced by unworthy motives, you freely and voluntarily offer yourself a candidate for the mysteries of Masonry?" Candidate answers, "I do. " Senior Deacon to candidate, "Do you sincerely declare, upon your honor before these gentlemen, that you are prompt to solicit the privileges of Masonry, by a favorable opinion conceived of the institution, a desire of knowledge, and a sincere wish of being serviceable to your fellow-creatures?" Candidate answers, "I do." Senior Deacon to candidate, "Do you sincerely declare, upon your honor before these gentlemen, that you will cheerfully conform to all the ancient established usages and customs of the fraternity?" Candidate answers, "I do." After the above questions are proposed and answered, and the result reported to the Master, he says, "Brethren, at the request of Mr. A. B., he has been proposed and accepted in the regular form. I therefore recommend him as a proper candidate for the Mysteries of Masonry, and worthy to partake of the privileges of the fraternity; and in consequence of a declaration of his intentions, voluntarily made, I believe he will cheerfully conform to the rules of the Order." The candidate, during the time, is divested of all his apparel (shirt excepted), and furnished with a pair of drawers, kept in the Lodge for the use of candidates; he is then blindfolded, his left foot bare, his right in a slipper, his left breast and arm naked, and a rope, called a cable-tow, 'round his neck and left arm (the rope is not put 'round the arm in all Lodges) in which posture the candidate is conducted to the door, where he is caused to give, or the conductor gives, three distinct knocks, which are answered by three from within; the conductor gives one more, which is also answered by one from within. The door is then partly opened, and the Junior Deacon generally asks, "Who comes there? Who comes there? Who comes there?" The conductor *alias* the Senior Deacon, answers, "A poor, blind candidate, who has long been desirous of having and receiving a part of the rights and benefits of this worshipful Lodge, dedicated (some say erected) to God, and held forth to the holy order of St. John, as all true fellows and brothers have done, who have gone this way before him." The Junior Deacon then asks, "Is it of his own free will and accord he makes this request? Is he duly and truly prepared? Worthy and well qualified? And properly avouched for?" [Pg 7] All of which being answered in the affirmative, the Junior Deacon says to the Senior Deacon, "By what further right does he expect to obtain this benefit?" The Senior Deacon replies, "By being a man, free born, of lawful age, and under the tongue of good report." The Junior Deacon then says, "Since this is the case you will wait till the Worshipful Master in the East is made acquainted with his request, and his answer returned." The Junior Deacon repairs to the Master, when the same questions are asked, and answers returned as at the door; after which the Master says, "Since he comes endowed with all these necessary qualifications, let him enter this worshipful Lodge in the name of the Lord, and take heed on what he enters." The candidate then enters, the Junior Deacon at the same time pressing his naked left breast with the point of the compass, and asks the candidate, "Did you feel anything?" Ans. —"I did." Junior Deacon to the candidate, "What was it?" Ans. —"A torture." The Junior Deacon then says, "As this is a torture to your flesh, so may it ever be to your mind and conscience, if ever you should attempt to reveal the secrets of Masonry unlawfully." The candidate is then conducted to the centre of the Lodge, where he and the Senior Deacon kneel, and the Deacon says the following prayer:

"Vouchsafe Thine aid, Almighty Father of the Universe, to this, our present convention; and grant that this candidate for Masonry may dedicate and devote his life to Thy service, and become a true and faithful brother among us! Endue him with a competency of Thy divine wisdom, that by the secrets of our art, he may be the better enabled to display the beauties of holiness, to the honor of Thy holy name. So mote it be. Amen!"

The Master then asks the candidate, "In whom do you put your trust?" The candidate answers, "In God." The Master then takes him by the right hand, and says, "Since in God you put your trust, arise, follow your leader, and fear no danger." The Senior Deacon then conducts the candidate three times regularly around the Lodge and halts at the Junior Warden in the South, where the same questions are asked, and answers returned as at the door.

As the candidate and the conductor are going around the room, the Master reads the following passage of Scripture, and takes the same time to read it that they do to go around the Lodge three times.

"Behold how good and how pleasant it is for brethren to dwell together in unity! It is like the precious ointment upon the head, that ran down upon the beard, even Aaron's beard, that went down to the skirts of his garment; as the dew of Hermon, and as the dew that descended upon the mountains of Zion, for there the Lord commanded the blessing, even life forevermore."

The candidate is then conducted to the Senior Warden in the West, where the same Questions are asked, and answers returned as before; from thence he is conducted to the Worshipful Master in the East, where the same questions are asked, and answers returned as before. The Master likewise demands of him from whence he came, and whither he is traveling. The candidate answers, "From the West, and traveling to the East." Master inquires, "Why do you leave the West and travel [Pg 8] to the East?" He answers, "In search of light. " Master then says "Since the candidate is traveling in search of light, you will please conduct him back to the West from whence he came, and put him in the care of the Senior Warden, who will teach him how to approach the East, the place of light, by advancing upon one upright regular step, to the first step, his feet forming the right angle of an oblong square, his body erect at the altar before the Master, and place him in a proper position to take upon himself the solemn oath or obligation of an Entered Apprentice Mason." The Senior Warden receives the candidate, and instructs him as directed. He first steps off with his left foot and brings up the heel of the right into the hollow thereof; the heel of the right foot against the ankle of the left, will, of course, form the right angle of an oblong square; the candidate then kneels on his left knee, and places his right foot so as to form a square with the left, he turns his foot around until the ankle bone is as much in front of him as the toes on the left; the candidate's left hand is then put under the Holy Bible, square and compass, and the right hand on them. This is the position in which a candidate is placed when he takes upon him the oath or obligation of an Entered Apprentice Mason. As soon as the candidate is placed in this position, the Worshipful Master approaches him, and says, "Mr. A. B., you are now placed in a proper position to take upon you the solemn oath or obligation of an Entered Apprentice Mason,
[2] 108
which I assure you is neither to affect your religion nor politics. If you are willing to take it, repeat your name, and say after me:

"I, A. B., of my own free will and accord, in presence of Almighty God, and this worshipful Lodge of Free and Accepted Masons, dedicated to God, and held forth to the holy order of St. John, do hereby and hereon most solemnly and sincerely promise and swear, that I will always hail, ever conceal, and never reveal any part or parts, art or arts, point or points of the secrets, arts and mysteries of ancient Free Masonry, which I have received, am about to receive, or may hereafter be instructed in, to any person or persons in the known world, except it be a true and lawful brother Mason, or within the body of a just and lawfully constituted Lodge of such, and not unto him, nor unto them whom I shall hear so to be, but unto them only after strict trial and due examination or lawful information. Furthermore, do I promise and swear that I will not write, print, stamp, stain, hew, cut, carve, indent, paint, or engrave it on anything moveable or immoveable, under the whole canopy of heaven, whereby, or whereon the least letter, figure, character, mark, stain, shadow, or resemblance of the same may become legible or intelligible to myself or any other person in the known world, whereby the secrets of Masonry may be unlawfully obtained through my unworthiness. To all which I do most solemnly and sincerely promise and swear, without the least equivocation, mental [Pg 9] reservation, or self-evasion of mind in me whatever; BINDING MYSELF UNDER NO LESS PENALTY THAN TO HAVE MY THROAT CUT ACROSS, MY TONGUE TORN OUT BY THE ROOTS, AND MY BODY BURIED IN THE ROUGH SANDS OF THE SEA AT LOW WATER MARK, WHERE THE TIDE EBBS AND FLOWS IN TWENTY-FOUR HOURS : so help me God, and keep me steadfast in the true performance of the same."

After the obligation, the Master addresses the candidate in the following manner: "Brother, to you the secrets of Masonry are about to be unveiled, and a brighter sun never shone lustre on your eyes; while prostrate before this sacred altar, do you not shudder at every crime? Have you not confidence in every virtue? May these thoughts ever inspire you with the most noble sentiments; may you ever feel that elevation of soul that shall scorn a dishonest act. Brother, what do you most desire?" The candidate answers, "Light." Master to brethren, "Brethren, stretch forth your hands and assist in bringing this new-made brother from darkness to light." The members having formed a circle round the candidate, the Master says, "And God said, Let there be light, and there was light." At the same time, all the brethren clap their hands and stamp on the floor with their right feet as heavy as possible, the bandage dropping from the candidate's eyes at the same instant, which, after having been so long blind, and full of fearful apprehensions all the time, this great and sudden transition from perfect darkness to a light brighter (if possible) than the meridian sun in a midsummer day, sometimes produces an alarming effect.

After the candidate is brought to light, the Master addresses him as follows: "Brother, on being brought to light, you first discover three great lights in Masonry by the assistance of three lesser; they are thus explained: The three great lights in Masonry are the Holy Bible, Square and Compass. The Holy Bible is given to us as a rule and guide for our faith and practice; the Square, to square our actions, and the Compass to keep us in due bounds with all mankind, but more especially with the brethren. Three lesser lights are three burning tapers, or candles placed on candlesticks (some say, or candles on pedestals), they represent the Sun, Moon, and Master of the Lodge, and are thus explained: As the sun rules the day, and the moon governs the night, so ought the Worshipful Master, with equal regularity, to rule and govern his Lodge, or cause the same to be done; you next discover me, as Master of this Lodge, approaching you from the East upon the first step of Masonry, under the sign and due-guard of an Entered Apprentice Mason, as already revealed to you. This is the manner of giving them; imitate me, as near as you can, keeping your position. First, step off with your left foot, and bring the heel of the right into the hollow thereof, so as to form a square." [This is the first step in Masonry.] The following is the sign of an Entered Apprentice Mason, and is the sign of distress in this degree; you are not to give it unless in distress. [It is given by holding your two hands traversely across each other, the right hand upwards, and one inch from the left.] The following is the due-guard of an Entered Apprentice Mason. [This is given by drawing your right hand across your throat, the thumb next to your throat, your arm as [Pg 10] high as the elbow, in a horizontal position.] "Brother, I now present you my right hand, in token of brotherly love and esteem, and with it the grip and name of the grip of an Entered Apprentice Mason." The right hands are joined together, as in shaking hands, and each sticks his thumb nail into the third joint or upper end of the forefinger; the name of the grip is Boaz , and is to be given in the following manner and no other: The Master gives the grip and word, and divides it for the instruction of the candidate; the questions are as follows: The Master and candidate holding each other by the grip as before described, the Master says, "What is this?" Candidate—"A grip." Master "A grip of what?" Candidate—"The grip of an Entered Apprentice Mason." Master—"Has it a name?" Candidate—"It has." Master—"Will you give it to me?" Candidate—"I did not so receive it, neither can I so impart it." Master—"What will you do with it?" Candidate—"Letter it, or halve it." Master—"Halve it and begin." Candidate—"You begin." Master—"Begin you." Candidate—"BO." Master—"AZ." Candidate—"BOAZ." Master says, "Right, Brother Boaz , I greet you. It is the name of the left hand pillar of the porch of King Solomon's Temple—arise, Brother Boaz, and salute the Junior and Senior Wardens as such, and convince them that you have been regularly initiated as an Entered Apprentice Mason, and have got the sign, grip, and word." The Master returns to his seat, while the Wardens are examining the candidate, and gets a lamb-skin or white apron, presents it to the candidate and observes, "Brother, I now present you with a lamb-skin, or white apron; it is an emblem of innocence, and the badge of a Mason; it has been worn by kings, princes, and potentates of the earth, who have never been ashamed to wear it; it is more honorable than the diamonds of kings, or pearls of princesses, when worthily worn; it is more ancient than the Golden Fleece or Roman Eagle; more honorable than the Star and Garter, or any other order that can be conferred upon you at this or any other time, except it be in the body of a just and fully constituted Lodge; you will carry it to the Senior Warden in the West, who will teach you how to wear it as an Entered Apprentice Mason." The Senior Warden ties the apron on, and turns up the flap, instead of letting it fall down in front of the apron. This is the way Entered Apprentice Masons wear, or ought to wear, their aprons until they are advanced. The candidate is now conducted to the Master in the East, who says, "Brother, as you are dressed, it is necessary you should have tools to work with; I will now present you with the working tools of an Entered Apprentice Mason, which are the twenty-four-inch gauge and common gavel; they are thus explained: The twenty-four-inch gauge is an instrument made use of by operative Masons to measure and lay out their work, but we, as Free and Accepted Masons, make use of it for the more noble and glorious purpose of dividing our time. The twenty-four inches on the gauge are emblematical of the twenty-four hours in the day, which we are taught to divide into three equal parts, whereby we find eight hours for the service of God and a worthy distressed brother; eight hours for our usual vocations; and eight for refreshment and sleep; the common gavel is an instrument made use of by operative Masons to break off the [Pg 11] corners of rough stones, the better to fit them for the builder's use; but we, as Free and Accepted Masons, use it for the more noble and glorious purpose of divesting our hearts and consciences of all the vices and superfluities of life, thereby fitting our minds as living and lively stones for that spiritual building, that house not made with hands, eternal in the Heavens. I also present you with a new name; it is CAUTION ; it teaches you, as you are barely instructed in the rudiments of Masonry, that you should be cautious over all your words and actions, particularly when before the enemies of Masonry. I shall next present you with three precious jewels, which are a LISTENING EAR , a SILENT TONGUE , and a FAITHFUL HEART . A listening ear teaches you to listen to the instructions of the Worshipful Master, but more especially that you should listen to the cries of a worthy distressed brother. A silent tongue teaches you to be silent while in the Lodge, that the peace and harmony thereof may not be disturbed, but more especially that you should be silent before the enemies of Masonry, that the craft may not be brought into disrepute by your imprudence. A faithful heart teaches you to be faithful to the instructions of the Worshipful Master at all times, but more especially that you should be faithful, and keep and conceal the secrets of Masonry, and those of a brother when given to you in charge as such, that they may remain as secure and inviolable in your breast as his own, before communicated to you. I further present you with checkwords two; their names are TRUTH and UNION , and are thus explained: Truth is a divine attribute, and the foundation of every virtue; to be good and true is the first lesson we are taught in Masonry; on this theme we contemplate, and by its dictates endeavor to regulate our conduct; hence, while influenced by this principle, hypocrisy and deceit are unknown among us, sincerity and plain dealing distinguish us, and the heart and tongue join in promoting each other's welfare, and rejoicing in each other's prosperity. Union is that kind of friendship which ought to appear conspicuous in every Mason's conduct. It is so closely allied to the divine attribute, truth, that he who enjoys the one is seldom destitute of the other. Should interest, honor, prejudice, or human depravity ever induce you to violate any part of the sacred trust we now repose in you, let these two important words, at the earliest insinuation, teach you to put on the check-line of truth, which will infallibly direct you to pursue that straight and narrow path which ends in the full enjoyment of the Grand Lodge above, where we shall all meet as Masons and members of the same family, in peace, harmony, and love; where all discord on account of politics, religion, or private opinion, shall be unknown, and banished from within our walls.

"Brother, it has been a custom from time immemorial to demand, or ask from a newly-made brother, something of a metallic kind, not so much on account of its intrinsic value, but that it may be deposited in the archives of the Lodge, as a memorial that you was herein made a Mason; a small trifle will be sufficient—anything of a metallic kind will do; if you have no money, anything of a metallic nature will be sufficient; even a button will do." [The candidate says he has nothing about him; it is known he has nothing.] "Search yourself," the Master [Pg 12] replies. He is assisted in searching—nothing is found. "Perhaps you can borrow a trifle," says the Master. [He tries to borrow, none will lend him; he proposes to go into the other room where his clothes are; he is not permitted: if a stranger, he is very much embarrassed.] Master to candidate, "Brother, let this ever be a striking lesson to you, and teach you, if you should ever see a friend, but more especially a brother, in a like penniless situation, to contribute as liberally to his relief as his situation may require, and your abilities will admit, without material injury to yourself or family." Master to Senior Deacon, "You will conduct the candidate back from whence he came, and invest him of what he has been divested, and let him return for further instruction. A zealous attachment to these principles will insure a public and private esteem. In the State, you are to be a quiet and peaceable subject, true to your government, and just to your country; you are not to countenance disloyalty, but faithfully submit to legal authority, and conform with cheerfulness to the government of the country in which you live. In your outward demeanor be particularly careful to avoid censure or reproach. Although your frequent appearance at our regular meetings is earnestly solicited, yet it is not meant that Masonry should interfere with your necessary vocations; for these are on no account to be neglected: neither are you to suffer your zeal for the institution to lead you into argument with those who, through ignorance, may ridicule it. At your leisure hours, that you may improve in Masonic knowledge, you are to converse with well-informed brethren, who will be always as ready to give, as you will be to receive information. Finally, keep sacred and inviolable the mysteries of the Order, as these are to distinguish you from the rest of the community, and mark your consequence among Masons. If, in the circle of your acquaintance, you find a person desirous of being initiated into Masonry, be particularly attentive not to commend him, unless you are convinced he will conform to our rules; that the honor, glory, and reputation of the institution may be firmly established, and the world at large convinced of its good effects." Here the initiation ends, and the candidate is congratulated by his Masonic friends.

After this, the business of the meeting proceeds according to the by-laws or regulations of the Lodge. Before adjourning, it is a very common practice to close a Lodge of Entered Apprentices, and open a Lodge of Fellow Crafts, and close that, and open a Master Mason's Lodge, all in the same evening.

Ceremony of Closing a Lodge of Entered Apprentices.

A brother having made a motion that the Lodge be closed, it being seconded and carried, the Master says to the Junior Deacon, "Brother Junior [giving one rap, which calls up both Deacons], the first as well as the last care of a Mason?" The Junior Deacon answers, "To see the Lodge tyled, Worshipful." Master to the Junior Deacon, "Attend to that part of your duty, and inform the Tyler that we are about to close this Lodge of Entered Apprentice Masons, and direct him to tyle accordingly." The Junior Deacon steps to the door and gives three [Pg 13] raps, which are answered by the Tyler with three more; the Junior Deacon then gives one, which is also answered by the Tyler by one. The Junior Deacon then opens the door, delivers his message, and resumes his place in the Lodge, and says, "The door is tyled, Worshipful." Master to Junior Deacon, "By whom?" Ans . "By a Master Mason without the door, armed with the proper implements of his office." Master to Junior Deacon, "His business there?" Ans . "To keep off all cowans and eavesdroppers, and see that none pass or repass without permission from the chair." Master to Junior Deacon, "Your duty there?" Ans . "To wait on the Worshipful Master and Wardens, act as their proxy in the active duties of the Lodge, and take care of the door." Master to Junior Deacon, "The Senior Deacon's place in the Lodge?" Ans . "At the right hand of the Worshipful Master in the East." Master to Senior Deacon, "Your duty there, Brother Senior?" Ans . "To wait on the Worshipful Master and Wardens, act as their proxy in the active duties of the Lodge, attend to the preparation and introduction of candidates; receive and clothe all visiting brethren." Master to the Senior Deacon, "The Secretary's place in the Lodge?" Ans . "At your left hand, Worshipful." Master to Secretary, "Your duty there, Brother Secretary?" The Secretary replies, "Duly to observe the Master's will and pleasure; record the proceedings of the Lodge; transmit a copy of the same to the Grand Lodge, if required; receive all moneys and money-bills from the hands of the brethren; pay them over to the Treasurer, and take his receipt for the same." Master to the Secretary, "The Treasurer's place in the Lodge?" Ans . "At the right hand of the Worshipful Master." Master to Treasurer, "Your business there, Brother Treasurer?" Treasurer answers, "Duly to observe the Worshipful Master's will and pleasure; receive all moneys and money-bills from the hands of the Secretary; keep a just and accurate account of the same; pay them out by order of the Worshipful Master and consent of the brethren." Master to the Treasurer, "The Junior Warden's place in the Lodge?" Ans . "In the South, Worshipful." Master to the Junior Warden, "Your business there, Brother Junior?" The Junior Warden says, "As the sun in the South, at high meridian, is the beauty and glory of the day, so stands the Junior Warden in the South at high twelve, the better to observe the time, call the crafts from labor to refreshment; superintend them during the hours thereof; see that none convert the purposes of refreshment into that of excess or intemperance; call them on again in due season; that the Worshipful Master may have honor, and they pleasure and profit thereby." The Master to the Junior Warden, "The Master's place in the Lodge?" Ans . "In the East, Worshipful." Master to Junior Warden, "His duty there?" Ans . "As the sun rises in the East to open and adorn the day, so presides the Worshipful Master in the East, to open and adorn his Lodge, set his crafts to work with good and wholesome laws, or cause the same to be done." Master to the Junior Warden, "The Senior Warden's place in the Lodge?" Ans . "In the West, Worshipful." Master to the Senior Warden, "Your business there, Brother Senior?" The Senior Warden replies, "As the sun sets in the West to close the day, so stands the Senior Warden in the West to assist the [Pg 14] Worshipful Master in opening and closing the Lodge; take care of the jewels and implements; see that none be lost; pay the craft their wages, if any be due; and see that none go away dissatisfied." The Master now gives three raps, when all the brethren rise, and the Master asks, "Are you all satisfied?" They answer in the affirmative by giving the due-guard. Should the Master discover that any declined giving it, inquiry is immediately made why it is so; and if any member is dissatisfied with any part of the proceedings, or with any brother, the subject is immediately investigated. Master to the brethren, "Attend to giving the signs; as I do, so do you give them downwards;" [which is by giving the last in opening, first in closing. In closing, on this degree, you first draw your right hand across your throat, as hereinbefore described, and then hold your two hands over each other as before described. This is the method pursued through all the degrees; and when opening on any of the upper degrees, all the signs of all the preceding degrees are given before you give the signs of the degree on which you are opening.] This being done, the Master proceeds, "I now declare this Lodge of Entered Apprentice Masons regularly closed in due and ancient form. Brother Junior Warden, please inform Brother Senior Warden, and request him to inform the brethren that it is my will and pleasure that this Lodge of Entered Apprentice Masons be now closed, and stand closed until our next regular communication, unless a case or cases of emergency shall require earlier convention, of which every member shall be notified; during which time it is seriously hoped and expected that every brother will demean himself as becomes a Free and Accepted Mason." Junior Warden to Senior Warden, "Brother Senior, it is the Worshipful Master's will and pleasure that this Lodge of Entered Apprentice Masons be closed, and stand closed until our next regular communication, unless a case or cases of emergency shall require earlier convention, of which every brother shall be notified; during which time it is seriously hoped and expected that every brother will demean himself as becomes a Free and Accepted Mason." Senior Warden to the brethren, "Brethren, you have heard the Worshipful Master's will and pleasure as communicated to me by Brother Junior; so let it be done." Master to the Junior Warden, "Brother Junior, how do Mason's meet?" Ans. "On the level." Master to Senior Warden, "How do Masons part?" Ans. "On the square." Master to the Junior and Senior Wardens, "Since we meet on the level, Brother Junior, and part on the square, Brother Senior, so let us ever meet and part in the name of the Lord." Master to the brethren, "Brethren, let us pray."

"Supreme Architect of the Universe! Accept our humble praises for the many mercies and blessings which Thy bounty has conferred upon us, and especially for this friendly and social intercourse. Pardon, we beseech Thee, whatever Thou hast seen amiss in us since we have been together; and continue to us Thy presence, protection and blessing. Make us sensible of the renewed obligations we are under to love Thee supremely, and to be friendly to each other. May all our irregular passions be subdued, and may we daily increase in faith, hope, and charity; but more especially in that charity which is the bond of peace, and [Pg 15] perfection of every virtue. May we so practice Thy precepts, that through the merits of the Redeemer we may finally obtain Thy promises, and find an acceptance through the gates and into the temple and city of our God. So mote it be. Amen."

It is often that the prayer is neglected and the following benediction substituted: May the blessing of heaven rest upon us, and all regular Masons! May brotherly love prevail, and every moral and social virtue cement us. So mote it be. Amen.

After the prayer the following charge ought to be delivered, but it is seldom attended to; in a majority of Lodges it is never attended to; Master to brethren, "Brethren, we are now about to quit this sacred retreat of friendship and virtue to mix again with the world. Amidst its concerns and employments, forget not the duties which you have heard so frequently inculcated, and so forcibly recommended in this Lodge. Remember that around this altar you have promised to befriend and relieve every brother who shall need your assistance. You have promised in the most friendly manner to remind him of his errors and aid a reformation. These generous principles are to extend further; every human being has a claim upon your kind offices. Do good unto all. Recommend it more 'especially to the household of the faithful.' Finally, brethren, be ye all of one mind, live in peace, and may the God of love and peace delight to dwell with and bless you."

In some Lodges, after the charge is delivered, the Master says, "Brethren, form on the square." Then all the brethren form a circle, and the Master, followed by every brother [except in using the words], says, "And God said, Let there be light, and there was light." At the same moment that the last of these words drops from the Master's lips, every member stamps with his right foot on the floor, and at the same instant brings his hands together with equal force, and in such perfect unison with each other, that persons situated so as to hear it would suppose it the precursor of some dreadful catastrophe. This is called " THE SHOCK ." The members of the Lodge then separate.

The above comprises all the secret forms and ceremonies in a Lodge of Entered Apprentice Masons; but if the candidate would thoroughly understand the whole, he must commit to memory the following "Lecture." Very few do this except the officers of the Lodge. The "Lecture" is nothing more nor less than a recapitulation of the preceding ceremonies and forms by way of question and answer, in order fully to explain the same. In fact, the ceremonies and forms (masonically called the WORK) and Lecture are so much the same that he who possesses a knowledge of the Lecture cannot be destitute of a knowledge of what the ceremonies and forms are. The ceremonies used in opening and closing are the same in all the degrees.

FIRST SECTION.

Lecture on the First Degree of Masonry.

Question—From whence came you as an Entered Apprentice Mason? Answer—From the Holy Lodge of St. John at Jerusalem.

[Pg 16] Q. What recommendations do you bring? A. Recommendations from the Worshipful Master, Wardens, and brethren of that Right Worshipful Lodge, who greet you.

Q. What comest thou hither to do? A. To learn to subdue my passions, and improve myself in the secret arts and mysteries of Ancient Freemasonry.

Q. You are a Mason, then, I presume? A. I am.

Q. How do you know that you are a Mason? A. By being often tried, never denied, and willing to be tried again.

Q. How shall I know you to be a Mason? A. By certain signs, and a token.

Q. What are signs? A. All right angles, horizontals and perpendiculars.

Q. What is a token? A. A certain friendly and brotherly grip, whereby one Mason may know another in the dark as well as in the light.

Q. Where were you first prepared to be a Mason? A. In my heart.

Q. Where secondly? A. In a room adjacent to the body of a just and lawfully constituted Lodge of such.

Q. How were you prepared? A. By being divested of all metals, neither naked nor clothed, barefoot nor shod, hoodwinked, with a cable-tow about my neck, in which situation I was conducted to the door of the Lodge.

Q. You being hoodwinked, how did you know it to be a door? A. By first meeting with resistance, and afterwards gaining admission.

Q. How did you gain admission? A. By three distinct knocks from without, answered by the same from within.

Q. What was said to you from within? A. Who comes there? Who comes there? Who comes there?

Q. Your answer? A. A poor, blind candidate, who has long been desirous of having and receiving a part of the rights and benefits of this Worshipful Lodge, dedicated to God, and held forth to the Holy Order of St. John, as all true fellows and brothers have done, who have gone this way before me.

Q. What further was said to you from within? A. I was asked if it was of my own free will and accord I made this request; if I was duly and truly prepared, worthy and well qualified; all of which being answered in the affirmative, I was asked by what further rights I expected to obtain so great a favor or benefit.

Q. Your answer? A. By being a man, free-born, of lawful age, and well recommended.

Q. What was then said to you? A. I was bid to wait till the Worshipful Master in the East was made acquainted with my request and his answer returned.

Q. After his answer was returned, what followed? A. I was caused to enter the Lodge.

Q. How? A. On the point of some sharp instrument pressing my naked left breast, in the name of the Lord.

Q. How were you then disposed of? A. I was conducted to the centre of the Lodge, and there caused to kneel for the benefit of a prayer.

[Pg 17] Q. After prayer, what was said to you? A. I was asked in whom I put my trust.

Q. Your answer? A. God.

Q. What followed? A. The Worshipful Master took me by the right hand and said, Since in God you put your trust, arise, follow your leader, and fear no danger.

Q. How were you then disposed of? A. I was conducted three times regularly around the Lodge, and halted at the Junior Warden in the South, where the same questions were asked, and answers returned at the door.

Q. How did the Junior Warden dispose of you? A. He ordered me to be conducted to the Senior Warden in the West, where the same questions were asked, and answers returned as before.

Q. How did the Senior Warden dispose of you? A. He ordered me to be conducted to the Worshipful Master in the East, where the same questions were asked, and answers returned as before, who likewise demanded of me from whence I came, and whither I was traveling.

Q. Your answer? A. From the West, and traveling to the East.

Q. Why do you leave the West and travel to the East? A. In search of light.

Q. How did the Worshipful Master then dispose of you? A. He ordered me to be conducted back to the West, from whence I came, and put in care of the Senior Warden, who taught me how to approach the East, the place of light, by advancing upon one upright regular step to the first step, my feet forming the right angle of an oblong square, my body erect at the altar before the Worshipful Master.

Q. What did the Worshipful Master do with you? A. He made an Entered Apprentice Mason of me.

Q. How? A. In due form.

Q. What was that due form? A. My left knee bare and bent, my right forming a square, my left hand supporting the Holy Bible, Square and Compass; I took upon me the solemn oath or obligation of an Entered Apprentice Mason.

Q. After you had taken your obligation, what was said to you? A. I was asked what I most desired.

Q. Your answer? A. Light.

Q. Was you immediately brought to light? A. I was.

Q. How? A. By the direction of the Master, and assistance of the brethren.

Q. What did you first discover after being brought to light? A. Three great lights in Masonry, by the assistance of three lesser.

Q. What were those three great lights in Masonry? A. The Holy Bible, Square and Compass.

Q. How are they explained? A. The Holy Bible is given to us as a guide for our faith and practice; the Square, to square our actions; and the Compass to keep us in due bounds with all mankind, but more especially with the brethren.

Q. What were those three lesser lights? A. Three burning tapers, or candles on candlesticks.

[Pg 18] Q. What do they represent? A. The Sun, Moon, and Master of the Lodge.

Q. How are they explained? A. As the Sun rules the day, and the Moon governs the night, so ought the Worshipful Master to use his endeavors to rule and govern his Lodge with equal regularity, or cause the same to be done.

Q. What did you next discover? A. The Worshipful Master approaching me from the East, under the sign and dueguard of an Entered Apprentice Mason, who presented me with his right hand in token of brotherly love and esteem, and proceeded to give me the grip and word of an Entered Apprentice Mason, and bid me arise and salute the Junior and Senior Wardens, and convince them that I had been regularly initiated as an Entered Apprentice Mason, and was in possession of the sign, grip, and word.

Q. What did you next discover? A. The Worshipful Master a second time approaching me from the East, who presented me with a lamb-skin, or white apron, which he said was an emblem of innocence, and the badge of a Mason; that it had been worn by kings, princes, and potentates of the earth, who had never been ashamed to wear it; that it was more honorable than the diamonds of kings, or pearls of princesses, when worthily worn; and more ancient than the Golden Fleece or Roman Eagle; more honorable than the Star or Garter, or any other order that could be conferred on me at that time, or any time thereafter, except it be in the body of a just and lawfully constituted Lodge of Masons; and bid me carry it to the Senior Warden in the West, who taught me how to wear it as an Entered Apprentice Mason.

Q. What were you next presented with? A. The working tools of an Entered Apprentice Mason.

Q. What were they? A. The twenty-four-inch gauge and common gavel.

Q. How were they explained? A. The twenty-four-inch gauge is an instrument made use of by operative masons to measure and lay out their work; but we, as Free and Accepted Masons, are taught to make use of it for the more noble and glorious purpose of dividing our time; the twenty-four inches on the gauge are emblematical of the twenty-four hours in the day, which we are taught so divide into three equal parts, whereby we find eight hours for the service of God and a worthy distressed brother; eight hours for our usual vocation, and eight hours for refreshment and sleep. The common gavel is an instrument made use of by operative masons to break off the corners of rough stones, the better to fit them for the builder's use; but we, as Free and Accepted Masons, are taught to make use of it for the more noble and glorious purpose of divesting our hearts and consciences of all the vices and superfluities of life, thereby fitting our minds as lively and living stone for that spiritual building, that house not made with hands, eternal in the heavens.

Q. What was you next presented with? A. A new name.

Q. What was it? A. Caution.

[Pg 19] Q. What does it teach? A. It teaches me, as I was barely instructed in the rudiments of Masonry, that I should be cautious over all my words and actions, especially when before its enemies.

Q. What were you next presented with? A. Three precious jewels.

Q. What were they? A. A listening ear, a silent tongue, and a faithful heart.

Q. What do they teach? A. A listening ear teaches me to listen to the instructions of the Worshipful Master, but more especially that I should listen to the calls and cries of a worthy distressed brother. A silent tongue teaches me to be silent in the Lodge, that the peace and harmony thereof may not be disturbed; but more especially that I should be silent when before the enemies of Masonry. A faithful heart, that I should be faithful to the instructions of the Worshipful Master at all times; but more especially that I should be faithful and keep and conceal the secrets of Masonry, and those of a brother, when delivered to me in charge as such, that they may remain as secure and inviolable in my breast as in his own, before communicated to me.

Q. What was you next presented with? A. Check-words two.

Q. What were they? A. Truth and Union.

Q. How explained? A. Truth is a divine attribute, and the foundation of every virtue. To be good and true are the first lessons we are taught in Masonry. On this theme we contemplate, and by its dictates endeavor to regulate our conduct; hence, while influenced by this principle, hypocrisy and deceit are unknown amongst us; sincerity and plain dealing distinguish us; and the heart and tongue join in promoting each other's welfare, and rejoicing in each other's prosperity.

Union is that kind of friendship that ought to appear conspicuous in the conduct of every Mason. It is so closely allied to the divine attribute, truth, that he who enjoys the one, is seldom destitute of the other. Should interest, honor, prejudice, or human depravity ever influence you to violate any part of the sacred trust we now repose in you, let these two important words, at the earliest insinuation, teach you to put on the check-line of truth, which will infallibly direct you to pursue that straight and narrow path which ends in the full enjoyment of the Grand Lodge above, where we shall all meet as Masons and members of one family; where all discord on account of religion, politics, or private opinion, shall be unknown and banished from within our walls.

Q. What followed? A. The Worshipful Master in the East made a demand of me of something of a metallic kind, which, he said, was not so much on account of its intrinsic value, as that it might be deposited in the archives of the Lodge as a memorial that I had herein been made a Mason.

Q. How did the Worshipful Master then dispose of you? A. He ordered me to be conducted out of the Lodge and invested of what I had been divested, and return for further instruction.

Q. After you returned, how was you disposed of? A. I was conducted to the northeast corner of the Lodge, and there caused to stand upright like a man, my feet forming a square, and received a solemn injunction, ever to walk and act uprightly before God and man, and in addition thereto received too following charge. [For this charge see pages 10-12.]

[Pg 20]

SECOND SECTION.

Question—Why was you divested of all metals when you was made a Mason? Answer—Because Masonry regards no man on account of his worldly wealth or honors; it is therefore the internal, and not the external qualifications that recommend a man to Masons.

Q. A second reason? A. There was neither the sound of an axe, hammer, or any other metal tool heard at the building of King Solomon's Temple.

Q. How could so stupendous a fabric be erected without the sound of axe, hammer, or any other metal tool? A. All the stones were hewed, squared, and numbered in the quarries where they were raised, all the timbers felled and prepared in the forests of Lebanon, and carried down to Joppa on floats, and taken from thence up to Jerusalem and set up with wooden mauls, prepared for that purpose; which, when completed, every part thereof fitted with that exact nicety, that it had more the resemblance of the handy workmanship of the Supreme Architect of the Universe than of human hands.

Q. Why was you neither naked nor clothed? A. As I was an object of distress at that time, it was to remind me, if ever I saw a friend, more especially a brother, in a like distressed situation, that I should contribute as liberally to his relief as his situation required, and my abilities would admit, without material injury to myself or family.

Q. Why was you neither barefoot nor shod? A. It was an ancient Israelitish custom adopted among Masons; and we read in the Book of Ruth concerning their mode and manner of changing and redeeming, and to confirm all things, a brother plucked off his shoe and gave it to his neighbor, and that was testimony in Israel. This, then, therefore, we do in confirmation of a token, and as a pledge of our fidelity; therefore signifying that we will renounce our own will in all things, and become obedient to the laws of our ancient institutions.

Q. Why was you hoodwinked? A. That my heart might conceive before my eyes beheld the beauties of Masonry.

Q. A second reason? A. As I was in darkness at that time, it was to remind me that I should keep the whole world so respecting Masonry.

Q. Why had you a cable-tow about your neck? A. In case I had not submitted to the manner and mode of my initiation, that I might have been led out of the Lodge without seeing the form and beauties thereof.

Q. Why did you give three distinct knocks at the door? A. To alarm the Lodge, and let the Worshipful Master, Wardens and brethren know that a poor blind candidate prayed admission.

Q. What do those three distinct knocks allude to? A. A certain passage in Scripture wherein it says, "Ask and it shall be given, seek and ye shall find, knock and it shall be opened unto you."

Q. How did you apply this to your then case in Masonry? A. I asked the recommendation of a friend to become a Mason; I sought admission through his recommendations and knocked, and the door of Masonry opened unto me.

Q. Why was you caused to enter on the point of some sharp instrument pressing your naked left breast in the name of the Lord? A. As [Pg 21] this was a torture to my flesh, so might the recollection of it ever be to my flesh and conscience, if ever I attempted to reveal the secrets of Masonry unlawfully.

Q. Why was you conducted to the centre of the Lodge, and there caused to kneel for the benefit of a prayer? A. Before entering on this, or any other great and important undertaking, it is highly necessary to implore a blessing from Deity.

Q. Why was you asked in whom you put your trust? A. Agreeably to the laws of our ancient institution, no Atheist could be made a Mason; it was, therefore, necessary that I should believe in Deity; otherwise, no oath or obligation could bind me.

Q. Why did the Worshipful Master take you by the right hand and bid you rise, follow your leader, and fear no danger? A. As I was in darkness at that time, and could neither forsee nor avoid danger, it was to remind me that I was in the hands of an affectionate friend, in whose fidelity I might with safety confide.

Q. Why was you conducted three times regularly round the Lodge? A. That the Worshipful Master, Wardens and brethren might see that I was duly and truly prepared.

Q. Why did you meet with those several obstructions on the way? A. This, and every other Lodge is, or ought to be, a true representation of King Solomon's Temple, which, when completed, had guards stationed at the East, West, and South gates.

Q. Why had they guards stationed at those several gates? A. To prevent any one from passing or repassing that was not duly qualified.

Q. Why did you kneel on your left knee and not on your right, or both? A. The left side has ever been considered the weakest part of the body; it was, therefore, to remind me that that part I was then taking upon me was the weakest part of Masonry, it being that only of an Entered Apprentice.

Q. Why was your right hand placed on the Holy Bible, Square and Compass, and not your left, or both? A. The right hand has ever been considered the seat of fidelity, and our ancient brethren worshipped Deity under the name of Fides , which has sometimes been represented by two right hands joined together; at others, by two human figures holding each other by the right hand; the right hand, therefore, we use in this great and important undertaking, to signify, in the strongest manner possible, the sincerity of our intentions in the business we are engaged.

Q. Why did the Worshipful Master present you with a lamb-skin, or a white apron? A. The lamb-skin has, in all ages, been deemed an emblem of innocence; he, therefore, who wears the lamb-skin, as a badge of a Mason, is thereby continually reminded of that purity of life and rectitude of conduct, which is so essentially necessary to our gaining admission into the Celestial Lodge above, where the Supreme Architect of the Universe presides.

Q. Why did the Master make a demand of you of something of a metallic nature? A. As I was in a poor and penniless situation at the time, it was to remind me if ever I saw a friend, but more especially a brother, [Pg 22] in a like poor and penniless situation, that I should contribute as liberally to his relief as my abilities would admit and his situation required, without injuring myself or family.

Q. Why was you conducted to the northeast corner of the Lodge, and there caused to stand upright, like a man, your feet forming a square, receiving, at the same time, a solemn charge to walk and act uprightly before God and man? A. The first stone in every Masonic edifice is, or ought to be, placed at the northeast corner; that being the place where an Entered Apprentice Mason receives his first instructions to build his future Masonic edifice upon.

THIRD SECTION.

Question—We have been saying a good deal about a Lodge, I want to know what constitutes a Lodge? Answer—A certain number of Free and Accepted Masons, duly assembled in a room or place, with the Holy Bible, Square and Compass, and other Masonic Implements, with a charter from the Grand Lodge, empowering them to work.

Q. Where did our ancient brethren meet before Lodges were erected? A. On the highest hills, and in the lowest vales.

Q. Why on the highest hills and in the lowest vales? A. The better to guard against cowans and enemies either ascending or descending, that the brethren might have timely notice of their approach, to prevent being surprised.

Q. What is the form of your Lodge? A. An oblong square.

Q. How long? A. From East to West.

Q. How wide? A. Between North and South.

Q. How high? A. From the surface of the earth to the highest heavens.

Q. How deep? A. From the surface to the centre.

Q. What supports your Lodge? A.

Three large columns or pillars.

Q. What are their names? A. Wisdom, Strength, and Beauty.

Q. Why so? A. It is necessary there should be wisdom to contrive, strength to support, and beauty to adorn, all great and important undertakings; but more especially this of ours.

Q. Has your Lodge any covering? A. It has; a clouded canopy, or starry-decked heaven, where all good Masons hope to arrive.

Q. How do you hope to arrive there? A. By the assistance of Jacob's ladder.

Q. How many principal rounds has it got? A. Three.

Q. What are their names? A. Faith, Hope, and Charity.

Q. What do they teach? A. Faith in God, hope in immortality, and charity to all mankind.

Q. Has your Lodge any furniture? A. It has; the Holy Bible, Square, and Compass.

Q. To whom do they belong? A. The Bible to God; the Square to the Master; and the Compass to the Craft.

Q. How explained? A. The Bible to God, it being the inestimable gift of God to man for his instruction, to guide him through the rugged paths of life; the Square to the Master, it being the proper emblem of [Pg 23] his office: the Compass to the Craft; by a due attention to which we are taught to limit our desires, curb our ambition, subdue our irregular appetites, and keep our passions and prejudices in due bounds with all mankind, but more especially with the brethren.

Q. Has your Lodge any ornaments? A. It has; the Mosaic, or checkered pavement; the indented tressel; that beautiful tesselated border which surrounds it, with the blazing star in the centre.

Q. What do they represent? A. The Mosaic, or checkered pavement, represents this world; which, though checkered over with good and evil, yet brethren may walk together thereon and not stumble; the indented tressel, with the blazing star in the centre, the manifold blessings and comforts with which we are surrounded in this life, but more especially those which we hope to enjoy hereafter; the blazing star, that prudence which ought to appear conspicuous in the conduct of every Mason, but more especially commemorative of the star which appeared in the East to guide the wise men to Bethlehem, to proclaim the birth and the presence of the Son of God.

Q. Has your Lodge any lights? A. It has; three.

Q. How are they situated? A. East, West, and South.

Q. Has it none in the North? A. It has not.

Q. Why so? A. Because this and every other Lodge is, or ought to be, a true representation of King Solomon's Temple, which was situated North of the ecliptic; the Sun and Moon, therefore, darting their rays from the South, no light was to be expected from the North; we, therefore, Masonically, term the North a place of darkness.

Q. Has your Lodge any jewels? A. It has; six; three movable and three immovable.

Q. What are the three movable jewels? A. The Square, Level, and Plumb.

Q. What do they teach? A. The Square, morality; the Level, equality; and the Plumb, rectitude of life and conduct.

Q. What are the three immovable jewels? A. The rough Ashlar, the perfect Ashlar, and the Tressel-Board.

Q. What are they? A. The rough Ashlar is a stone in its rough and natural state; the perfect Ashlar is also a stone, made ready by the working tools of the Fellow Craft to be adjusted in the building; and the Tressel-Board is for the master workman to draw his plans and designs upon.

Q. What do they represent? A. The rough Ashlar represents man in his rude and imperfect state by nature; the perfect Ashlar also represents man in that state of perfection to which we all hope to arrive, by means of a virtuous life and education, our own endeavors, and the blessing of God. In erecting our temporal building, we pursue the plans and designs laid down by the master workman on his Tressel-Board: but in erecting our spiritual building, we pursue the plans and designs laid down by the Supreme Geometrician of the Universe, in the Book of Life, which we, Masonically, term our spiritual Tressel-Board.

Q. Who did you serve? A. My Master.

Q. How long? A. Six days.

[Pg 24] Q. What did you serve him with? A. Freedom, Fervency, and Zeal.

Q. What do they represent? A. Chalk, Charcoal, and Earth.

Q. Why so? A. There is nothing freer than chalk, the slightest touch of which leaves a trace behind; nothing more fervent than heated charcoal; it will melt the most obdurate metals; nothing more zealous than the earth to bring forth.

Q. How is your Lodge situated? A. Due East and West.

Q. Why so? A. Because the Sun rises in the East and sets in the West.

Q. A second reason? A. The gospel was first preached in the East and is spreading to the West.

Q. A third reason? A. The liberal arts and sciences began in the East and are extending to the West.

Q. A fourth reason? A. Because all the churches and chapels are, or ought to be, so situated.

Q. Why are all churches and chapels so situated? A. Because King Solomon's Temple was so situated.

Q. Why was King Solomon's Temple so situated? A. Because Moses, after conducting the children of Israel through the Red Sea, by divine command, erected a tabernacle to God, and placed it due East and West, which was to commemorate, to the latest posterity, that miraculous East wind that wrought their mighty deliverance; and this was an exact model of Solomon's Temple; since which time, every well regulated and governed Lodge is, or ought to be, so situated.

Q. To whom did our ancient brethren dedicate their Lodges? A. To King Solomon.

Q. Why so? A. Because King Solomon was our most ancient Grand Master.

Q. To whom do modern Masons dedicate their Lodges? A. To St. John the

Baptist and St. John the Evangelist.

Q. Why so? A. Because they were the two most ancient Christian patrons of Masonry; and, since their time, in every well-regulated and governed Lodge there has been a certain point within a circle, which circle is bounded on the East and the West by two perpendicular parallel lines, representing the anniversary of St. John the Baptist and St. John the Evangelist, who were two perfect parallels, as well in Masonry as Christianity, on the vertex of which rests the Book of the Holy Scriptures, supporting Jacob's Ladder, which is said to reach the watery clouds, and, in passing round this circle, we naturally touch on both these perpendicular parallel lines, as well as the Book of the Holy Scriptures; and while a Mason keeps himself thus circumscribed, he cannot materially err.

END OF THE LECTURE, AND OF THE FIRST DEGREE.

It is proper to add here that very few Masons ever learn the Lecture. Of course, it is necessary that the officers of the Lodge should understand their own particular part, and that is generally all they learn.

THE SECOND OR FELLOW CRAFT MASON'S DEGREE.

This degree is usually called "passing. " The ceremonies of opening and closing the Lodge are precisely the same as in the first degree; except two [Pg 25] knocks are used in this degree, and the door is entered by the benefit of a password. It is Shibboleth , and explained in the Lecture. The candidate, as before, is taken into the preparation room and prepared in the manner following: All his clothing taken off, except his shirt; furnished with a pair of drawers; his right breast bare; his left foot in a slipper; the right bare; a cable-tow twice 'round his neck; semi-hoodwinked; in which situation he is conducted to the door of the Lodge, where he gives two knocks, when the Senior Warden rises and says, "Worshipful, while we are peaceably at work on the second degree of Masonry, under the influence of faith, hope, and charity, the door of our Lodge is alarmed." Master to Junior Deacon, "Brother Junior, inquire the cause of that alarm." [In many Lodges they come to the door, knock, are answered by the Junior Deacon, and come in without being noticed by the Senior Warden or Master.] The Junior Deacon gives two raps on the inside of the door. The candidate gives one without. It is answered by the Junior Deacon with one; when the door is partly opened by the Junior Deacon, who inquires, "Who comes here? Who comes here?" The Senior Deacon, who is, or ought to be, the conductor, answers, "A worthy brother, who has been regularly initiated as an Entered Apprentice Mason, served a proper time as such, and now wishes for further light in Masonry, by being passed to the degree of Fellow Craft. " Junior Deacon to Senior Deacon, "Is it of his own free will and accord he makes this request?" Senior Deacon replies, "It is." Junior Deacon to Senior Deacon, "Is he duly and truly prepared?" Ans. "He is." Junior Deacon to Senior Deacon, "Is he worthy and well qualified?" Ans. "He is." Junior Deacon to Senior Deacon, "Has he made suitable proficiency in the preceding degree?" Ans. "He has." Junior Deacon to Senior Deacon, "By what further rights does he expect to obtain this benefit?" Ans. "By the benefit of a pass-word." Junior Deacon to Senior Deacon, "Has he a pass-word?" Ans. "He has not, but I have it for him." Junior Deacon to Senior Deacon, "Give it to me." The Senior Deacon whispers in the Junior Deacon's ear, " Shibboleth. " The Junior Deacon says, "The pass is right; since this is the case, you will wait until the Worshipful Master in the East is made acquainted with his request, and his answer returned." The Junior Deacon then repairs to the Master and gives two knocks, as at the door, which are answered by two by the Master; when the same questions are asked, and answers returned, as at the door. After which, the Master says, "Since he comes endued with all these necessary qualifications, let him enter this Worshipful Lodge in the name of the Lord, and take heed on what he enters." He enters; the angle of the Square is pressed hard against his naked right breast, at which time the Junior Deacon says, "Brother, when you entered this Lodge the first time, you entered on the point of the Compass pressing your naked left breast, which was then explained to you. You now enter it on the angle of the Square, pressing your naked right breast; which is to teach you to act upon the square with all mankind, but more especially with the brethren." The candidate is then conducted twice regularly 'round the Lodge and halted at the Junior Warden in the South, where he gives two raps, and is [Pg 26] answered by two, when the same questions are asked, and answers returned as at the door; from thence he is conducted to the Senior Warden, where the same questions are asked, and answers returned as before; he is then conducted to the Master in the East, where the same questions are asked, and answers returned as before; the Master likewise demands of him from whence he came, and whither he was traveling; he answers, "From the West, and traveling to the East." The Master says, "Why do you leave the West, and travel to the East?" The candidate answers, "In search of more light." The Master then says to the Senior Deacon, "Since this is the case, you will please conduct the candidate back to the West, from whence he came, and put him in the care of the Senior Warden, who will teach him how to approach the East, 'the place of light,' by advancing upon two upright regular steps to the second step (his heel is in the hollow of the right foot in this degree), his feet forming the right angle of an oblong square, and his body erect at the altar before the Worshipful Master, and place him in a proper position to take the solemn oath or obligation of a Fellow Craft Mason. " The Master then leaves his seat and approaches the kneeling candidate (the candidate kneels on the right knee, the left forming a square; his left arm, as far as the elbow, in a horizontal position, and the rest of the arm in a vertical position, so as to form a square; his arm supported by the Square held under his elbow), and says, "Brother, you are now placed in a proper position to take on you the solemn oath or obligation of a Fellow Craft Mason, which, I assure you, as before, is neither to affect your religion nor politics; if you are willing to take it, repeat your name, and say after me:

"I, A. B., of my own free will and accord, in the presence of Almighty God, and this Worshipful Lodge of Fellow Craft Masons, dedicated to God, and held forth to the Holy Order of St. John, do hereby and hereon most solemnly and sincerely promise and swear, in addition to my former obligation, that I will not give the degree of a Fellow Craft Mason to any one of an inferior degree, nor to any one being in the known world, except it be to a true and lawful brother, or brethren Fellow Craft Masons, or within the body of a just and lawfully constituted Lodge of such; and not unto him nor unto them whom I shall hear so to be, but unto him and them only whom I shall find so to be, after strict trial and due examination, or lawful information. Furthermore, do I promise and swear, that I will not wrong this Lodge, nor a brother of this degree, to the value of two cents, knowingly, myself, nor suffer it to be done by others, if in my power to prevent it. Furthermore, do I promise and swear, that I will support the Constitution of the Grand Lodge of the United States, and of the Grand Lodge of this State, under which this Lodge is held, and conform to all the by-laws, rules, and regulations of this, or any other Lodge, of which I may at any time hereafter become a member, as far as in my power. Furthermore, do I promise and swear, that I will obey all regular signs and summons given, handed, sent, or thrown to me by the hand of a brother Fellow Craft Mason, or from the body of a just and lawfully constituted Lodge of such; provided it be within the length of my cable-tow, or a square and angle of my work. Furthermore, do I promise and swear, that I will be aiding and assisting all poor and penniless brethren Fellow Crafts, their widows and orphans, wheresoever disposed 'round the globe, they applying to me as such, as far as in my power, without injuring myself or family. To all which I do most solemnly and sincerely promise and swear, without the least hesitation, mental reservation, or self-evasion of mind in me whatever; binding myself under no [Pg 27] less penalty than to have my left breast torn open, and my heart and vitals taken from thence and thrown over my left shoulder, and carried into the valley of Jehosaphat, there to become a prey to the wild beasts of the fields, and vultures of the air, if ever I should prove wilfully guilty of violating any part of this my solemn oath or obligation of a Fellow Craft Mason; so keep me God, and keep me steadfast in the due performance of the same."

The Master then says, "Detach your hands and kiss the book, which is the Holy Bible, twice." The bandage is now (by one of the brethren) dropped over the other eye, and the Master says, "Brother (at the same time laying his hand on the top of the candidate's head), what do you most desire?" The candidate answers, after his prompter, "More light." The Master says, "Brethren, form on the square, and assist in bringing our new-made brother from darkness to light; 'And God said, Let there be light, and there was light.'" At this instant all the brethren clap their hands, and stamp on the floor, as in the preceding degree. The Master says to the candidate, "Brother, what do you discover different from before?" The Master says, after a short pause, "You now discover one point of the Compass elevated above the Square, which denotes light in this degree; but as one is yet in obscurity, it is to remind you that you are yet one material point in the dark respecting Masonry." The Master steps off from the candidate three or four steps, and says, "Brother, you now discover me as a Master of this Lodge, approaching you from the East, under the sign and due-guard of a Fellow Craft Mason; do as I do, as near as you can, keeping your position." The sign is given by drawing your right hand flat, with the palm of it next to your breast, across your breast, from the left to the right side, with some quickness, and dropping it down by your side; the due-guard is given by raising the left arm until that part of it between the elbow and shoulder is perfectly horizontal, and raising the rest of the arm in a vertical position, so that that part of the arm below the elbow, and that part above it, forms a square; this is called the due-guard of a Fellow Craft Mason. The two given together are called the sign and due-guard of a Fellow Craft Mason, and they are never given separate; they would not be recognized by a Mason if given separately. The Master, by the time he gives his steps, sign, and due-guard, arrives at the candidate, and says, "Brother, I now present you with my right hand, in token of brotherly love and confidence, and with it the pass-grip and word of a Fellow Craft Mason." The pass, or more properly the pass-grip, is given by taking each other by the right hand, as though going to shake hands, and each putting his thumb between the fore and second finger, where they join the hands, and pressing the thumb between the joints. This is the pass-grip of a Fellow Craft Mason; the name of it is Shibboleth . Its origin will be explained in the Lecture; the pass-grip some give without lettering or syllabling, and others give it in the same way they do the real grip. The real grip of a Fellow Craft Mason is given by putting the thumb on the joint of the second finger, where it joins the hand, and crooking your thumb so that each can stick the nail of his thumb into the joint of the other. This is the real grip of a Fellow Craft Mason; the name of it is Jachin ; it is given in the following manner: If [Pg 28] you wish to examine a person, after having taken each other by the grip, ask him, "What is this?" A. "A grip." Q. "A grip of what?" A. "The grip of a Fellow Craft Mason." Q. "Has it a name?" A. "It has." Q. "Will you give it to me?" A. "I did not so receive it, neither can I so impart it." Q. "What will you do with it?" A. "I'll letter it or halve it." Q. "Halve it, and you begin. " A. "No; begin you." Q. "You begin." A. "JA." Q. "CHIN." A. "JACHIN." Q.

"Right, Brother Jachin, I greet you."

After the Master gives the candidate the pass-grip and grip, and their names, he says, "Brother, you will rise and salute the Junior and Senior Wardens as such, and convince them that you have been regularly passed to the degree of a Fellow Craft Mason, and have got the sign and pass-grip, real grip, and their names." [I do not here express it as expressed in Lodges generally; the Master usually says you will rise and salute the Wardens, &c., and convince them, &c., that you have got the sign, pass-grip, and word. It is obviously wrong, because the first thing he gives is the sign, then the due-guard, then the pass-grip, and their names.] While the Wardens are examining the candidate, the Master gets an apron, and returns to the candidate, and says, "Brother, I now have the honor of presenting you with a lamb-skin, or white apron, as before, which I hope you will continue to wear, with honor to yourself, and satisfaction to the brethren; you will please carry it to the Senior Warden in the West, who will teach you how to wear it as a Fellow Craft Mason." The Senior Warden ties on his apron, and turns up one corner of the lower end of the apron, and tucks it under the apron string. The Senior Deacon then conducts his pupil to the Master, who has by this time resumed his seat in the East, where he has, or ought to have, the floor carpet to assist him in his explanations. Master to the candidate, "Brother, as you are dressed, it is necessary you should have tools to work with; I will, therefore, present you with the tools of a Fellow Craft Mason. They are the Plumb, Square, and Level. The Plumb is an instrument made use of by operative masons to raise perpendiculars; the Square, to square their work; and the Level, to lay horizontals; but we, as Free and Accepted Masons, are taught to use them for more noble and glorious purposes; the Plumb teaches us to walk uprightly, in our several stations, before God and man; squaring our actions by the square of virtue; and remembering that we are traveling on the level of time to that 'undiscovered country, from whose bourne no traveler has returned.' I further present you with three precious jewels; their names are Faith, Hope, and Charity; they teach us to have faith in God, hope in immortality, and charity to all mankind." The Master to the Senior Deacon, "You will now conduct the candidate out of this Lodge, and invest him with what he has been divested." After he is clothed, and the necessary arrangements made for his reception, such as placing the columns and floor carpet, if they have any, and the candidate is reconducted back to the Lodge; as he enters the door, the Senior Deacon observes, "We are now about to return to the middle chamber of King Solomon's Temple." When within the door, the Senior Deacon proceeds, "Brother, we have worked [Pg 29] in speculative Masonry, but our forefathers wrought both in speculative and operative Masonry. They worked at the building of King Solomon's Temple, and many other Masonic edifices; they wrought six days; they did not work on the seventh, because in six days God created the heavens and the earth, and rested on the seventh day. The seventh, therefore, our ancient brethren consecrated as a day of rest; thereby enjoying more frequent opportunities to contemplate the glorious works of creation, and to adore their great Creator." Moving a step or two, the Senior Deacon proceeds, "Brother, the first thing that attracts our attention are two large columns, or pillars, one on the left hand, and the other on the right; the name of the one on the left hand is Boaz, and denotes strength; the name of the one on the right hand is Jachin, and denotes establishment; they collectively allude to a passage in Scripture, wherein God has declared in his word, 'In strength shall this house be established.' These columns are eighteen cubits high, twelve in circumference, and four in diameter; they are adorned with two large chapiters, one on each, and these chapiters are ornamented with net work, lily work, and pomegranates; they denote unity, peace, and plenty. The net work, from its connection, denotes union; the lily work, from its whiteness, purity and peace; and the pomegranate, from the exuberance of its seed, denotes plenty. They also have two large globes, or balls, one on each; these globes or balls contain, on their convex surfaces, all the maps and charts of the celestial and terrestrial bodies; they are said to be thus extensive to denote the universality of Masonry, and that a Mason's charity ought to be equally extensive. Their composition is molten, or cast brass; they were cast on the banks of the river Jordan, in the clay-ground between Succoth and Zaradatha, where King Solomon ordered these and all other holy vessels to be cast; they were cast hollow; and were four inches, or a hand's breadth thick; they were cast hollow, the better to withstand inundations and conflagrations; they were the archives of Masonry, and contained the constitution, rolls, and records." The Senior Deacon having explained the columns, he passes between them, advances a step or two, observing as he advances, "Brother, we will pursue our travels; the next thing that we come to is a long, winding staircase, with three, five, seven steps, or more. The three first allude to the three principal supports in Masonry, viz., wisdom, strength, and beauty; the five steps allude to the five orders in architecture, and the five human senses; the five orders in architecture are the Tuscan, Doric, Ionic, Corinthian, and Composite; the five human senses are Hearing, Seeing, Feeling, Smelling, and Tasting; the three first of which have ever been highly essential among Masons: Hearing, to hear the word; Seeing, to see the sign; and Feeling, to feel the grip, whereby one Mason may know another in the dark as well as in the light. The seven steps allude to the seven sabbatical years; seven years of famine; seven years in building the temple; seven golden candlesticks; seven wonders of the world; seven planets; but more especially the seven liberal arts and sciences, which are Grammar, Rhetoric, Logic, Arithmetic, Geometry, Music, and Astronomy; for this, and many other reasons, the number seven has ever been held in high [Pg 30] estimation among Masons." Advancing a few steps, the Senior Deacon proceeds, "Brother, the next thing we come to is the outer door of the middle chamber of King Solomon's Temple, which is partly open, but closely tyled by the Junior Warden" [It is the Junior Warden in the South who represents the Tyler at the outer door of the middle chamber of King Solomon's Temple], who, on the approach of the Senior Deacon and candidate, inquires, "Who comes here? Who comes here?" The Senior Deacon answers, "A Fellow Craft Mason." Junior Warden to Senior Deacon, "How do you expect to gain admission?" A. "By a pass, and token of a pass." Junior Warden to Senior Deacon, "Will you give them to me?" [The Senior Deacon, or the candidate (prompted by him), gives them; this and many other tokens, or grips, are frequently given by strangers when first introduced to each other. If given to a Mason, he will immediately return it; they can be given in any company unobserved, even by Masons, when shaking hands. A pass, and token of a pass ; the pass is the word Shibboleth ; the token, alias the pass-grip, is given, as before described, by taking each other by the right hand, as if shaking hands, and placing the thumb between the forefinger and second finger, at the third joint, or where they join the hand, and pressing it hard enough to attract attention. In the Lecture it is called a token, but generally called the pass-grip. It is an undeniable fact that Masons express themselves so differently, when they mean the same thing, that they frequently wholly misunderstand each other.]

After the Junior Warden has received the pass Shibboleth , he inquires, "What does it denote?" A. "Plenty." Junior Warden to Senior Deacon, "Why so?" A. "From an ear of corn being placed at the water-ford." Junior Warden to Senior Deacon, "Why was this pass instituted?" A. "In consequence of a quarrel which had long existed between Jephthah, Judge of Israel, and the Ephraimites, the latter of whom had long been a stubborn, rebellious people, whom Jephthah had endeavored to subdue by lenient measures, but to no effect. The Ephraimites being highly incensed against Jephthah, for not being called to fight and share in the rich spoils of the Ammonitish war, assembled a mighty army, and passed over the river Jordan to give Jephthah battle; but he, being apprised of their approach, called together the men of Israel, and gave them battle, and put them to flight; and to make his victory more complete, he ordered guards to be placed at the different passes on the banks of the river Jordan, and commanded, if the Ephraimites passed that way, that they should pronounce the word Shibboleth ; but they, being of a different tribe, pronounced it Sibboleth , which trifling defect proved them spies, and cost them their lives; and there fell that day, at the different passes on the banks of the river Jordan, forty and two thousand. This word was also used by our ancient brethren to distinguish a friend from a foe, and has since been adopted as a proper pass-word, to be given before entering any well-regulated and governed Lodge of Fellow Craft Masons." Since this is the case, you will pass on to the Senior Warden in the West for further examination. As they approach the Senior Warden in the West, the Senior Deacon says to the candidate, "Brother, the next thing we [Pg 31] come to is the inner door of the middle chamber of King Solomon's Temple, which we find partly open, but more closely tyled by the Senior Warden;" when the Senior Warden inquires, "Who comes here? Who comes here?" The Senior Deacon answers, "A Fellow Craft Mason." Senior Warden to Senior Deacon, "How do you expect to gain admission?" A. "By the grip and word." The Senior Warden to the Senior Deacon, "Will you give them to me?" They are then given as hereinbefore described. The word is Jachin . After they are given, the Senior Warden says, "They are right; you can pass on to the Worshipful Master in the East." As they approach the Master, he inquires, "Who comes here? Who comes here?" Senior Deacon answers, "A Fellow Craft Mason." The Master then says to the candidate, "Brother you have been admitted into the middle chamber of King Solomon's Temple for the sake of the letter G. It denotes Deity, before whom we all ought to bow with reverence, worship, and adoration. It also denotes Geometry, the fifth science: it being that on which this degree was principally founded. By Geometry we may curiously trace nature through her various windings to her most concealed recesses; by it we may discover the power, the wisdom, and the goodness of the Grand Artificer of the Universe, and view with delight the proportions which connect this vast machine; by it we may discover how the planets move in their different orbits, and demonstrate their various revolutions; by it we account for the return of a season, and the variety of scenes which each season displays to the discerning eye. Numberless worlds surround us, all formed by the same Divine Architect, which roll through this vast expanse, and all conducted by the same unerring law of nature. A survey of nature, and the observations of her beautiful proportions, first determined man to imitate the divine plan, and study symmetry and order. The architect began to design; and the plans which he laid down, being improved by experience and time, have produced works which are the admiration of every age. The lapse of time, the ruthless hand of ignorance, and the devastations of war, have laid waste and destroyed many valuable monuments of antiquity, on which the utmost exertions of human genius have been employed. Even the Temple of Solomon, so spacious and magnificent, and constructed by so many celebrated artists, escaped not the unsparing ravages of barbarous force. The ATTENTIVE EAR received the sound from the INSTRUCTIVE TONGUE ; and the mysteries of Freemasonry are safely lodged in the repository of FAITHFUL BREASTS . Tools and implements of architecture, and symbolic emblems, most expressive, are selected by the fraternity to imprint on the mind wise and serious truths; and thus, through a succession of ages, are transmitted, unimpaired, the most excellent tenets of our institution."

Here the labor ends of the Fellow Craft's degree. It will be observed that the candidate has received, in this place, the second section of the Lecture on this degree. This course is not generally pursued, but it is much the most instructive method; and when it is omitted, I generally conclude that it is for want of a knowledge of the Lecture. Monitorial writers (who are by no means coeval with Masonry) all write, or copy, very much after each other, and they have all inserted in their books all [Pg 32] those clauses of the several Lectures which are not considered by the wise ones as tending to develop the secrets of Masonry. In some instances, they change the phraseology a little; in others, they are literal extracts from the Lectures. This, it is said, is done to facilitate the progress of learners, or young Masons; when, in fact, it has the contrary effect.

The following charge is, or ought to be, delivered to the candidate after he has got through the ceremonies; but he is generally told, "It is in the Monitor, and you can learn it at your leisure." "Brother, being advanced to the second degree of Masonry, we congratulate you on your preferment. The internal, and not the external, qualifications of a man are what Masonry regards. As you increase in knowledge, you will improve in social intercourse. It is unnecessary to recapitulate the duties which, as a Mason, you are bound to discharge; or enlarge on the necessity of a strict adherence to them, as your own experience must have established their value. Our laws and regulations you are strenuously to support; and be always ready to assist in seeing them duly executed. You are not to palliate or aggravate the offences of your brethren; but in the decision of every trespass against our rules, you are to judge with candor, admonish with friendship, and reprehend with justice. The study of the liberal arts, that valuable branch of education, which tends so effectually to polish and adorn the mind, is earnestly recommended to your consideration; especially the science of Geometry, which is established as the basis of our art. Geometry, or Masonry, originally synonymous terms, being of a divine moral nature, is enriched with the most useful knowledge; while it proves the wonderful properties of nature, it demonstrates the more important truths of morality. Your past behavior and regular deportment have merited the honor which we have now conferred, and, in your new character, it is expected that you will conform to the principles of the Order, by steadily persevering in the practice of every commendable virtue. Such is the nature of your engagements as a Fellow Craft, and to these duties you are bound by the most sacred ties."

I will now proceed with the Lecture on this degree; it is divided into two sections.

FIRST SECTION.

Question—Are you a Fellow Craft Mason? A. I am; try me.

Q. By what will you be tried? A. By the Square.

Q. Why by the Square? A. Because it is an emblem of virtue.

Q. What is a Square? A. An angle extending to ninety degrees, or the fourth part of a circle.

Q. Where was you prepared to be made a Fellow Craft Mason? A. In a room adjacent to the body of a just and lawfully constituted Lodge of such, duly assembled in a room or place, representing the middle chamber of King Solomon's Temple.

Q. How was you prepared? A. By being divested of all metals; neither naked nor clothed; barefooted nor shod; hoodwinked; with a [Pg 33] cable-tow twice 'round my neck; in which situation I was conducted to the door of the Lodge, where I gave two distinct knocks.

Q. What did those two distinct knocks allude to? A. To the second degree in Masonry, it being that on which I was about to enter.

Q. What was said to you from within? A. Who comes there? Who comes there?

Q. Your answer? A. A worthy brother, who has been regularly initiated as an Entered Apprentice Mason; served a proper time as such; and now wishes for further light in Masonry, by being passed to the degree of a Fellow Craft.

Q. What was then said to you from within? A. I was asked if it was of my own free will and accord I made this request; if I was duly and truly prepared, worthy and well qualified; and had made suitable proficiency in the preceding degree; all of which being answered in the affirmative, I was asked by what further rights I expected to obtain so great a benefit.

Q. Your answer? A. By the benefit of a pass-word.

Q. What is that pass-word? A. Shibboleth.

Q. What further was said to you from within? A. I was bid to wait till the Worshipful Master in the East was made acquainted with my request and his answer returned.

Q. After his answer was returned, what followed? A. I was caused to enter the Lodge.

Q. How did you enter? A. On the angle of the Square presented to my naked right breast, in the name of the Lord.

Q. How were you then disposed of? A. I was conducted twice regularly around the Lodge, and halted at the Junior Warden in the South, where the same questions were asked, and answers returned as at the door.

Q. How did the Junior Warden dispose of you? A. He ordered me to be conducted to the Senior Warden in the West, where the same questions were asked, and answers returned as before.

Q. How did the Senior Warden dispose of you? A. He ordered me to be conducted to the Worshipful Master in the East, where the same questions were asked, and answers returned as before, who likewise demanded of me from whence I came, and whither I was traveling.

Q. Your answer? A. From the West, and traveling to the East.

Q. Why do you leave the West and travel to the East? A. In search of more light.

Q. How did the Worshipful Master then dispose of you? A. He ordered me to be conducted back to the West, from whence I came, and put in care of the

Senior Warden who taught me how to approach the East, by advancing upon two upright regular steps to the second step, my feet forming the right angle of an oblong square, and my body erect; at the altar before the Worshipful Master.

Q. What did the Worshipful Master do with you? A. He made a Fallow Craft Mason of me.

Q. How? A. In due form.

[Pg 34] Q. What was that due form? A. My right knee bare bent; my left knee forming a square; my right hand on the Holy Bible, Square, and Compass; my left arm forming an angle, supported by the Square, and my hand in a vertical position; in which posture I took upon me the solemn oath, or obligation, of a Fellow Craft Mason. [See pages 26 and 27 for obligation.]

Q. After your oath, or obligation, what was said to you? A. I was asked what I most desired.

Q. Your answer? A. More light.

Q. On being brought to light, what did you discover different from before? A. One point of the Compass elevated above the Square, which denoted light in this degree; but as one point was yet in obscurity, it was to remind me that I was yet one material point in the dark respecting Masonry.

Q. What did you next discover? A. The Worshipful Master approaching me from the East, under the sign and dueguard of a Fellow Craft Mason, who presented me with his right hand in token of brotherly love and confidence, and proceeded to give me the pass-grip and word of a Fellow Craft Mason, and bid me arise and salute the Junior and Senior Wardens, and convince them that I had been regularly passed to the degree of a Fellow Craft, and had the sign, grip, and word of a Fellow Craft Mason.

Q. What next did you discover? A. The Worshipful Master approaching me a second time from the East, who presented me a lamb-skin, or white apron, which, he said, he hoped I would continue to wear with honor to myself and satisfaction and advantage to my brethren.

Q. What was you next presented with? A. The working tools of a Fellow Craft Mason.

Q. What are they? A. The Plumb, Square, and Level.

Q. What do they teach? [I think this question ought to be, "How explained?"] A. The Plumb is an instrument made use of by operative Masons to raise perpendiculars; the Square, to square the work, and the Level, to lay horizontals; but we, as Free and Accepted Masons, are taught to make use of them for more noble and glorious purposes. The Plumb admonishes us to walk uprightly, in our several stations, before God and man; squaring our actions by the square of virtue; and remembering that we are all traveling upon the level of time, to that undiscovered country, from whose bourne no traveler returns.

Q. What was you next presented with? A. Three precious jewels.

Q. What were they? A. Faith, Hope, and Charity.

Q. What do they teach? A. Faith in God, hope in immortality, and charity to all mankind.

Q. How was you then disposed of? A. I was conducted out of the Lodge, and invested of what I had been divested.

SECOND SECTION.

Question—Have you ever worked as a Fellow Craft Mason? Answer—I have, in speculative; but our forefathers wrought both in speculative and operative Masonry.

[Pg 35] Q. Where did they work? A. At the building of King Solomon's Temple, and many other Masonic edifices.

Q. How long did they work? A. Six days.

Q. Did they not work on the Seventh? A. They did not.

Q. Why so? A. Because in six days God created the heavens and the earth, and rested on the seventh day; the seventh day, therefore, our ancient brethren consecrated as a day of rest from their labors; thereby enjoying more frequent opportunities to contemplate the glorious works of creation, and adore their great Creator.

Q. Did you ever return to the sanctum sanctorum, or holy of holies, of King Solomon's Temple? A. I did.

Q. By what way? A. Through a long porch, or alley.

Q. Did anything particular strike your attention on your return? A. There did; viz.: Two large columns, or pillars, one on the left hand, and the other on the right.

Q. What was the name of the one on the left hand? A. Boaz , to denote strength.

Q. What was the name of the one on the right hand? A. Jachin , denoting establishment.

Q. What do they collectively allude to? A. A passage in Scripture, wherein God has declared in his word, "In strength shall this house be established. "

Q. What were their dimensions? A. Eighteen cubits in height, twelve in circumference, and four in diameter.

Q. Were they adorned with anything? A. They were; with two large chapiters, one on each.

Q. Were they ornamented with anything? A. They were; with wreaths of net work, lily work, and pomegranates.

Q. What do they denote? A. Unity, Peace, and Plenty.

Q. Why so? A. Net work, from its connection, denotes union; lily work, from its whiteness and purity, denotes peace; and pomegranates, from the exuberance of its seed, denotes plenty.

Q. Were those columns adorned with anything further? A. They were; viz.: Two large globes, or balls, one on each.

Q. Did they contain anything? A. They did; viz.; All the maps and charts of the celestial and terrestrial bodies.

Q. Why are they said to be so extensive? A. To denote the universality of Masonry, and that a Mason's charity ought to be equally extensive.

Q. What was their composition? A. Molten, or cast brass.

Q. Who cast them? A. Our Grand Master, Hiram Abiff.

Q. Where were they cast? A. On the banks of the river Jordan, in the clay ground between Succoth and Zaradatha, where King Solomon ordered these and all other holy vessels to be cast.

Q. Were they cast solid or hollow? A. Hollow.

Q. What was their thickness? A. Four inches, or a hand's breadth.

Q. Why were they cast hollow? A. The better to withstand inundations or conflagrations; were the archives of Masonry, and contained the constitution, rolls, and records.

[Pg 36] Q. What did you next come to? A. A long, winding staircase, with three, five, seven steps, or more.

Q. What does the three steps allude to? A. The three principal supports in Masonry, viz., Wisdom, Strength, and Beauty.

Q. What does the five steps allude to? A. The five orders in architecture, and the five human senses.

Q. What are the five orders in architecture? A. The Tuscan, Doric, Ionic, Corinthian, and Composite.

Q. What are the five human senses? A. Hearing, Seeing, Feeling, Smelling, and Tasting; the first three of which have ever been deemed highly essential among Masons: Hearing, to hear the word; Seeing, to see the sign; and Feeling, to feel the grip, whereby one Mason may know another in the dark as well as in the light.

Q. What does the seven steps allude to? A. The seven sabbatical years; seven years of famine; seven years In building the temple; seven golden candlesticks; seven wonders of the world; seven planets; but more especially the seven liberal arts and sciences, which are Grammar, Rhetoric, Logic, Arithmetic, Geometry, Music, and Astronomy; for these, and many other reasons, the number seven has ever been held in high estimation among Masons.

Q. What did you next come to? A. The outer door of the middle chamber of King Solomon's Temple, which I found partly open, but closely tyled by the Junior Warden.

Q. How did you gain admission? A. By a pass, and token of a pass.

Q. What was the name of the pass? A. Shibboleth.

Q. What does it denote? A. Plenty.

Q. Why so? A. From an ear of corn being placed at the water-ford.

Q. Why was this pass instituted? A. In consequence of a quarrel which had long existed between Jephthah, Judge of Israel, and the Ephraimites, the latter of whom had long been a stubborn, rebellious people, whom Jephthah had endeavored to subdue by lenient measures, but to no effect. The Ephraimites being highly incensed against Jephthah, for not being called to fight and share in the rich spoils of the Ammonitish war, assembled a mighty army, and passed over the river Jordan to give Jephthah battle; but he, being apprised of their approach, called together the men of Israel, and gave them battle, and put them to flight; and to make his victory more complete, he ordered guards to be placed at the different passes on the banks of the river Jordan, and commanded, if the Ephraimites passed that way, that they should pronounce the word Shibboleth ; but they, being of a different tribe, pronounced it Sibboleth , which trifling defect proved them spies, and cost them their lives; and there fell that day, at the different passes on the banks of the river Jordan, forty and two thousand. This word was also used by our ancient brethren to distinguish a friend from a foe, and has since been adopted as a proper pass-word, to be given before entering any well-regulated and governed Lodge of Fellow Craft Masons.

Q. What did you next discover? A. The inner door of the middle chamber of King Solomon's Temple, which I found partly open, but closely tyled by the Senior Warden.

[Pg 37] Q. How did you gain admission? A. By the grip and word.

Q. How did the Senior Warden dispose of you? A. He ordered me to be conducted to the Worshipful Master in the East, who informed me that I had been admitted into the middle chamber of King Solomon's Temple for the sake of the letter G.

Q. Does it denote anything? A. It does; Deity —before whom we should all bow with reverence, worship, and adoration. It also denotes Geometry, the fifth science; it being that on which this degree was principally founded.

Thus ends the second degree of Masonry.

THE THIRD, OR MASTER MASON'S DEGREE.

The traditional account of the death, several burials, and resurrection of Hiram Abiff, the widow's son (as hereafter narrated), admitted as facts, this degree is certainly very interesting. The Bible informs us that there was a person of that name employed at the building of King Solomon's Temple; but neither the Bible, the writings of Josephus, nor any other writings, however ancient, of which I have any knowledge, furnish any information respecting his death. It is very singular that a man so celebrated as Hiram Abiff was, and arbiter between Solomon, King of Israel, and Hiram, King of Tyre, universally acknowledged as the third most distinguished man then living, and in many respects, the greatest man in the world, should pass off the stage of action, in the presence of King Solomon, three thousand, three hundred grand overseers, and one hundred and fifty thousand workmen, with whom he had spent a number of years, and neither King Solomon, his bosom friend, nor any other among his numerous friends, even recorded his death, or anything about him.

A person who has received the two preceding degrees, and wishes to be raised to the sublime degree of a Master Mason, is (the Lodge being opened as in the preceding degrees) conducted from the preparation room to the door (the manner of preparing him is particularly explained in the Lecture), where he gives three distinct knocks, when the Senior Warden rises and says, "Worshipful, while we are peaceably at work on the third degree of Masonry, under the influence of humanity, brotherly love, and affection, the door of our Lodge appears to be alarmed." The Master to the Junior Deacon, "Brother Junior, inquire the cause of that alarm. " The Junior Deacon then steps to the door and answers the three knocks that have been given by three more (the knocks are much louder than those given on any occasion, other than that of the admission of candidates in the several degrees); one knock is then given without, and answered by one from within, when the door is partly opened, and the Junior Deacon asks, "Who comes there? Who comes there? Who comes there?" The Senior Deacon answers, "A worthy brother, who has been regularly initiated as an Entered Apprentice Mason, passed to the degree of a Fellow Craft, and now wishes for further light in Masonry, by being raised to the sublime degree of a Master Mason." Junior Deacon to Senior Deacon, "Is it of his own free will and [Pg 38] accord he makes this request?" A. "It is." Junior Deacon to Senior Deacon, "Is he worthy and well qualified?" A. "He is." Junior Deacon to Senior Deacon, "Has he made suitable proficiency in the preceding degree?" A. "He has." Junior Deacon to Senior Deacon, "By what further rights does he expect to obtain this benefit?" A. "By the benefit of a pass-word." Junior Deacon to Senior Deacon, "Has he a pass-word?" A. "He has not, but I have it for him." Junior Deacon to Senior Deacon, "Will you give it to me?" The Senior Deacon then whispers in the ear of the Junior Deacon, " Tubal Cain ." Junior Deacon says, "The pass is right; since this is the case, you will wait till the Worshipful Master be made acquainted with his request, and his answer returned." The Junior Deacon then repairs to the Master, and gives three knocks, as at the door; after answering which, the same questions are asked and answers returned, as at the door; when the Master says, "Since he comes endued with all these necessary qualifications, let him enter this Worshipful Lodge in the name of the Lord, and take heed on what he enters." The Junior Deacon returns to the door and says, "Let him enter this Worshipful Lodge in the name of the Lord, and take heed on what he enters." In entering, both points of the Compass are pressed against his naked right and left breasts, when the Junior Deacon stops the candidate and says, "Brother, when you first entered this Lodge, you was received on the point of the Compass pressing your naked left breast, which was then explained to you; when you entered it the second time, you were received on the angle of the Square, which was also explained to you; on entering it now, you are received on the two extreme points of the Compass pressing your naked right and left breasts, which are thus explained: As the most vital points of man are contained between the two breasts, so are the most valuable tenets of Masonry contained between the two extreme points of the Compass, which are 'Virtue, Morality, and Brotherly Love. '" The Senior Deacon then conducts the candidate three times regularly around the Lodge. [I wish the reader to observe, that on this, as well as every other degree, the Junior Warden is the first of the three principal officers that the candidate passes, traveling with the Sun, when he starts around the Lodge, and as he passes the Junior Warden, Senior Warden, and Master, the first time going around, they each give one rap; the second time, two raps; and the third time, three raps. The number of raps given on those occasions are the same as the number of the degree, except the first degree, on which three are given, I always thought improperly.] During the time the candidate is traveling around the room, the Master reads the following passage of Scripture, the conductor and candidate traveling, and the Master reading, so that the traveling and reading terminates at the same time:

"Remember now thy Creator in the days of thy youth, while the evil days come not, nor the years draw nigh, when thou shalt say, I have no pleasure in them: while the Sun, or the Moon, or the Stars be not darkened, nor the clouds return after the rain; in the day when the keepers of the house shall tremble, and the strong men shall bow themselves, and the grinders cease because they are few, and those that look out of the windows be darkened, and the doors shall be shut in the streets; [Pg 39] when the sound of the grinding is low, and he shall rise up at the voice of the bird, and all the daughters of music shall be brought low. Also, when they shall be afraid of that which is high, and fears shall be in the way, and the almond tree shall flourish, and the grasshopper shall be a burden, and desire shall fail, because man goeth to his long home, and the mourners go about the streets. Or ever the silver cord be loosed, or the golden bowl be broken, or the pitcher be broken at the fountain, or the wheel at the cistern. Then shall the dust return to the earth, as it was; and the spirit return unto God who gave it."

The conductor and candidate halt at the Junior Warden in the South, where the same questions are asked and answers returned, as at the door; he is then conducted to the Senior Warden, where the same questions are asked and answers returned as before; from thence he is conducted to the Worshipful Master in the East, who asks the same questions and receives the same answers as before; and who likewise asks the candidate from whence he came, and whither he is traveling? Ans. "From the West, and traveling to the East." Q. "Why do you leave the West and travel to the East?" A. "In search of more light." The Master then says to the Senior Deacon, "You will please conduct the candidate back to the West, from whence he came, and put him in the care of the Senior Warden, and request him to teach the candidate how to approach the East, by advancing upon three upright regular steps to the third step, his feet forming a square, his body erect at the altar before the Worshipful Master, and place him in a proper position to take upon him the solemn oath or obligation of a Master Mason." The Master then comes to the candidate and says, "Brother, you are now placed in a proper position (the Lecture explains it) to take upon you the solemn oath or obligation of a Master Mason, which I assure you, as before, is neither to affect your religion nor politics. If you are willing to take it, repeat your name, and say after me:

"I, A. B., of my own free will and accord, in the presence of Almighty God, and this Worshipful Lodge of Master

Masons erected to God, and dedicated to the Holy Order of St. John, do hereby and hereon most solemnly and sincerely promise and swear, in addition to my former obligations, that I will not give the degree of a Master Mason to any one of an inferior degree, nor to any other being in the known world, except it be to a true and lawful brother, or brethren Master Masons, or within the body of a just and lawfully constituted Lodge of such; and not unto him, nor unto them, whom I shall hear so to be, but unto him and them only whom I shall find so to be, after strict trial and due examination, or lawful information received. Furthermore, do I promise and swear, that I will not give the Master's word, which I shall hereafter receive, neither in the Lodge, nor out of it, except it be on the five points of fellowship, and then not above my breath. Furthermore, do I promise and swear, that I will not give the grand hailing sign of distress, except I am in real distress, or for the benefit of the craft when at work; and should I ever see that sign given, or the word accompanying it, and the person who gave it appearing to be in distress, I will fly to his relief at the risk of my life, should there be a greater probability of saving his life than of losing my own. Furthermore, do I promise and swear, that I will not wrong this Lodge, nor a brother of this degree, to the value of one cent, knowingly, myself, nor suffer it to be done by others, if in my power to prevent it. Furthermore, do I promise and swear, that I will not be at the initiating, passing, and raising a candidate at one communication, without a regular dispensation from the Grand Lodge for the same. Furthermore, do I promise and swear, that I will not be at the initiating, passing, or raising a candidate in a clandestine Lodge, I knowing it to [Pg 40] be such. Furthermore, do I promise and swear, that I will not be at the initiating of an old man in dotage, a young man in nonage, an atheist, irreligious libertine, idiot, madman, hermaphrodite, nor woman. Furthermore, do I promise and swear, that I will not speak evil of a brother Master Mason, neither behind his back, nor before his face, but will apprise him of all approaching danger, if in my power. Furthermore, do I promise and swear, that I will not violate the chastity of a Master Mason's wife, mother, sister, or daughter, I knowing them to be such, nor suffer it to be done by others, if in my power to prevent it. Furthermore, do I promise and swear, that I will support the constitution of the Grand Lodge of the State of ———, under which this Lodge is held, and conform to all the by-laws, rules, and regulations of this, or any other Lodge, of which I may, at any time hereafter, become a member. Furthermore, do I promise and swear, that I will obey all regular signs, summons, or tokens given, handed, sent, or thrown to me from the hand of a brother Master Mason, or from the body of a just and lawfully constituted Lodge of such: provided it be within the length of my cable-tow. Furthermore, do I promise and swear, that a Master Mason's secrets, given to me in charge as such, and I knowing them to be such, shall remain as secure and inviolable in my breast as in his own, when communicated to me, murder and treason excepted; and they left to my own election. Furthermore, do I promise and swear, that I will go on a Master Mason's errand, whenever required, even should I have to go barefoot and bareheaded, if within the length of my cable-tow. [3] Furthermore, do I promise and swear, that I will always remember a brother Master Mason when on my knees, offering up my devotions to Almighty God. Furthermore, do I promise and swear, that I will be aiding and assisting all poor indigent Master Masons, their wives and orphans, wheresoever disposed 'round the globe, as far as in my power, without injuring myself or family materially. Furthermore, do I promise and swear, that if any part of this my solemn oath or obligation be omitted at this time, that I will hold myself amenable thereto, whenever informed. To all which I do most solemnly and sincerely promise and swear, with a fixed and steady purpose of mind in me, to keep and perform the same, binding myself under no less penalty than to have my body severed in two in the midst, and divided to the North and South, my bowels burnt to ashes in the centre, and the ashes scattered before the four winds of heaven, that there might not the least tract or trace of remembrance remain among men or Masons of so vile and perjured a wretch as I should be, were I ever to prove wilfully guilty of violating any part of this my solemn oath or obligation of a Master Mason; so help me God, and keep me steadfast in the due performance of the same."

The Master then asks the candidate, "What do you most desire?" The candidate answers after his prompter, "More light." The bandage which was tied 'round his head in the preparation room is, by one of the brethren who stands behind him for that purpose, loosened and put over both eyes, and he is immediately brought to light in the same manner as in the preceding degree, except three stamps on the floor, and three claps of the hands are given in this degree. On being brought to light, the Master says to the candidate, "You first discover, as before, three great lights in Masonry, by the assistance of three lesser, with this difference, both points of the Compass are elevated above the Square, which denotes to you that you are about to receive all the light that can be conferred on you in a Mason's Lodge." The Master steps back from the candidate and says, "Brother, you now discover me as Master of [Pg 41] this Lodge, approaching you from the East, under the sign and due-guard of a Master Mason." The sign is given by raising both hands and arms to the elbows perpendicularly, one on either side of the head, the elbows forming a square. The words accompanying this sign in case of distress are, "O Lord, my God, is there no help for the widow's son?" As the last words drop from your lips, you let your hands fall in that manner best calculated to indicate solemnity. King Solomon is said to have made this exclamation on the receipt of the information of the death of Hiram Abiff. Masons are all charged never to give the words except in the dark, when the sign cannot be seen. Here Masons differ very much; some contend that Solomon gave this sign, and made this exclamation when informed of Hiram's death, and work accordingly in their Lodges. Others say the sign was given, and the exclamation made at the grave when Solomon went there to raise Hiram, and, of course, they work accordingly; that is to say, the Master who governs a Lodge holding the latter opinion, gives the sign, &c., at the grave, when he goes to raise the body, and vice versa. The due-guard is given by putting the right hand to the left side of the bowels, the hand open, with the thumb next to the belly, and drawing it across the belly and let it fall; this is done tolerably quick. After the Master has given the sign and dueguard, which does not take more than a minute, he says, "Brother, I now present you with my right hand in token of brotherly love and affection, and with it the pass-grip and word." The passgrip is given by pressing the thumb between the joints of the second and third fingers, where they join the hand, and the word or name is Tubal Cain . It is the pass-word to the Master's degree. The Master, after having given the candidate the pass-grip and word, bids him rise and salute the Junior and Senior Wardens, and convince them that he is an obligated Master Mason, and is in possession of the pass-grip and word. While the Wardens are examining the candidate, the Master returns to the East and gets an apron, and as he returns to the candidate, one of the Wardens (sometimes both) says to the Master, "Worshipful, we are satisfied that Brother —— is an obligated Master Mason." The Master then says to the candidate, "Brother, I now have the honor to present you with a lamb-skin, or white apron, as before, which, I hope, you will continue to wear with credit to yourself, and satisfaction and advantage to the brethren; you will please carry it to the Senior Warden in the West, who will teach you how to wear it as a Master Mason."

The Senior Warden ties on his apron, and lets the flap fall down before in its natural and common situation.

The Master returns to his seat, and the candidate is conducted to him. Master to candidate, "Brother, I perceive you are dressed; it is, of course, necessary you should have tools to work with; I will now present you with the working tools of a Master Mason, and explain their uses to you. The working tools of a Master Mason are all the implements of Masonry indiscriminately, but more especially the Trowel. The Trowel is an instrument made use of by operative Masons to spread the cement which unites a building into one common mass; but we, as Free and Accepted Masons, are taught to make use of it for the more noble [Pg 42] and glorious purpose of spreading the cement of brotherly love and affection; that cement which unites us into one sacred band or society of friends and brothers, among whom no contention should ever exist, but that noble contention, or rather emulation, of who can best work, or best agree. I also present you with three precious jewels; their names are Humanity, Friendship, and Brotherly Love. Brother, you are not yet invested with all the secrets of this degree, nor do I know whether you ever will, until I know how you withstand the amazing trials and dangers that await you. You are now about to travel to give us a specimen of your fortitude, perseverance, and fidelity, in the preservation of what you have already received; fare you well, and may the Lord be with you, and support you through your trials and difficulties." [In some Lodges they make him pray before he starts.] The candidate is then conducted out of the Lodge, clothed, and returns; as he enters the door, his conductor says to him, "Brother, we are now in a place representing the SANCTUM SANCTORUM , or HOLY OF HOLIES , of King Solomon's Temple. It was the custom of our Grand Master, Hiram Abiff, every day at high twelve, when the crafts were from labor to refreshment, to enter into the sanctum sanctorum and offer up his devotions to the ever living God. Let us, in imitation of him, kneel and pray." They then kneel, and the conductor says the following prayer:

"Thou, O God, knowest our downsitting and uprising, and understandest our thoughts afar off; shield and defend us from the evil intentions of our enemies, and support us under the trials and afflictions we are destined to endure while traveling through this vale of tears. Man that is born of a woman is of few days and full of trouble. He cometh forth as a flower, and is cut down; he fleeth also as a shadow, and continueth not. Seeing his days are determined, the number of his months are with Thee: Thou hast appointed his bounds that he cannot pass; turn from him, that he may rest till he shall accomplish his day. For there is hope of a tree, if it be cut down, that it will sprout again, and that the tender branch thereof will not cease. But man dieth and wasteth away; yea, man giveth up the ghost, and where is he? As the waters fail from the sea, and flood decayeth and drieth up, so man lieth down and riseth not up till the heavens shall be no more. Yet, O Lord! have compassion on the children of Thy creation; administer unto them comfort in time of trouble, and save them with an everlasting salvation. Amen. So mote it be."

They then rise, and the conductor says to the candidate, "Brother, in further imitation of our Grand Master, Hiram Abiff, let us retire at the South gate." They then advance to the Junior Warden (who represents Jubela , one of the ruffians), who exclaims, "Who comes here?" [The room is dark, or the candidate hoodwinked.] The conductor answers, "Our Grand Master, Hiram Abiff." "Our Grand Master, Hiram Abiff!" exclaims the ruffian, "he is the very man I wanted to see (seizing the candidate by the throat at the same time, and jerking him about with violence); give me the Master Mason's word, or I'll take your life." The conductor replies, "I cannot give it now, but if you will wait till the Grand Lodge assembles at Jerusalem, if you are worthy, you shall then receive it, otherwise you cannot." The ruffian then gives the candidate a blow with the twenty-four-inch gauge across the throat, on which he fled to the West gate, where he was accosted by the second ruffian, [Pg 43] Jubelo, with more violence, and on his refusing to comply with his request, he gave him a severe blow with the Square across his breast; on which he attempted to make his escape at the East gate, where he was accosted by the third ruffian, Jubelum, with still more violence, and refusing to comply with his request, the ruffian gave him a violent blow with the common gavel on the forehead, which brought him to the floor, on which one of them exclaimed, "What shall we do, we have killed our Grand Master, Hiram Abiff?" Another answers, "Let us carry him out at the East gate and bury him in the rubbish till low twelve, and then meet and carry him a westerly course and bury him." The candidate is then taken up in a blanket, on which he fell, and carried to the West end of the Lodge, and covered up and left; by this time the Master has resumed his seat (King Solomon is supposed to arrive at the Temple at this juncture), and calls to order, and asks the Senior Warden the cause of all that confusion; the Senior Warden answers, "Our Grand Master, Hiram Abiff, is missing, and there are no plans or designs laid down on the Tressle-Board for the crafts to pursue their labor." The Master, alias King Solomon, replies, "Our Grand Master missing; our Grand Master has always been very punctual in his attendance; I fear he is indisposed; assemble the crafts, and search in and about the Temple, and see if he can be found." They all shuffle about the floor a while, when the Master calls them to order, and asks the Senior Warden, "What success?" He answers, "We cannot find our Grand Master, my Lord." The Master then orders the Secretary to call the roll of workmen, and see whether any of them are missing. The Secretary calls the roll, and says, "I have called the roll, my Lord, and find that there are three missing, viz.: Jubela, Jubelo and Jubelum." His Lordship then observes, "This brings to my mind a circumstance that took place this morning—twelve Fellow Crafts, clothed in white gloves and aprons, in token of their innocence, came to me and confessed that they twelve, with three others, had conspired to extort the Master Mason's word from their Grand Master, Hiram Abiff, and in case of refusal to take his life; they twelve had recanted, but feared the other three had been base enough to carry their atrocious designs into execution. " Solomon then ordered twelve Fellow Crafts to be drawn from the bands of the workmen, clothed in white aprons, in token of their Innocence, and sent three East, three West, three North, and three South, in search of the ruffians, and, if found, to bring them forward. Here the members all shuffle about the floor awhile, and fall in with a reputed traveler, and inquire of him if he had seen any traveling men that way; he tells them that he had seen three that morning near the coast of Joppa, who from their dress and appearance were Jews, and were workmen from the Temple, inquiring for a passage to Ethiopia, but were unable to obtain one, in consequence of an embargo which had recently been laid on all the shipping, and had turned back into the country. The Master now calls them to order again, and asks the Senior Warden, "What success?" He answers by relating what had taken place. Solomon observes, "I had this embargo laid to prevent the ruffians from making their escape;" and adds, "you will go and search [Pg 44] again, and search till you find them, if possible; and if they are not found, the twelve who confessed shall be considered as the reputed murderers, and suffer accordingly." The members all start again, and shuffle about awhile, until one of them, as if by accident, finds the body of Hiram Abiff, alias the candidate and hails his traveling companions, who join him, and while they are humming out something over the candidate, the three reputed ruffians, who are seated in a private corner near the candidate, are heard to exclaim in the following manner—first, Jubela, "O that my throat had been cut across, my tongue torn out, and my body buried in the rough sands of the sea at low-water mark, where the tide ebbs and flows twice in twenty-four hours, ere I had been accessory to the death of so good a man as our Grand Master, Hiram Abiff."

The second, Jubelo, "O that my left breast had been torn open, and my heart and vitals taken from thence, and thrown over my left shoulder, carried into the valley of Jehosaphat, and there to become a prey to the wild beasts of the field, and vultures of the air, ere I had conspired the death of so good a man as our Grand Master, Hiram Abiff. "

The third, Jubelum, "O that my body had been severed in two in the midst, and divided to the North and South, my bowels burnt to ashes in the centre, and the ashes scattered by the four winds of heaven, that there might not the least track or trace of remembrance remain among men or Masons of so vile and perjured a wretch as I am. Ah, Jubela and Jubelo, it was I that struck him harder than you both—it was I that gave him the fatal blow—it was I that killed him outright."

The three Fellow Crafts who had stood by the candidate all this time listening to the ruffians, whose voices they recognized, says one to the other, "What shall we do, there are three of them, and only three of us?" "It is," said one in reply, "our cause is good, let us seize them;" on which they rush forward, and carry them to the Master, to whom they relate what had passed. The Master then addresses them in the following manner (they in many Lodges kneel, or lie down, in token of their guilt and penitence): "Well, Jubela, what have you got to say for yourself—guilty or not guilty?" A. "Guilty, my Lord." " Jubelo, guilty or not guilty?" A. "Guilty, my Lord." " Jubelum, guilty or not guilty?" A. "Guilty, my Lord." The Master to the three Fellow Crafts who took them, "Take them without the West gate of the Temple, and have them executed according to the several imprecations of their own mouths." They are then hurried off to the West end of the room. Here this part of the farce ends. The Master then orders fifteen Fellow Crafts to be elected from the bands of the workmen, and sent three East, three West, three North, three South; and three in and about the Temple, in search of their Grand Master, Hiram Abiff [In some Lodges they only send twelve, when their own Lectures say fifteen were sent], and charges them if they find the body, to examine carefully on and about it for the Master's word, or a key to it. The three that traveled a Westerly course come to the candidate and finger about him a little, and are called to order by the Master, when they report that they have [Pg 45] found the grave of their Grand Master, Hiram Abiff, and, on moving the earth till they came to the body, they involuntarily found their hands raised in this position [showing it at the same time; it is the due-guard of this degree], to guard their nostrils against the offensive affluvia which arose from the grave; and that they had searched carefully on and about the body for the Master's word, but had not discovered anything but a faint resemblance of the letter G on the left breast. The Master, on the receipt of this information (raising himself), raises his hand three several times above his head (as herein before described), and exclaims twice, "Nothing but a faint resemblance of the letter G! that is not the Master's word, nor a key to it, I fear the Master's word is forever lost!" [The third exclamation is different from the others—attend to it; it has been described in pages 40 and 41.] "Nothing but a faint resemblance of the letter G! that is not the Master's word, nor a key to it." "O Lord, my God, is there no help for the widow's son?" The Master then orders the Junior Warden to summon a Lodge of Entered Apprentice Masons, and repair to the grave to raise the body of their Grand Master, by the Entered Apprentice's grip. They go to the candidate and take hold of his forefinger and pull it, and return and tell the Master that they could not raise him by the Entered Apprentice's grip; that the skin cleaved from the bone. A Lodge of Fellow Crafts are then sent, who act as before, except that they pull the candidate's second finger. The Master then directs the Senior Warden [generally] to summon a Lodge of Master Masons, and says, "I will go with them myself in person, and try to raise the body by the Master's grip, or lion's paw." [Some say by the strong grip, or the lion's paw.] They then all assemble around the candidate, the Master having declared the first word spoken after the body was raised, should be adopted as a substitute for the Master's word, for the government of Master Mason's Lodges in all future generations; he proceeds to raise the candidate, alias the representative of the dead body of Hiram Abiff. He [the candidate] is raised on what is called the five points of fellowship, which are foot to foot, knee to knee, breast to breast, hand to back, and mouth to ear. This is done by putting the inside of your right foot to the inside of the right foot of the person to whom you are going to give the word, the inside of your knee to his, laying your right breast against his, your left hands on the back of each other, and your mouths to each other's right ear [in which position you are alone permitted to give the word], and whisper the word Mah-hah-bone . The Master's grip is given by taking hold of each other's right hand, as though you were going to shake hands, and sticking the nails of each of your fingers into the joint of the other's wrist, where it unites with the hand. In this position the candidate is raised, he keeping his whole body stiff, as though dead. The Master, in raising him, is assisted by some of the brethren, who take hold of the candidate by the arms and shoulders. As soon as he is raised to his feet they step back, and the Master whispers the word Mah-hah-bone in his ear, and causes the candidate to repeat it, telling him at the same time that he must never give it in any manner other than that in which he receives it. He is also told that Mah-hah-bone [Pg 46] signifies marrow in the bone. They then separate, and the Master makes the following explanation respecting the five points of fellowship. Master to candidate, "Brother, foot to foot teaches you that you should, whenever asked, go on a brother's errand, if within the length of your cable-tow, even if you should have to go barefoot and bareheaded. Knee to knee, that you should always remember a Master Mason in your devotion to Almighty God. Breast to breast, that you should keep the Master Mason's secrets, when given to you in charge as such, as secure and inviolable in your breast, as they were in his own, before communicated to you. Hand to back, that you should support a Master Mason behind his back, as well as before his face. Mouth to ear, that you should support his good name as well behind his back as before his face."

After the candidate is through with what is called the work part, the Master addresses him in the following manner: "Brother, you may suppose from the manner you have been dealt with tonight, that we have been fooling with you, or that we have treated you different from others, but I assure you that is not the case. You have, this night, represented one of the greatest men that ever lived, in the tragical catastrophe of his death, burial, and resurrection; I mean Hiram Abiff, the widow's son, who was slain by three ruffians at the building of King Solomon's Temple, and who, in his inflexibility, integrity, and fortitude, never was surpassed by man. The history of that momentous event is thus related. Masonic tradition informs us that at the building of King Solomon's Temple, fifteen Fellow Crafts discovering that the Temple was almost finished, and not having the Master Mason's word, became very impatient, and entered into a horrid conspiracy to extort the Master Mason's word from their Grand Master, Hiram Abiff, the first time they met him alone, or take his life, that they might pass as Masters in other countries, and receive wages as such; but before they could accomplish their designs, twelve of them recanted, but the other three were base enough to carry their atrocious designs into execution. Their names were Jubela , Jubelo , and Jubelum .

"It was the custom of our Grand Master, Hiram Abiff, every day at high twelve, when the crafts were from labor to refreshment, to enter into the sanctum sanctorum, and offer his devotions to the ever living God, and draw out his plans and designs on the Tressle-Board for the crafts to pursue their labor. On a certain day (not named in any of our traditional accounts), Jubela, Jubelo and Jubelum placed themselves at the South, West, and East gates of the Temple, and Hiram having finished his devotions and labor, attempted (as was his usual custom) to retire at the South gate, where he was met by Jubela, who demanded of him the Master Mason's word (some say the secrets of a Master Mason), and on his refusal to give it, Jubela gave him a violent blow with a twenty-four-inch gauge across the throat; on which Hiram fled to the West gate, where he was accosted in the same manner by Jubelo, but with more violence. Hiram told him that he could not give the word then, because Solomon, King of Israel, Hiram, King of Tyre, and himself had entered into a solemn league that the word never should be given, [Pg 47] unless they three were present; but if he would have patience till the Grand Lodge assembled at Jerusalem, if he was then found worthy he should then receive it, otherwise he could not; Jubelo replied in a very peremptory manner, "If you do not give me the Master's word, I'll take your life;" and on Hiram's refusing to give it, Jubelo gave him a severe blow with the Square across the left breast, on which he fled to the East gate, where he was accosted by Jubelum, in the same manner, but with still more violence. Here Hiram reasoned as before; Jubelum told him that he had heard his caviling with Jubela and Jubelo long enough, and that the Master's word had been promised to him from time to time for a long time; that he was still put off, and that the Temple was almost finished, and he was determined to have the word or take his life. "I want it so that I may be able to get wages as a Master Mason in any country to which I may go for employ, after the Temple is finished, and that I may be able to support my wife and children." Hiram persisting in his refusal, he gave Hiram a violent blow with the gavel on the forehead, which felled him to the floor and killed him; they took the body and carried it out of the West gate, and buried it in the rubbish till low twelve at night (which is twelve o'clock), when they three met agreeably to appointment, and carried the body a westerly course, and buried it at the brow of a hill, in a grave, dug due East and West, six feet perpendicular, and made their escape. King Solomon coming up to the Temple at low six in the morning (as was his usual custom), found the crafts all in confusion, and on inquiring the cause, was informed that their Grand Master, Hiram Abiff, was missing, and there was no plans or designs laid down on the Tressle-Board, for the crafts to pursue their labor. Solomon ordered search to be made inland about the Temple for him; no discovery being made, he then ordered the Secretary to call the roll of workmen to see if any were missing; it appearing that there were three, viz.: Jubela, Jubelo and Jubelum, Solomon observed, "This brings to my mind a circumstance that took place this morning. Twelve Fellow Crafts came to me, dressed in white gloves and aprons, in token of their innocence, and confessed that they twelve, with three others, had conspired to extort the Master Mason's word from their Grand Master, Hiram Abiff, and in case of his refusal to take his life; they twelve had recanted, but feared the three others had been base enough to carry their atrocious designs into execution." Solomon immediately ordered twelve Fellow Crafts to be selected from the bands of the workmen, clothed in white gloves and aprons, in token of their innocence, and sent three East, three West, three North, and three South, in search of the ruffians, and, if found, to bring them up before him. The three that traveled a westerly course, coming near the coast of Joppa, fell in with a wayfaring man, who informed them that he had seen three men pass that way that morning, who, from their appearance and dress, were workmen from the Temple, inquiring for a passage to Ethiopia, but were unable to obtain one, in consequence of an embargo which had recently been laid on all the shipping, and had turned back into the country. After making further and more diligent search, and making no further discovery, they returned to the Temple and reported [Pg 48] to Solomon the result of their pursuit and inquiries. On which Solomon directed them to go again, and search until they found their Grand Master, Hiram Abiff, if possible; and if he was not found, the twelve who had confessed should be considered as the murderers, and suffer accordingly.

They returned again in pursuit of the ruffians, and one of the three that traveled a westerly course, being more weary than the rest, sat down at the brow of a hill to rest and refresh himself; and, in attempting to rise, caught hold of a sprig of cassia, which easily gave, and excited his curiosity, and made him suspicious of a deception; on which he hailed his companions, who immediately assembled, and, on examination, found that the earth had been recently moved; and on moving the rubbish, discovered the appearance of the grave, and while they were confabulating about what measures to take, they heard voices issuing from a cavern in the clefts of the rocks, on which they immediately repaired to the place, where they heard the voice of Jubela exclaim: "O that my throat had been cut across, my tongue torn out, and my body buried in the rough sands of the sea at low-water mark, where the tide ebbs and flows twice in twenty-four hours, ere I had been accessory to the death of so good a man as our Grand Master, Hiram Abiff"—on which they distinctly heard the voice of Jubelo exclaim, "O that my left breast had been torn open, and my heart and vitals taken from thence, and thrown over my left shoulder, carried into the valley of Jehosaphat, there to become a prey to the wild beasts of the field, and vultures of the air, ere I had conspired to take the life of so good a man as our Grand Master, Hiram Abiff"—when they more distinctly heard the voice of Jubelum exclaim, "O that my body had been severed in two in the midst, and divided to the North and the South, my bowels burnt to ashes in the centre, and the ashes scattered by the four winds of heaven, that there might not remain the least trace of remembrance among men or Masons of so vile and perjured a wretch as I am, who wilfully took the life of so good a man as our Grand Master, Hiram Abiff. Ah, Jubela and Jubelo, it was I that struck him harder than you both—it was I that gave him the fatal blow—it was I that killed him outright!" on which they rushed forward, seized, bound, and carried them before King Solomon, who, after hearing the testimony of the three Fellow Crafts, and the three ruffians having pleaded guilty, order them to be taken out at the West gate of the Temple, and executed agreeably to the several imprecations of their own mouths. King Solomon then ordered fifteen Fellow Crafts to be elected from the bands of the workmen, clothed with white gloves and aprons, in token of their innocence, and sent three East, three West, three North, three South; and three in and about the Temple, in search of the body of our Grand Master, Hiram Abiff; and the three that traveled a westerly course found it under a sprig of cassia, where a worthy brother sat down to rest and refresh himself; and on removing the earth till they came to the coffin, they involuntarily found their hands raised, as hereinbefore described, to guard their nostrils against the offensive effluvia that 'rose from the [Pg 49] grave. It is also said that the body had lain there fourteen days; some say fifteen.

The body was raised in the manner herein before described, carried up to the Temple, and buried as explained in the closing clauses of the Lecture. Not one-third part of the preceding history of this degree is ever given to a candidate. A few general, desultory, unconnected remarks are made to him, and he is generally referred to the manner of raising, and to the Lecture, for information as to the particulars. Here follows a charge which ought to be, and sometimes is, delivered to the candidate after hearing the history of the degree.

An Address to be Delivered to the Candidate after the History Has Been Given.

"Brother, your zeal for the institution of Masonry, the progress you have made in the mystery, and your conformity to our regulations, have pointed you out as a proper object of our favor and esteem.

"You are bound by duty, honor, and gratitude to be faithful to your trust; to support the dignity of your character on every occasion; and to enforce, by precept and example, obedience to the tenets of the Order.

"In the character of a Master Mason you are authorized to correct the errors and irregularities of your uninformed brethren, and to guard them against a breach of fidelity.

"To preserve the reputation of the fraternity unsullied, must be your constant care, and for this purpose, it is your province to recommend to your inferiors, obedience and submission; to your equals, courtesy and affability; to your superiors, kindness and condescension. Universal benevolence you are always to inculcate; and, by the regularity of your own behavior, afford the best example for the conduct of others less informed. The ancient landmarks of the Order, entrusted to your care, you are carefully to preserve; and never suffer them to be infringed, or countenance a deviation from the established usages and customs of the fraternity.

"Your virtue, honor, and reputation are concerned in supporting, with dignity, the character you now bear. Let no motive, therefore, make you swerve from your duty, violate your vow, or betray your trust: but be true and faithful, and imitate the example of that celebrated artist whom you this evening represent: thus you will render yourself deserving the honor which we have conferred, and merit the confidence that we have reposed."

Here follows the Lecture on this degree, which is divided into three sections.

FIRST SECTION.

Question—Are you a Master Mason? Answer—I am; try me; disprove me if you can.

Q. Where were you prepared to be made a Master Mason? A. In a room adjacent to the body of a just and lawfully constituted Lodge of such, duly assembled in a room, representing the SANCTUM SANCTORUM, or HOLY OF HOLIES, of King Solomon's Temple.

Q. How were you prepared? A. By being divested of all metals; neither naked nor clothed; barefooted nor shod; with a cable-tow three times about my naked body; in which posture I was conducted to the door of the Lodge, where I gave three distinct knocks.

[Pg 50] Q. What did those three distinct knocks allude to? A. To the third degree in Masonry; it being that on which I was about to enter.

Q. What was said to you from within? A. Who comes there? Who comes there? Who comes there?

Q. Your answer? A. A worthy brother, who has been regularly initiated as an Entered Apprentice Mason, passed to the degree of a Fellow Craft, and now wishes for further light in Masonry, by being raised to the sublime degree of a Master Mason.

Q. What further was said to you from within? A. I was asked if it was of my own free will and accord I made this request; if I was duly and truly prepared; worthy and well qualified; and had made suitable proficiency in the preceding degree; all of which being answered in the affirmative, I was asked by what further rights I expected to obtain that benefit.

Q. Your answer? A. By the benefit of a pass-word.

Q. What was that pass-word? A. Tubal Cain.

Q. What was next said to you? A. I was bid to wait till the Worshipful Master in the East was made acquainted with my request, and his answer returned.

Q. After his answer was returned, what followed? A. I was caused to enter the Lodge on the two extreme points of the Compass pressing my right and left breasts, in the name of the Lord.

Q. How were you then disposed of? A. I was conducted three times regularly around the Lodge and halted at the Junior Warden in the South, where the same questions were asked and answers returned, as at the door.

Q. How did the Junior Warden dispose of you? A. He ordered me to be conducted to the Senior Warden in the West, where the same questions were asked and answers returned as before.

Q. How did the Senior Warden dispose of you? A. He ordered me to be conducted to the Worshipful Master in the East, where the same questions were asked, and answers returned as before; who likewise demanded of me from whence I came, and whither I was traveling.

Q. Your answer? A. From the West, and traveling to the East.

Q. Why do you leave the West and travel to the East? A. In search of light.

Q. How did the Worshipful Master dispose of you? A. He ordered me to be conducted back to the West, from whence I came, and put in care of the Senior Warden, who taught me how to approach the East, by advancing upon three upright regular steps to the third step, my feet forming a square, and my body erect at the altar before the Worshipful Master.

Q. What did the Worshipful Master do with you? A. He made an obligated Master Mason of me.

Q. How? A. In due form.

Q. What was that due form? A. Both my knees bare bent, they forming a square; both hands on the Holy Bible, Square, and Compass; in which posture I took upon me the solemn oath or obligation of a true Master Mason.

[Pg 51] Q. After your obligation, what was said to you? A. What do you most desire.

Q. Your answer? A. More light. [The bandage around the head is now dropped over the eyes.]

Q. Did you receive light? A. I did.

Q. On being brought to light on this degree, what did you first discover? A. Three great lights in Masonry, by the assistance of three less, and both points of the Compass elevated above the Square, which denoted to me that I had received, or was about to receive, all the light that could be conferred on me in a Master's Lodge.

Q. What did you next discover? A. The Worshipful Master approaching me from the East, under the sign and dueguard of a Master Mason, who presented me with his right hand in token of brotherly love and confidence, and proceeded to give me the pass-grip and word of a Master Mason [the word is the name of the pass-grip], and bid me rise and salute the Junior and Senior Wardens, and convince them that I was an obligated Master Mason, and had the sign, pass-grip, and word (Tubal Cain).

Q. What did you next discover? A. The Worshipful Master approaching me a second time from the East, who presented me with a lamb-skin, or white apron, which, he said, he hoped I would continue to wear with honor to myself, and satisfaction and advantage to the brethren.

Q. What were you next presented with? A. The working tools of a Master Mason.

Q. What are they? A. All the implements of Masonry indiscriminately, but more especially the Trowel.

Q. How explained? A. The Trowel is an instrument made use of by operative Masons to spread the cement which unites a building into one common mass; but we, as Free and Accepted Masons, are taught to make use of it for the more noble and glorious purposes of spreading the cement of brotherly love and affection; that cement which unites us into one sacred band, or society of brothers, among whom no contention should ever exist, but that noble emulation of who can best work, or best agree.

Q. What were you next presented with? A. Three precious jewels.

Q. What are they? A. Humanity, Friendship, and Brotherly Love.

Q. How were you then disposed of? A. I was conducted out of the Lodge, and invested of what I had been divested, and returned again in due season.

SECOND SECTION.

Question—Did you ever return to the SANCTUM SANCTORUM , or HOLY OF HOLIES , of King Solomon's Temple? Answer—I did.

Q. Was there anything in particular took place on your return? A. There was, viz., I was accosted by three ruffians, who demanded of me the Master Mason's word.

Q. Did you ever give it to them? A. I did not, but bid them wait, with time and patience, till the Grand Lodge assembled at Jerusalem, and [Pg 52] then, if they were found worthy, they should receive it, otherwise they could not.

Q. In what manner was you accosted? A. In attempting to retire at the South gate, I was accosted by one of them, who demanded of me the Master Mason's word, and, on my refusing to comply with his request, he gave me a blow with the twenty-four-inch gauge across my breast, on which I fled to the West gate, where I was accosted by the second with more violence, and, on my refusing to comply with his request, he gave me a severe blow with the Square across my breast; on which I attempted to make my escape at the East gate, where I was accosted by the third with still more violence, and, on my refusing to comply with his request, he gave me a violent blow with the common gavel on the forehead, and brought me to the floor.

Q. Whom did you represent at that time? A. Our Grand Master, Hiram Abiff, who was slain at the building of King Solomon's Temple.

Q. Was his death premeditated? A. It was—by fifteen Fellow Crafts, who conspired to extort from him the Master Mason's word; twelve of whom recanted, but the other three were base enough to carry their atrocious designs into execution.

Q. What did they do with the body? A. They carried it out at the West gate of the Temple, and buried it till low twelve at night, when they three met agreeably to appointment, and carried it a westerly course from the Temple, and buried it under the brow of a hill, in a grave six feet, due East and West, six feet perpendicular, and made their escape.

Q. What time was he slain? A. At high twelve at noon, when the crafts were from labor to refreshment.

Q. How came he to be alone at that

time? A. Because it was the usual custom of our Grand Master, Hiram Abiff, every day at high twelve, when the crafts were from labor to refreshment, to enter into the SANCTUM SANCTORUM, or HOLY OF HOLIES, and offer up his adorations to the ever-living God, and draw out his plans and designs on his Tressle-Board, for the crafts to pursue their labor.

Q. At what time was he missing? A. At low six in the morning, when King Solomon came up to the Temple, as usual, to view the work, and found the crafts all in confusion; and, on inquiring the cause, he was informed that their Grand Master, Hiram Abiff, was missing, and no plans or designs were laid down on the Tressle-Board for the crafts to pursue their labor.

Q. What observations did King Solomon make at that time? A. He observed that our Grand Master, Hiram Abiff, had always been very punctual in attending, and feared that he was indisposed, and ordered search to be made in and about the Temple, to see if he could be found.

Q. Search being made, and he not found, what further remarks did King Solomon make? A. He observed he feared some fatal accident had befallen our Grand Master, Hiram Abiff; that morning twelve Fellow Crafts, clothed in white gloves and aprons, in token of their innocence, had confessed that they twelve with three others, had conspired to extort the Master Mason's word from their Grand Master, Hiram Abiff, [Pg 53] or take his life; that they twelve had recanted, but feared the other three had been base enough to carry their atrocious designs into execution.

Q. What followed? A. King Solomon ordered the roll of workmen to be called, to see if there were any missing.

Q. The roll being called, were there any missing? A. There were three, viz., Jubela, Jubelo, and Jubelum.

Q. Were the ruffians ever found? A. They were.

Q. How? A. By the wisdom of King Solomon, who ordered twelve Fellow Crafts to be selected from the bands of the workmen, clothed in white gloves and aprons, in token of their innocence, and sent three East, three West, three North, and three South, in search of the ruffians, and, if found, to bring them forward.

Q. What success? A. The three that traveled a westerly course from the Temple, coming near the coast of Joppa, were informed by a wayfaring man, that three men had been seen that way that morning, who, from their appearance and dress, were workmen from the Temple, inquiring for a passage to Ethiopia, but were unable to obtain one, in consequence of an embargo which had recently been laid on all the shipping, and had turned back into the country.

Q. What followed? A. King Solomon ordered them to go and search again, and search till they were found, if possible; and if they were not found, that the twelve who had confessed should be considered as the reputed murderers, and suffer accordingly.

Q. What success? A. One of the three that traveled a westerly course from the Temple, being more weary than the rest, sat down under the brow of a hill to rest and refresh himself; and, in attempting to rise, caught hold of a sprig of cassia, which easily gave way, and excited his curiosity, and made him suspicious of a deception; on which he hailed his companions, who immediately assembled, and, on examination, found that the earth had recently been moved; and on moving the rubbish, discovered the appearance of a grave, and while they were confabulating about what measures to take, they heard voices issuing from a cavern in the clefts of the rocks, on which they immediately repaired to the place, where they heard the voice of Jubela exclaim: "O that my throat had been cut across, my tongue torn out, and my body buried in the rough sands of the sea at low-water mark, where the tide ebbs and flows twice in twenty-four hours, ere I had been accessory to the death of so good a man as our Grand Master, Hiram Abiff"—on which they distinctly heard the voice of Jubelo exclaim, "O that my left breast had been torn open, and my heart and vitals taken from thence, and thrown over my left shoulder, carried into the valley of Jehosaphat, there to become a prey to the wild beasts of the field, and vultures of the air, ere I had conspired to take the life of so good a man as our Grand Master, Hiram Abiff"—when they more distinctly heard the voice of Jubelum exclaim, "O that my body had been severed in two in the midst, and divided to the North and the South, my bowels burnt to ashes in the centre, and the ashes scattered by the four winds of heaven, that there might not [Pg 54] remain the least track or trace of remembrance among men or Masons of so vile and perjured a wretch as I am, who wilfully took the life of so good a man as our Grand Master, Hiram Abiff. Ah, Jubela and Jubelo, it was I that struck him harder than you both—it was I that gave him the fatal blow—it was I that killed him outright!" on which they rushed forward, seized, bound, and carried them up before King Solomon.

Q. What did King Solomon do with them? A. He ordered them to be executed agreeably to the several imprecations of their own mouths.

Q. Was the body of our Grand Master, Hiram Abiff, ever found? A. It was.

Q. How? A. By the wisdom of King Solomon, who ordered fifteen (in some Lodges they say twelve) Fellow Crafts to be selected from the bands of the workmen, and sent three East, three West, three North, and three South; and three in and about the Temple, in search of the body.

Q. Where was it found? A. Under that sprig of cassia, where a worthy brother sat down to rest and refresh himself.

Q. Was there anything particular took place on the discovery of the body? A. There was, viz.: On removing the earth till they came to the coffin, they involuntarily found their hands raised in this position to guard their nostrils against the offensive effluvia that 'rose from the grave.

Q. How long had the body lain there? A. Fourteen days.

Q. What did they do with the body? A. Raised it in a Masonic form, and carried it up to the Temple for more decent interment.

Q. Where was it buried? A. Under the SANCTUM SANCTORUM , or HOLY OF HOLIES , of King Solomon's Temple, over which they erected a marble monument, with this inscription delineated thereon: A virgin weeping over a broken column, with a book open before her; in her right hand a sprig of cassia; in her left, an urn; Time standing behind her, with his hands infolded in the ringlets of her hair.

Q. What do they denote? A. The weeping virgin denotes the unfinished state of the Temple; the broken column, that one of the principal supporters of Masonry had fallen; the open book before her, that his memory was on perpetual record; the sprig of cassia, the timely discovery of his grave; the urn in her left hand, that his ashes were safely deposited under the SANCTUM SANCTORUM , or HOLY OF HOLIES , of King Solomon's Temple; and Time standing behind her, with his hands infolded in the ringlets of her hair, that time, patience, and perseverance will accomplish all things.

THIRD SECTION.

Question—What does a Master's Lodge represent? Answer—The SANCTUM SANCTORUM , or HOLY OF HOLIES , of King Solomon's Temple.

Q. How long was the Temple building? A. Seven years; during which it rained not in the daytime, that the workmen might not be obstructed in their labor.

[Pg 55] Q. What supported the Temple? A. Fourteen hundred and fifty-three columns, and two thousand, nine hundred and six pilasters, all hewn from the finest Parian marble.

Q. What further supported it? A. Three grand columns, or pillars.

Q. What were they called? A. Wisdom, Strength, and Beauty.

Q. What did they represent? A. The pillar of Wisdom represented Solomon, King of Israel, whose wisdom contrived the mighty fabric; the pillar of Strength, Hiram, King of Tyre, who strengthened Solomon in his glorious undertaking; the pillar of Beauty, Hiram Abiff, the widow's son, whose cunning craft and curious workmanship beautified and adorned the Temple.

Q. How many were there employed in the building of King Solomon's Temple? A. Three Grand Masters; three thousand, three hundred Masters, or overseers of the work; eighty thousand Fellow Crafts, and seventy thousand Entered Apprentices; all those were classed and arranged in such a manner, by the wisdom of Solomon, that neither envy, discord, nor confusion were suffered to interrupt that universal peace and tranquility that pervaded the work at that important period.

Q. How many constitutes an Entered Apprentice's Lodge? A. Seven; one Master and six Entered Apprentices.

Q. Where did they usually meet? A. On the ground floor of King Solomon's Temple.

Q. How many constitutes a Fellow Craft's Lodge? A. Five; two Masters and three Fellow Crafts.

Q. Where did they usually meet? A. In the middle chamber of King Solomon's Temple.

Q. How many constitutes a Master's Lodge? A. Three Master Masons.

Q. Where did they usually meet? A. In the SANCTUM SANCTORUM , or HOLY OF HOLIES , of King Solomon's Temple.

Q. Have you any emblems on this degree? A. We have several, which are divided into two classes.

Q. What are the first class? A. The pot of incense; the bee-hive; the book of constitutions, guarded by the Tyler's sword; the sword, pointing to a naked heart; the all-seeing eye; the anchor and ark; the forty-seventh problem of Euclid; the hour-glass; the scythe; and the three steps usually delineated on the Master's carpet, which are thus explained: The pot of INCENSE is an emblem of a pure heart, which is always an acceptable sacrifice to the Deity; and as this glows with fervent heat, so should our hearts continually glow with gratitude to the great and beneficent Author of our existence, for the manifold blessings and comforts we enjoy. The BEE-HIVE is an emblem of industry, and recommends the practice of that virtue to all created beings, from the highest seraph in heaven to the lowest reptile of the dust. It teaches us that as we came into the world rational and intelligent beings, so we should ever be industrious ones; never sitting down contented while our fellow-creatures around us are in want, when it is in our power to relieve them, without inconvenience to ourselves. When we take a survey of nature, we behold man, in his infancy, more helpless and indigent than the brute creation; he lies languishing for days, weeks, months, and [Pg 56] years, totally incapable of providing sustenance for himself; of guarding against the attacks of the field, or sheltering himself from the inclemencies of the weather. It might have pleased the great Creator of heaven and earth to have made man independent of all other beings, but as independence is one of the strongest bonds of society, mankind were made dependent on each other for protection and security, as they thereby enjoy better opportunities of fulfilling the duties of reciprocal love and friendship. Thus was man formed for social and active life, the noblest part of the work of God; and he, who will so demean himself as not to be endeavoring to add to the common stock of knowledge and understanding, may be deemed a DRONE in the HIVE of nature, a useless member of society, and unworthy of our protection as Masons. The BOOK OF CONSTITUTIONS, GUARDED BY THE TYLER'S SWORD , reminds us that we should be ever watchful and guarded, in our thoughts, words, and actions, and particularly when before the enemies of Masonry; ever bearing in remembrance those truly masonic virtues, SILENCE and CIRCUMSPECTION . The SWORD , POINTING TO A NAKED HEART , demonstrates that justice will sooner or later overtake us; and, although our thoughts, words, and actions may be hidden from the eyes of men, yet that ALL-SEEING EYE , whom the SUN , MOON , and STARS obey, and under whose watchful care even comets perform their stupendous revolutions, pervades the inmost recesses of the human heart, and will reward us according to our merits. The ANCHOR and ARK are emblems of a well-grounded hope and well-spent life. They are emblematical of that divine ARK which safely wafts us over this tempestuous sea of troubles, and that ANCHOR which shall safely moor us in a peaceful harbor, where the wicked cease from troubling, and the weary shall find rest. The forty-seventh problem of Euclid —this was an invention of our ancient friend and brother, the great Pythagoras, who, in his travels through Asia, Africa, and Europe, was initiated into several orders of priesthood, and raised to the sublime degree of a Master Mason.

This wise philosopher enriched his mind abundantly in a general knowledge of things, and more especially in Geometry or Masonry; on this subject he drew out many problems and theorems; and among the most distinguished, he erected this, which, in the joy of his heart, he called Eureka , in the Grecian language signifying, I have found it ; and upon the discovery of which he is said to have sacrificed a hecatomb. It teaches Masons to be general lovers of the arts and sciences. The HOUR-GLASS is an emblem of human life. Behold! how swiftly the sands run, and how rapidly our lives are drawing to a close. We cannot, without astonishment behold the little particles which are contained in this machine; how they pass away almost imperceptibly, and yet, to our surprise, in the short space of an hour they are all exhausted.

Thus wastes man to-day; he puts forth the tender leaves of hope; to-morrow, blossoms, and bears his blushing honors thick upon him; the next day comes a frost, which nips the shoot, and when he thinks his greatness is still ripening, he falls, like autumn leaves, to enrich our mother earth. The SCYTHE is an emblem of time, which cuts the brittle thread of life, and launches us into eternity. Behold! what havoc the [Pg 57] scythe of time makes among the human race; if, by chance, we should escape the numerous evils incident to childhood and youth, and, with health and vigor, arrive to the years of manhood, yet withal, we must soon be cut down by the all-devouring scythe of time, and be gathered into the land where our fathers had gone before us. The THREE STEPS , usually delineated upon the Master's carpet, are emblematical of the three principal stages of human life, viz.: Youth, Manhood, and Age. In youth, as Entered Apprentices, we ought industriously to occupy our minds in the attainment of useful knowledge; in manhood, as Fellow Crafts, we should apply our knowledge to the discharge of our respective duties to God, our neighbors, and ourselves; so that in age, as Master Masons, we may enjoy the happy reflections consequent on a well-spent life, and die in the hope of a glorious immortality.

Q. What are the second class of emblems? A. The spade, coffin, death-head, marrow bones, and sprig of cassia, which are thus explained: The SPADE opens the vault to receive our bodies, where our active limbs will soon moulder to dust. The COFFIN , DEATH-HEAD , and MARROW BONES are emblematical of the death and burial of our Grand Master, Hiram Abiff, and are worthy our serious attention. The SPRIG OF CASSIA is emblematical of that immortal part of man which never dies; and when the cold winter of death shall have passed, and the bright summer's morn of the resurrection appears, the Son of Righteousness shall descend, and send forth his angels to collect our ransomed dust; then, if we are found worthy, by his pass-word we shall enter into the Celestial Lodge above, where the Supreme Architect of the Universe presides, where we shall see the King in the beauty of holiness, and with him enter into an endless fraternity.

Here ends the first three degrees of Masonry, which constitutes a Master Mason's Lodge. A Master Mason's Lodge and a Chapter of Royal Arch Masons are two distinct bodies, wholly independent of each other. The members of a Chapter are privileged to visit all Master Mason's Lodges when they please; and may be, and often are, members of both at the same time; and all the members of a Master Mason's Lodge who are Royal Arch Masons, though not members of any Chapter, may visit any Chapter. I wish the reader to understand that neither all Royal Arch Masons nor Master Masons are members of either Lodge or Chapter; there are tens of thousands who are not members, and scarcely ever attend, although privileged to do so.

A very small proportion of Masons, comparatively speaking, ever advance any further than the third degree, and consequently never get the great word which was lost by Hiram's untimely death. Solomon, King of Israel, Hiram, King of Tyre, and Hiram Abiff, the widow's son, having sworn that they, nor either of them, would ever give the word, except they three were present (and it is generally believed that there was not another person in the world, at that time, that had it), consequently the word was lost, and supposed to be forever; but the sequel will show it was found, after a lapse of four hundred and seventy years; notwithstanding, the word Mah-hah-bone , which was substituted by Solomon, still continues to be used by Master Masons, and no doubt will, [Pg 58] as long as Masonry attracts the attention of men; and the word which was lost is used in the Royal Arch Degree. What was the word of the Royal Arch Degree before they found the Master's word, which was lost at the death of Hiram Abiff, and was not found for four hundred and seventy years? Were there any Royal Arch Masons before the Master's word was found? I wish some masonic gentleman would solve these two questions.

The ceremonies, histories, and the Lecture, in the preceding degree are so similar that perhaps some one of the three might have been dispensed with, and the subject well understood by most readers, notwithstanding there is a small difference between the work and history, and between the history and the Lecture.

I shall now proceed with the Mark Master's degree, which is the first degree in the Chapter. The Mark Master's degree, the Past Master's, and the Most Excellent Master's, are Lodges of Mark Master Masons, Past Master, and Most Excellent Master; yet, although called Lodges, they are called component parts of the Chapter. Ask a Mark Master Mason if he belongs to the Chapter; he will tell you he does, but that he has only been marked. It is not an uncommon thing, by any means, for a Chapter to confer all four of the degrees in one night, viz:—the Mark Master, Past Master, Most Excellent Master, and Royal Arch degrees.

Test-Oath and Word.

The following "test-oath and word" were invented and adopted by the "Grand Lodge" of the State of New York, at their Session in June, 1827, for the purpose of guarding against Book Masons. They are given in a Master's Lodge. They were obtained from a gentleman in high standing in society, and among Masons, but a friend to Anti-Masonry. He was a member of the "Grand Lodge," and present when they were adopted.

A person wishing to be admitted into the Lodge, presents himself at the door; the Tyler (or some brother from within) demands or asks, "Do you wish to visit this Lodge?" The candidate for admission says, "If thought worthy." Tyler —"By what are you recommended?" Ans. —"By fidelity." Tyler says, "Prove that;" at the same time advances and throws out his hand or arm to an angle of about forty-five degrees obliquely forward, the hand open, and thumb upward. The candidate then advances, and places the back of his LEFT HAND against the PALM of the Tyler's RIGHT HAND —still extended puts his mouth to the Tyler's ear and whispers, L-O-S, and pronounces LOS.
Test-Oath. —"I, A. B., of my own free will and accord, in the presence of Almighty God, solemnly and sincerely promise and swear that I will not communicate the secret test-word, annexed to this obligation, to any but a true and lawful Master Mason, and that in the body of a lawful Lodge of such, in actual session, or at the door of a Lodge, for the purpose of gaining admission; under the penalty of being forever disgraced and dishonored as a man, and despised, degraded, and expelled as a Mason."

[Pg 59]

FOURTH, OR MARK MASTER'S DEGREE.

Ceremonies Used in Opening a Lodge of Mark Master Masons.

One rap calls the Lodge to order; one calls up the Junior and Senior Deacons; two raps call up the subordinate officers; and three, all the members of the Lodge. The Right Worshipful Master having called the Lodge to order, and all being seated, the Right Worshipful Master says to the Junior Warden, "Brother Junior, are they all Mark Master Masons in the South?" Junior Warden answers, "They are, Right Worshipful." R. W. M.—"I thank you, brother. " R. W. M.—"Brother Senior, are they all Mark Master Masons in the West?" Senior Warden—"They are, Right Worshipful." R. W. M.—"They are in the East." At the same time gives a rap with the mallet which calls up both Deacons. R. W. M.—"Brother Junior, the first care of a Mason?" "To see the Lodge tyled, Right Worshipful." R. W. M.—"Attend to that part of the duty, and inform the Tyler that we are about to open a Lodge of Mark Master Masons, and direct him to tyle accordingly." Junior Deacon steps to the door and gives four raps, which are answered by four without by the Tyler; the Junior Deacon then gives one, which is answered by the Tyler with one; the door is then partly opened, and the Junior Deacon then delivers his message and resumes his station, gives the due-guard of a Mark Master Mason, and says, "The door is tyled, Right Worshipful." R. W. M.—"By whom?" J. D.—"By a Mark Master Mason without the door, armed with the proper implements of his office." R. W. M.—"His duty there?" J. D.—"To keep off all cowans and eavesdroppers, see that none pass or repass without permission from the Right Worshipful Master." R. W. M.—"Brother Junior, your place in the Lodge?" J. D.—"At the right hand of the Senior Warden in the West." R. W. M.—"Your business there, Brother Junior?" J. D.—"To wait on the Right Worshipful Master and Wardens, act as their proxy in the active duties of the Lodge, and take care of the door." R. W. M.—"The Senior Deacon's place in the Lodge?" J. D.—"At the right hand of the Worshipful Master in the East." R. W. M.—"I thank you, brother." He then gives two raps with the mallet, and the subordinate officers rise. R. W. M.—"Your duty there, Brother Senior?" S. D.—"To wait on the Right Worshipful Master and Wardens, act as their proxy in the active duties of the Lodge, attend to the preparation and introduction of candidates, and welcome and clothe all visiting brethren." R. W. M.—"The Secretary's place in the Lodge, Brother Junior?" J. D.—"At the right hand of the Worshipful Master in the East." R. W. M.—"I thank you, brother. Your duty there, Brother Secretary?" Sec.—"The better to observe the Right Worshipful Master's will and pleasure; record the proceedings of the Lodge; transmit the same to the Grand Lodge, if required; receive all monies and money-bills from the hands of the brethren, pay them over to the Treasurer, and take his receipt for the same." R. W. M.—"The Treasurer's place in the Lodge?" Sec. —"At the right hand of the Right Worshipful Master." R. W. M.—"I thank you, brother. Your duty there, Brother Treasurer?" Treasurer—"Duly to observe the Right Worshipful Master's will and pleasure; receive all [Pg 60] monies and money-bills from the hands of the Secretary; give a receipt for the same; keep a just and true account of the same; pay them out by order of the Right Worshipful Master and consent of the brethren." R. W. M.—"The Junior Overseer's place in the Lodge, Brother Treasurer?" Treas.—"At the right hand of the Junior Warden in the South, Right Worshipful." R. W. M.—"I thank you, brother. Your business there, Brother Junior Overseer?" J. O.—"To inspect all material brought up for the building of the Temple; approve or disapprove of the same; and, if approved, pass it on to the Senior Overseer for further inspection." R. W. M.—"The Senior Overseer's place in the Lodge?" J. O.—"At the right hand of the Senior Warden in the West, Right Worshipful." R. W. M.—"I thank you, brother. Your business there, Brother Senior Overseer?" S. O.—"To inspect all materials brought up for the building of the Temple; and, if approved, pass it on to the Master Overseer at the East gate for further inspection." R. W. M.—"The Master Overseer's place in the Lodge, Brother Senior Overseer?" S. O.—"At the right hand of the Right Worshipful Master in the East." R. W. M.—"I thank you, brother. Your business there, Brother Master Overseer?" M. O.—"To assist in the inspection of all materials brought up for the building of the Temple; and if disapproved, to call a council of my brother Overseers." R. W. M.—"The Junior Warden's place in the Lodge, Brother Master Overseer?" M. O.—"In the South, Right Worshipful." R. W. M.—"I thank you, brother. Your business there, Brother Junior?" J. W.—"As the sun in the South, at high meridian, is the beauty and glory of the day, so stands the Junior Warden in the South, the better to observe the time, call the crafts from labor to refreshment, superintend them during the hours thereof, see that none convert the hours of refreshment into that of intemperance or excess, and call them on again in due season, that the Right Worshipful Master may have honor, and they pleasure and profit thereby." R. W. M.—"The Senior Warden's place in the Lodge?" J. W.—"In the West, Right Worshipful." R. W. M.—"I thank you, brother. Your duty there, Brother Senior?" S. W.—"As the sun sets in the West to close the day, so stands the Senior Warden in the West, to assist the Right Worshipful in opening and closing the Lodge; take care of the jewels and implements; see that none be lost; pay the craft their wages, if any be due; and see that none go away dissatisfied." R. W. M.—"The Master's place in the Lodge?" S. W.—"In the East, Right Worshipful." R. W. M.—"His duty there?" S. W.—"As the sun rises in the East to open and adorn the day, so presides the Right Worshipful Master in the East to open and adorn his Lodge, set his crafts to work, and govern them with good and wholesome laws, or cause the same to be done." R. W. M.—"I thank you, brother." Gives three raps with the mallet, which calls up all the brethren, takes off his hat and says, "In like manner, so do I, strictly prohibiting all profane language, private committees, or any other disorderly conduct, whereby the peace and harmony of this Lodge may be interrupted, while engaged in its lawful pursuits; under no less penalty than the by-laws enjoin, or a majority of the brethren present may see cause to inflict. Brethren, attend to giving the signs." [Pg 61] The Right Worshipful Master (all the brethren imitating him) extends his left arm from his body, so as to form an angle of about forty-five degrees, and holds his right hand transversely across his left, the palms thereof about an inch apart. This is called the first sign of a Mason—is the sign of distress in the first degree, and alludes to the position a candidate's hands are placed when he takes the obligation of an Entered Apprentice Mason; he then draws his right hand across his throat, the hand open, with his thumb next his throat, drops it down by his side. This is called the due-guard of an Entered Apprentice Mason, and alludes to the penal part of the obligation. Next he places the palm of his open right hand upon his left breast, and, at the same time, throws up his left hand, and so extends his left arm as to form a right angle; from the shoulder to the elbow it is horizontal, from the elbow to the tip of the finger it is perpendicular. This is the sign and due-guard of a Fellow Craft Mason, and also alludes to the penal part of the obligation, which is administered in this degree. After this, the Right Worshipful Master draws his right hand across his bowels, with his hand open, and thumb next his body, and drops it down by his side. This is the sign or due-guard of a Master Mason, and, like the others, alludes to the penalty of this degree. He then throws up the grand hailing sign of distress; this is given by raising both hands and arms to the elbow, perpendicularly, one on each side of the head, the elbows forming a square, his arms then drop by his side; he then clutches the third and little fingers of his right hand; with his thumb extended at the same time, his middle and forefingers, brings up his hand in such a manner as to have the side of the middle finger touch the rim of the right ear, then lets it drop, and, as it falls, brings the outward side of the little finger of the left hand across the wrist of the right, then lets them fall by his sides. This is the sign or dueguard of a Mark Master Mason, and also alludes to the penal part of the obligation in this degree. Here it is proper to remark that in the opening of any Lodge of Masons, they commence giving the signs of an Entered Apprentice, and go through all the signs of the different degrees, in regular gradation, until they arrive to the one which they are opening, and commence at the sign of the degree in which they are at work, and descend to the last when closing. After going through all the signs, as before described, the Right Worshipful Master declares the Lodge opened in the following manner: "I now declare this Lodge of Mark Master Masons duly opened for the dispatch of business." The Senior Warden declares it to the Junior Warden, and he to the brethren. The Right Worshipful Master then repeats a charge: "Wherefore, brethren, lay aside all malice and guile," &c., &c.

The Lodge being opened and ready for business, the Right Worshipful Master directs the Secretary to read the minutes of the last meeting, which generally brings to view the business of the present. If there are any candidates to be brought forward, that is generally the first business. A Master Mason, wishing for further light in Masonry, sends a petition to the Chapter, and requests to be advanced to the honorary degree of Mark Master Mason; if there is no serious objection to the petition, it is entered on the minutes, and a committee of several appointed [Pg 62] to inquire into his character, and report to the next regular communication: at that time, if the committee report in his favor, and no serious objection is made against him otherwise, a motion is made that the ballot pass; if carried, the Deacons pass the ballot boxes; these boxes are the same as in the preceding degrees. When the balls are received, the box is presented to the Right Worshipful Master, Senior and Junior Wardens. R. W. M.—"Clear in the West, Brother Senior?" S. W.—"Clear, Right Worshipful." R. W. M.—"Clear in the South, Brother Junior?" J. W.—"Clear, Right Worshipful." Right Worshipful Master says, "Clear in the East." This being the case, the candidate is accepted; but if there is one black ball in that end of the box which has the white tube, and the Senior Warden pronouncing "Not clear," all stop, and inquiry is made, and the ballot passes again; and, if blacked a third time, the candidate is rejected. It being otherwise, the Senior Deacon, who is the candidate's conductor, passes out of the Lodge into the adjoining room, where the candidate is in waiting, and there the conductor is furnished with a small oblong square, six inches long; the candidate is presented with a large white marble keystone, weighing, probably, twenty pounds, and is ordered, by his conductor, to take it by the little end, between his first and second fingers and thumb of his right hand. The door is then opened without ceremony, and they pass directly to the Junior Overseer's station at the South gate, which is nothing more than the Junior Warden's seat, and the conductor gives four raps, with his block of timber, on a pedestal in front of the Junior Overseer's station. J. O.—"Who comes here?" Cond.—"Two brother Fellow Crafts, with materials for the Temple." J. O.—"Have you a specimen of your labor?" Cond.—"I have." J. O.—"Present it." The conductor then presents the piece of timber before described; the Junior Overseer receives it, and applies a small trying square to its different angles, and they agreeing with the angles of the square, he says, "This is good work, square work, such work as we are authorized to receive." Returns the block of timber, and turning his eye upon the candidate, asks, "Who is this you have with you?" Cond.—"A brother Fellow Craft." J. O.—"Have you a specimen of your labor?" Cand.—"I have." J. O.—"Present it." The candidate then presents the keystone; the Junior Overseer receives it, and applies his square to all its angles, and they not agreeing with the angles of the square, he says, "What have you here, brother? this is neither an oblong nor a square, neither has it the regular mark of the craft upon it, but from its singular form and beauty, I am unwilling to reject it; pass on to the Senior Overseer at the West gate for further inspection." They then pass on to the Senior Overseer's station at the West gate, which is the Senior Warden's seat, and give four raps, as before, on the pedestal which stands in front of the Senior Overseer. S. O.—"Who comes here?" Cond.—"Two brother Fellow Crafts, with materials for the Temple." S. O.—"Have you a specimen of your labor?" Cond.—"I have." S. O. —"Present it." The conductor, as before, presents the block of timber; the Senior Overseer applies his square to it, and finding it agrees with the angles of his square, says, "This is good work, square work, such [Pg 63] work as we are authorized to receive; who is this you have with you?" Cond.—"A brother Fellow Craft." S. O.—"Have you a specimen of your labor?" Cand.—"I have." S. O.—"Present it." The candidate then presents the keystone, and he applies it, but not fitting, he says, "This is neither an oblong nor a square, neither has it the regular mark of the craft upon it; it is a curious wrought stone, and on account of its singular form and beauty, I am unwilling to reject it; pass on to the Master Overseer at the East gate for further inspection." They pass to to his station at the East gate, and give four raps. M. O.—"Who comes here?" Cond.—"Two brethren, Fellow Crafts, with their materials for the Temple." M. O.—"Have you a specimen of your labor?" Cond.—"I have." M. O.—"Present it." The conductor presents his billet of wood to him, applies his square to it, and, like the other Overseers, says, "This is good work, square work, such work as we are authorized to receive; who is this you have with you?" Cond. —"A brother Fellow Craft." M. O.—"Have you a specimen of your labor?" Cand.—"I have." M. O.—"Present it." [It ought here to be remarked that when the candidate is presented with the keystone, and takes it between his thumb and two fingers, it hangs suspended by his side, and he is requested to carry his work plumb, and the conductor taking good care to see that he does it, by the time he arrives at the Master Overseer's station at the East gate, and when the Master Overseer says "Present it," the candidate is extremely willing to hand over the keystone to him for inspection; for, by this time, it becomes very painful to hold any longer the stone which he has in charge.] The Master Overseer having received the keystone, he applies his square to the different angles of it, and, being found not to be square, he, like the other Overseers, says, "This is neither an oblong nor a square, neither has it the regular mark of the craft upon it." He then looks sternly upon the candidate and demands, "Is this your work?" Cand.—"It is not." M. O.—"Is this your mark?" Cand.—"It is not." M. O.—"Where did you get it?" Cond.—"I picked it up in the quarry. " M. O.—"Picked it up in the quarry? this explains the matter; what! been loitering away your time this whole week, and now brought up another man's work to impose upon the Grand Overseers! this deserves the severest punishment. [Motions the candidate to stand.] Brother Junior and Senior Overseers, here is work brought up for inspection which demands a council." The Junior, Senior, and Master Overseers then assemble in council. M. O., presenting the stone—"Did a Fellow Craft present this to you for inspection, Brother Junior?" J. O.—"A Fellow Craft came to my office and presented this stone for inspection; I examined it, and found it was neither an oblong nor a square, neither, had it the regular mark of the craft upon it; but on account of its singular form and beauty, I was unwilling to reject it, and ordered it to the Senior Overseer at the West gate for further inspection." M. O.—"Brother Senior, was this stone presented to you for inspection?" S. O.—"It was; I know of no use for it in the Temple; I tried it with the square, and observed it was neither an oblong nor a square, neither had it the regular mark of the craft upon it; but on account of its singular form and beauty, I was unwilling to reject it, and, therefore, directed it [Pg 64] to the Master Overseer at the East gate for further inspection." M. O.—"It was also presented to me for inspection, but I do not know of any use which it can be in the building." S. O.—"I know of no use for it." J. O.—"I know of no use for it." M. O.—"Brother Senior, what shall we do with it?" S. O.—"Heave it over among the rubbish." The Master and Senior Overseers then take the stone between them, and after waving it backward and forward four times, they heave it over in such a manner that the one letting go while the stone is arriving at the highest point, it brings the stone in a quarterly direction over the other's left shoulder; the Junior Overseer, being stationed in a suitable position, at this moment receives the stone, and carries it away into the preparation room. R. W. M.—"Brother Senior Warden, assemble the crafts to receive wages." At this command the brethren all arise, and form a procession single file; the candidate is placed at the head of the procession, and when stationed, is told that "the last shall be first, and the first last." The procession being formed, they commence singing the following song: "Mark Masters all appear," &c., and, at the same time, commence a circular march (against the course of the sun) around the room, giving all the signs during their march, beginning with that of Entered Apprentice, and ending at that of Mark Master. They are given in the following manner: The first revolution each brother, when opposite the Right Worshipful Master, gives the first sign in Masonry. The second revolution, when opposite the Master, the second; and so on, until they give all the signs to that of Mark Master. While the ceremony is going on in the Lodge, the Senior Grand Warden procures a sufficient number of cents and passes into the preparation room, and opens a lattice window in the door which communicates to the Lodge room, and when the craftsmen arrive to the Mark Master Mason's sign, each of them, in their last revolution, puts his hand through the window in the door and gives a token (this is given by shutting the third and little fingers, extending the fore and middle fingers, and placing the thumb over them in a suitable manner to receive the penny or cent), and receives a penny or cent from the Senior Grand Warden. Matters are so timed in the march, that when they come to that part of the song which says, "Caution them to beware of the right hand," it comes the turn of the candidate to put his hand through the aperture of the door and receive his penny, but not being able to give the token, he is detected as an impostor, and the Senior Grand Warden, instead of giving him his penny, seizes him by the hand and draws his arm full length through the door and holds him securely, exclaiming at the same time, "An impostor! an impostor!" Others, who are in the room with the Senior Grand Warden, cry out, "Chop off his hand! chop off his hand!" At this moment the conductor steps to the candidate and intercedes warmly in his behalf. Cond.—"Spare him! spare him!" S. G. W.—"He is an impostor. He has attempted to receive wages without being able to give the token. The penalty must be inflicted." Cond.—"He is a brother Fellow Craft, and on condition that you will release him, I will be responsible that he shall be taken before the Right Worshipful Master, where all the circumstances shall be made known, and, if he condemns [Pg 65] him, I will see that the penalty is inflicted." S. G. W.—"On these conditions, I release him." The candidate is released, and taken before the Right Worshipful Master. Cond.—"This young Fellow Craft has brought up work for inspection, which was not his own, and has attempted to receive wages for it; he was detected at the Senior Grand Warden's apartment as an impostor, and I became responsible, on condition of his release, that he should appear before the Right Worshipful, and, if, after a fair trial, you should pronounce him guilty, that I should see the penalty of an impostor inflicted upon him." R. W. M.—"Brother Junior Overseer, did this man bring up work to your station for inspection?" J. O.—"He did. I inspected it, and observed that it was neither an oblong nor a square, neither had it the regular mark of the craft upon it; but on account of its singular form and beauty, I was unwilling to reject it; therefore, I ordered it passed to the Senior Overseer's station at the West gate for further inspection." R. W. M.—"Brother Senior Overseer, did this young man bring up work to you for inspection?" S. O.—"He did; and I, for similar reasons offered by Brother Junior Overseer, was unwilling to reject it, and ordered it passed on to the Master Overseer at the East gate for further inspection." R. W. M.—"Brother Master Overseer, did this young man bring up work to you for inspection?" M. O.—"He did. I inspected the work, and observed that it was neither an oblong nor a square, neither had it the regular mark of the craft upon it; I then asked him if it was his work. He admitted that it was not. I asked him where he got it; he said he picked it up in the quarry. I rebuked him severely for his attempt to impose upon the Grand Overseers, and for loitering away his time, and then bringing up another man's work for inspection. I then called a council of my brother Overseers, and we, knowing no use for the work, hove it over among the rubbish." R. W. M.—"Senior Grand Warden, did the young man attempt to receive wages at your apartment?" S. G. W.—"He did, and I detected him as an impostor, and was about to inflict the penalty, but the conductor becoming responsible, that if I would release him, he would see the impostor taken before the Right Worshipful, and, if found guilty, that the penalty should be inflicted, I released him." R. W. M.—"Young man, it appears that you have been loitering away your time this whole week, and have now brought up another man's work for inspection, to impose upon the Grand Overseers, and what is more, you have attempted to receive wages for labor which you never performed; conduct like this deserves prompt punishment. The penalty of an impostor is that of having his right hand chopped off. This young man appears as though he deserved a better fate, and as though he might be serviceable in the building of the Temple. Are you a Fellow Craft?" Cand.—"I am." R. W. M.—"Can you give us any proof of it?" Candidate gives the sign of a Fellow Craft. R. W. M.—"He is a Fellow Craft. Have you ever been taught how to receive wages?" Cand.—"I have not." R. W. M.—"This serves, in a measure, to mitigate his crime. If you are instructed how to receive wages, will you do better in future, and never again attempt to impose on the Grand Overseers, and, above all, never attempt to receive wages for [Pg 66] labor which you never performed." Cand.—"I will." R. W. M.—"The penalty is remitted." The candidate is then taken into the preparation room and divested of his outward apparel, and all money and valuables, his breast bare, and a cable-tow four times around his body; in which condition he is conducted to the door, when the conductor gives four distinct knocks, upon the hearing of which the Senior Warden says to the Right Worshipful, "While we are peaceably at work on the fourth degree of Masonry, the door of our Lodge appears to be alarmed." R. W. M.—"Brother Junior, see the cause of that alarm." The Junior Warden then steps to the door and answers the alarm by four knocks, the conductor and himself each giving another; the door is then partly opened, and the Junior Warden then asks, "Who comes there?" Cond.—"A worthy brother, who has been regularly initiated as an Entered Apprentice, served a proper time as such; passed to the degree of Fellow Craft; raised to the sublime degree of a Master Mason; and now wishes further light in Masonry, by being advanced to the more honorable degree of a Mark Master Mason." J. W.—"Is it of his own free will and accord he makes this request?" Cond.—"It is." J. W.—"Is he duly and truly prepared?" Cond.—"He is." J. W.—"Has he wrought in the quarry, and exhibited specimens of his skill in the preceding degrees?" Cond.—"He has." J. W.—"By what further right or benefit does he expect to obtain this favor?" Cond.—"By the benefit of a pass-word." J. W.—"Has he a pass-word?" Cond.—"He has not, but I have it for him." J. W.—"Give it to me." Conductor whispers in his ear, " Joppa ." J. W.—"The password is right. You will let him wait until the Right Worshipful Master is made acquainted with his request and his answer returned." The Junior Warden returns him to the Right Worshipful Master, where the same questions are asked and answers returned, as at the door. The Right Worshipful Master then says, "Since he comes endowed with the necessary qualifications, let him enter in the name of the Lord, and take heed on what he enters. [Previous to the candidate's entering, one of the brethren, who is best qualified for the station, is selected and furnished with an engraving chisel and mallet, and placed near the door, so that when the candidate enters, it is on the edge of an engraving chisel, under the pressure of the mallet. As this is the business of no particular officer, we have, for convenience, styled him executioner.] Brother, it becomes my duty to put a mark on you, and such a one, too, as you will probably carry to your grave." Places the edge of the chisel near his left breast and makes several motions with the mallet, as though he was about to strike upon the head of the chisel. Executioner—"This is a painful undertaking; I do not feel able to perform it, Right Worshipful (turning to the Right Worshipful Master); this task is too painful; I feel that I cannot perform it; I wish the Right Worshipful would select some other brother to perform it in my stead." R. W. M.—"I know the task is unpleasant, and a painful one; but as you have undertaken to perform it, unless some other brother will volunteer his service and take your place, you must proceed." Exec—"Brother (calling the name), will you volunteer your service and take my place?" Brother—"I cannot consent to do it [Pg 67] (after several solicitations and refusals)." Exec.—"Right Worshipful, no brother feels willing to volunteer his services, and I declare I feel unwilling and unable to perform it." R. W. M.—"As no brother feels disposed to take your station, it becomes your duty to perform it yourself." Exec. (taking his station) "Brethren, support the candidate (several take hold of the candidate); brother (naming some physician or surgeon), will you assist?" Doctor (stepping up)—"Brethren, it becomes necessary that we should have a bowl, or some other vessel, to receive the blood." A bowl is presented, having the appearance of blood upon it, and is held in a suitable position to receive the blood; the surgeon places his fingers on the left breast of the candidate, and gives counsel where it would be advisable to inflict the wound. The executioner then places the edge of the chisel near the spot and draws back the mallet, and while making several false motions, says, "Operative Masons make use of the engraving chisel and mallet to cut, hew, carve, and indent their work; but we, as Free and Accepted Masons, make use of them for a more noble and glorious purpose; we use them to cut, hew, carve, and indent the mind;" giving, at the instant the last word is pronounced, a severe blow with the mallet upon the head of the chisel, without the least injury to the candidate, which often terrifies him to an alarming degree. The candidate is then conducted four times around the Lodge, and each time, as he passes the station of the Master, Senior and Junior Wardens, they each give one loud rap with their mallet; the Master, in the meantime, reads the following passages of Scripture: Psalms cxviii. 22. "The stone which the builders refused is become the headstone of the corner." Matt. xxi. 42. "Did ye never read in the Scriptures the stone which the builders rejected, the same is become the head of the corner?" Luke xx. 17. "What is this, then, that is written: The stone which the builders rejected, the same is become the head of the corner?" Acts iv. 11. "This is the stone which was set at nought of you builders which is become the head of the corner." The reading of them is so timed as to be completed just as the candidate arrives at the Junior Warden's post; here he stops, and the same questions are asked and answers returned, as at the door; the same passes at the Senior Warden and Master, who orders the candidate to be conducted back to the Senior Warden in the West, by him to be taught to approach the East by four upright regular steps, his feet forming a square, and body erect at the altar; the candidate then kneels and receives the obligation, as follows:

"I, A. B., of my own free will and accord, in presence of Almighty God, and this Right Worshipful Lodge of Mark Master Masons, do hereby and hereon, in addition to my former obligations, most solemnly and sincerely promise and swear, that I will not give the degree of a Mark Master Mason to anyone of an inferior degree, nor to any other person in the known world, except it be to a true and lawful brother or brethren of this degree, and not unto him nor unto them whom I shall hear so to be, but unto him and them only whom I shall find so to be, after strict trial and due examination, or lawful information given. Furthermore, do I promise and swear, that I will support the constitution of the General Grand Royal Arch Chapter of the United States of America, also the Grand Royal Arch Chapter of this State, under which this Lodge is held, and conform to all the by-laws, rules and regulations of this or any other Lodge of Mark Master Masons, of which I may at [Pg 68] any time hereafter become a member. Furthermore, do I promise and swear that I will obey all regular signs and summons given, handed, sent, or thrown to me from the hand of a brother Mark Master Mason, or from the body of a just and legally constituted Lodge of such, provided it be within the length of my cable tow. Furthermore do I promise and swear, that I will not wrong this Lodge, or a brother of this degree, to the value of his wages (or one penny), myself, knowingly, nor suffer it to be done by others, if in my power to prevent it. Furthermore, do I promise and swear, that I will not sell, swap, barter or exchange my mark, which I shall hereafter choose, nor send it a second time to pledge until it is lawfully redeemed from the first. Furthermore, do I promise and swear, that I will receive a brother's mark when offered to me requesting a favor, and grant him his request, if in my power and if it is not in my power to grant his request, I will return him his mark with the value thereof, which is half a shekel of silver, or quarter of a dollar. To all of which I do most solemnly and sincerely promise and swear, with a fixed and steady purpose of mind in me, to keep and perform the same, binding myself under no less penalty than to have my right ear smote off, that I may forever be unable to hear the word, and my right hand chopped off, as the penalty of an impostor, if I should ever prove wilfully guilty of violating any part of this my solemn oath or obligation of a Mark Master Mason. So help me God, and make me steadfast to keep and perform the same."

"Detach your hand and kiss the book"

The Master then produces the same keystone, concerning which so much has already been said, and says to the candidate, "We read in a passage of Scripture—Rev. II 17 'To him that overcometh will I give to each of the hidden manna, and will give him a white stone, and in the stone a new name written, which no man knoweth save him that receiveth it'" He then presents the stone to the candidate and says, 'I now present you with a white stone, on which is written a new name; we give the words that form this circle (the letters are so engraved on the stone as to form a circle), the initials are H T W S S T K S—Hiram Tyran, Widow's Son, sent to King Solomon. These, placed in this form were the mark of our Grand Master, Hiram Abiff. At present they are used as the general MARK of this degree, and in the centre of them each brother places his own individual MARK .' The stone is removed, and the candidate still remains on his knees at the altar, the Master then takes the jewel containing his mark from his neck and presents it to the candidate—requests of him some favor, such as the loan of five, ten, or twenty dollars. The candidate having left all his money and valuables in the preparation room, answers, "I cannot do it. I have no money about me," and offers to return the MARK to the Master, but he refuses to take it, and says to the candidate, "Have you not just sworn that you will receive a brother Mark Master's mark when offered to you, requesting a favor, and if not in your power to grant the favor, you would return him his mark with the value of it? Is this the way you mind your obligations? Here I presented my mark with a request for a small favor; you say you cannot grant it, and offer to return my MARK alone? Where is the quarter of a dollar you have sworn to return with it?" The candidate, much embarrassed, answers, "I cannot do even that. I have no money about me. It was all taken from me in the preparation room. " The Master asks, "Are you quite sure you have none?" Candidate answers, "I am, it is all in the other room." [Pg 69] Master—"You have not examined; perhaps some friend has, in pity to your destitute situation, supplied you with that amount unknown to yourself; feel in all your pockets, and if you find, after a thorough search, that you have really none, we shall have less reason to think that you meant wilfully to violate your obligation." The candidate examines his pockets and finds a quarter of a dollar, which some brother had slyly placed there; this adds not a little to his embarrassment; he protests he had no intention of concealing it; really supposed he had none about him, and hands it to the Master, with his mark. The Master receives it and says to the candidate, "Brother, let this scene be a striking lesson to you: should you ever hereafter have a mark presented you by a worthy brother, asking a favor, before you deny him make diligent search, and be quite sure of your inability to serve him; perhaps you will then find, as in the present instance, that some unknown person has befriended you, and you are really in a better situation than you think yourself." The candidate then rises and is made acquainted with the grips, words, and signs of this degree. The pass-grip of this degree is made by extending the right arms and clasping the fingers of the right hands, as one would naturally do to assist another up a steep ascent; the pass-word is "Joppa;" the real grip is made by locking the little fingers of the right hand, bringing the knuckles together, placing the ends of the thumbs against each other; the word is "Mark well." The signs have been described. After the grips, words, and signs are given and explained (see Lectures), the Master says, "Brother, I now present you with the tools of a Mark Master (here he points them out in the carpet, or in the chart), which are the chisel and mallet; they are thus explained: The chisel morally demonstrates the advantages of discipline and education; the mind, like the diamond in its original state, is rude and unpolished, but as the effect of the chisel on the external coat soon presents to view the latent beauties of the diamond, so education discovers the latent beauties of the mind, and draws them forth to range the large field of matter and space, to display the summit of human knowledge, our duty to God and man. The mallet morally teaches to correct irregularities, and to reduce man to a proper level; so that by quiet deportment, he may, in the school of discipline, learn to be content. What the mallet is to the workmen, enlightened reason is to the passions; it curbs ambition, it depresses envy, it moderates anger, and it encourages good dispositions, whence arises among good Masons that comely order,

'Which nothing earthly gives, or can destroy,
The soul's calm sunshine, and the heartfelt joy.'"

The Worshipful Master then delivers a charge to the candidate, which completes the ceremony of advancement to this degree.

Ceremonies Generally Gone Through in Closing a Lodge of Mark Masons.

The Worshipful Master says, "Brother Junior Warden, assemble the brethren, and form a procession for the purpose of closing the Lodge." [Pg 70] The brethren then assemble and commence a circular march, singing the song, "Mark Masons all appear." After the song is completed, the brethren compare the wages they have received, and finding that all have received alike (one penny or cent), they begin to murmur among themselves, some pretending to think they ought to have more, as they have done all the labor. They finally throw down their wages upon the altar, declaring if they cannot be dealt justly with, they will have none. The Worshipful Master calls to order, and demands the cause of the confusion. Some brother answers, "Worshipful, we are not satisfied with the manner of paying the workmen, for we find those who have done nothing, and even the candidate just received, is paid just as much as we, who have borne the heat and burden of the day." Master says, "It is perfectly right." Brother—"It cannot be right—it is very unreasonable." Master—"Hear what the law says on the subject." He then reads the following parable—Matt. XX. 1-16. "For the kingdom of heaven is like unto a man that is a householder, which went out early in the morning to hire laborers into his vineyard. And when he had agreed with the laborers for a penny a day, he sent them into his vineyard. And he went out about the third hour, and saw others standing idle in the market-place, and said unto them, 'Go ye also into the vineyard, and whatsoever is right, I will give you.' And they went their way. Again he went out about the sixth and ninth hour, and did likewise. And about the eleventh hour he went out and found others standing idle, and saith unto them, 'Why stand ye here all the day idle?' They say unto him, 'Because no man hath hired us.' He saith unto them, 'Go ye also into the vineyard, and whatsoever is right, that shall ye receive.' So when even was come, the lord of the vineyard said unto his steward, 'Call the laborers, and give them their hire, beginning from the last unto the first.' And when they came that were hired about the eleventh hour, they received every man a penny. But when the first came, they supposed that they should have received more, and they likewise received every man a penny. And when they had received it, they murmured against the good man of the house, saying, 'These last have wrought but one hour, and thou hast made them equal unto us, which have borne the burden and heat of the day.' But he answered one of them and said, 'Friend, I do thee no wrong; didst thou not agree with me for a penny? Take that thine is, and go thy way; I will give unto this last even as unto thee. Is it not lawful for me to do what I will with mine own? Is thine eye evil because I am good? So the last shall be first, and the first last; for many be called, but few chosen.'" The brethren then declare themselves satisfied; the signs are given from Mark Master down to the Entered Apprentice, and the Master declares the Lodge closed.

Lecture on the Fourth Degree of Masonry, or Mark Master's Degree.

FIRST SECTION.

Question—Are you a Mark Master Mason? Answer—I am; try me.

Q. By what will you be tried? A. By the engraving chisel and mallet.

[Pg 71] Q. Why by the engraving chisel and mallet? A. Because they are the proper masonic implements of this degree.

Q. On what was the degree founded? A. On a certain keystone which belonged to the principal arch of King Solomon's Temple.

Q. Who formed this keystone? A. Our worthy Grand Master, Hiram Abiff.

Q. What were the preparatory steps relative to your advancement to this degree? A. I was caused to represent one of the Fellow Craft at the building of King Solomon's Temple, whose custom it was, on the eve of every sixth day, to carry up their work for inspection.

Q. Why was you caused to represent these Fellow Crafts? A. Because our worthy Grand Master, Hiram Abiff, had completed this keystone agreeable to the original plan, and before he gave orders to have it carried up to the Temple, was slain by three ruffians, as already represented in the preceding degrees; and it so happened that on the eve of a certain sixth day, as the craft were carrying up work for inspection, a young Fellow Craft discovered this stone in the quarry, and from its singular form and beauty, supposing it to belong to some part of the Temple, carried it up for inspection.

Q. Who inspected it? A. The Grand Overseers, placed at the East, West, and South gates.

Q. How did they inspect it? A. On its being presented to the Junior Overseer at the South gate, he observed that it was neither an oblong or a square, neither had it the regular mark of the craft upon it; but from its singular form and beauty was unwilling to reject it, therefore ordered it to be passed to the Senior Overseer at the West gate for further inspection; who, for similar reasons, suffered it to pass to the Master Overseer at the East gate, who held a consultation with his brother Overseers, and they observed, as before, that it was neither an oblong or square, neither had it the regular mark of the craft upon it; and neither of them being Mark Master Masons, supposed it of no use in the building, and hove it over among the rubbish.

Q. How many Fellow Crafts were there engaged at the building of the Temple? A. Eighty thousand.

Q. Were not the Master Overseers liable to be imposed upon by receiving bad work from the hands of such a vast number of workmen? A. They were not.

Q. How was this imposition prevented? A. By the wisdom of King Solomon, who wisely ordered that the craftsman who worked should choose him a particular mark and place it upon all his work; by which it was known and distinguished when carried up to the building, and, if approved, to receive wages.

Q. What was the wages of a Fellow Craft? A. A penny a day.

Q. Who paid the craftsmen? A. The Senior Grand Warden.

Q. Was not the Senior Grand Warden liable to be imposed upon by impostors in paying off such a vast number of workmen? A. He was not.

Q. How was this imposition prevented? A. By the wisdom of King Solomon, who also ordered that every craftsman applying to receive wages, should present his right hand through a lattice window of the [Pg 72] door of the Junior Grand Warden's apartment, with a copy of his mark in the palm thereof, at the same time giving a token.

Q. What was that token? (This was before explained.)

Q. What did it allude to? A. To the manner of receiving wages; it was also to distinguish a true craftsman from an impostor.

Q. What is the penalty of an impostor? A. To have his right hand chopped off.

SECOND SECTION.

Question—Where was you prepared to be made a Mark Master Mason? A. In the room adjoining the body of a just and lawfully constituted Lodge of such, duly assembled in a room or place, representing a workshop that was erected near the ruins of King Solomon's Temple.

Q. How was you prepared? A. By being divested of all my outward apparel and all money; my breast bare, with a cable-tow four times about my body, in which situation I was conducted to the door of a Lodge, where I gave four distinct knocks.

Q. What do these four distinct knocks allude to? A. To the fourth degree of Masonry; it being that on which I was about to enter.

Q. What was said to you from within? A. Who comes there?

Q. Your answer? A. A worthy brother, who has been regularly initiated as an Entered Apprentice, served a proper time as such; passed to the Fellow Craft; raised to the sublime degree of a Master Mason; and now wishes further light in Masonry, by being advanced to the more honorable degree of a Mark Master Mason.

Q. What further was said to you from within? A. I was asked if it was of my own free will and accord I made this request; if I was duly and truly prepared; worthy and well qualified; had wrought in the quarries, and exhibited specimens of my skill and proficiency in the preceding degrees; all of which being answered in the affirmative, I was asked by what further right or benefit I expected to gain this favor.

Q. Your answer? A. By the benefit of a pass-word.

Q. What was that pass-word? A. Joppa.

Q. What did it allude to? A. The city of Joppa, the place where the materials were landed for building king Solomon's Temple, after being prepared in the forest of Lebanon, and carried there on floats (by sea). [Masonic tradition informs us that the banks of this place are so perpendicular that it was impossible to ascend them without assistance from above, which was effected by brethren stationed there, with this strong grip; this has been explained; which, together with the word Joppa, has since been adopted as a proper pass to be given before entering any well-regulated Lodge of Mark Master Masons.]

Q. What further was said to you from within? A. I was bid to wait till the Right Worshipful Master in the East was made acquainted with my request and his answer returned.

Q. When his answer was returned, what followed? A. I was caused to enter the Lodge.

Q. On what did you enter? A. On the edge of the engraving chisel, under the pressure of the mallet, which was to demonstrate the moral [Pg 73] precepts of this degree, and make a deep and lasting impression on my mind and conscience.

Q. How was you then disposed of? A. I was conducted four times regularly around the Lodge and halted at the Junior Warden's in the South, where the same questions were asked, and answers returned as at the door.

Q. How did the Junior Warden dispose of you? A. He ordered me to be conducted to the Senior Warden in the West, where the same questions were asked, and the same answers returned as before.

Q. How did the Senior Warden dispose of you? A. He ordered me to be conducted to the Right Worshipful Master in the East, where the same questions were asked, and answers returned as before; who likewise demanded of me from whence I came, and whither I was traveling.

Q. Your answer? A. From the West, and traveling to the East.

Q. Why do you leave the West and travel to the East? A. In search of light.

Q. How did the Right Worshipful Master dispose of you? A. He ordered me to be conducted back to the West, from whence I came, and put in the care of the Senior Warden, who taught me how to approach the East, the place of light, by advancing upon four upright regular steps to the fourth step, my feet forming a square, and my body erect at the altar before the Right Worshipful Master.

Q. What did the Right Worshipful Master do with you? A. He made a Mark Master Mason of me.

Q. How? A. In due form.

Q. What was that due form? A. Both knees bent, they forming a square, both my hands on the Holy Bible, Square, and Compass, my body being erect; in which posture I took upon me the solemn oath or obligation of a Mark Master Mason.

Q. Have you that oath or obligation? A. I have.

Q. Will you give it me? A. I will, with your assistance. [Here, as in the preceding degree, you repeat after the Right Worshipful Master, I, A. B., etc. See pages 67 and 68.]

Q. After your oath or obligation, what follows? A. Information was brought that the Temple was almost completed, but the craft was all in confusion for want of a certain keystone, which none of them had been instrumental to make.

Q. What followed? A. King Solomon believing in confidence, that our worthy Grand Master, Hiram Abiff, had completed this keystone agreeable to the original plan, ordered inquiry to be made among the Master Overseers, if a stone bearing a particular mark had been presented to them for inspection; and on inquiry being made, it was found that there had.

Q. What followed? A. King Solomon ordered search to be made for the stone, when it was found, and afterwards applied to its intended use.

Q. What color was the stone? A. White.

Q. What did it allude to? A. To a passage in Scripture, where it says, "To him that overcometh will I give to eat of the hidden manna, and I [Pg 74] will give him a white stone, and in the stone a new name written, which no man knoweth saving him that receiveth."

Q. What was that new name? A. The letters on the stone and the initials of the words for which they stand, viz.: H. T. W. S. S. T. K. S.

Q. Of what use is this new name to you in Masonry? A. It was the original mark of our worthy Grand Master, Hiram Abiff, and is the general mark of this degree, and the letters form the circle, in the centre of which every brother of this degree places his particular mark, to which his obligation alludes.

Q. What followed? A. I was more fully instructed with the secrets of this degree.

Q. Of what do they consist? A. Of signs and tokens.

Q. Have you a sign? A. I have.

Q. What is it called? A. Heave over.

Q. What does it allude to? A. To the manner of heaving over work that the Overseers said was unfit for the Temple; also the manner the keystone was hove over.

Q. Have you any other sign? A. I have (at the same time giving it).

Q. What is that? A. The due-guard of a Mark Master Mason.

Q. What does it allude to? A. To the penalty of my obligation; which is, that my right ear should be smote off, that I might forever be unable to hear the word, and my right hand be chopped off, as the penalty of an impostor, if I should ever prove wilfully guilty of revealing any part of my obligation.

Q. Have you any further sign? A. I have.

Q. What is that? A. The grand sign, or sign of distress.

Q. What does it allude to? A. To the manner the Fellow Crafts carry their work up to the Temple for inspection; also the manner I was taught to carry my work, on my advancement to this degree.

Q. Have you any other sign? A. I have not; but I have a token (gives it to him).

Q. What is this? A. The pass-grip of a Mark Master Mason.

Q. What is the name of it? A. " Joppa. "

Q. What does it allude to? A. The city of Joppa.

Q. Have you any other token? A. I have.

Q. What is this? A. The real grip of a Mark Master Mason.

Q. What is the name of it? A. Mark well.

Q. What does it allude to? A. To a passage of Scripture, where it says, "Then he brought me back the way of the gate of the outward sanctuary, which looketh towards the East, and it was shut; and the Lord said unto me, son of man, mark well, and behold with thine eyes, and hear with thine ears, all that I say unto thee concerning all the ordinances of the house of the Lord, and the laws thereof, and mark well the entering in of the house, with the going forth of the sanctuary."

Q. Who founded this degree? A. Our three ancient Grand Masters, viz.: Solomon, King of Israel, Hiram, King of Tyre, and Hiram Abiff.

Q. Why was it founded? A. Not only as an honorary reward, to be conferred on all who have proved themselves meritorious in the preceding degrees, but to render it impossible for a brother to suffer for [Pg 75] the immediate necessities of life, when the price of his mark will procure them.

Q. A brother pledging his mark and asking a favor, who does he represent? A. Our worthy Grand Master, Hiram Abiff, who was a poor man, but on account of his great skill and mysterious conduct at the building of King Solomon's Temple, was most eminently distinguished.

Q. A brother receiving a pledge and granting a favor, whom does he represent? A. King Solomon, who was a rich man, but renowned for his benevolence.

THE PAST MASTER'S DEGREE.

This degree is very simple. It is necessary that a Master Mason should take this degree before he can, constitutionally, preside over a Lodge of Master Masons as Master of it; and when a Master Mason is elected Master of a Lodge, who has not previously received the Past Master's degree, it is then conferred upon him, often without any other ceremony than that of administering the obligation.

This Lodge is opened and closed in the same manner that the Lodges of the first three degrees are; the candidate petitions and is balloted for in the same manner, but he is received into the Lodge in a very different manner. He is conducted into the Lodge without any previous preparation, when the presiding officer rises and says, "Brethren, it is inconvenient for me to serve you any longer as Master of this Lodge. I wish you would select some other brother for that purpose." The candidate is nominated, the usual forms of balloting for officers are then dispensed with, and a vote of the Lodge is taken by yeas and nays. The candidate is elected, and generally refuses to serve, but he is eventually prevailed on to accept; whereupon the presiding officer addresses the Master-elect in the words following, viz.:

"Brother, previous to your investiture, it is necessary that you assent to those ancient charges and regulations, which point out the duty of a Master of a Lodge.

1. You agree to be a good man and true, and strictly to obey the moral law.

2. You agree to be a peaceable subject, and cheerfully to conform to the laws of the country in which you reside.

3. You promise not to be concerned in any plots or conspiracies against government; but patiently to submit to the decisions of the supreme legislature.

4. You agree to pay a proper respect to the civil magistrate, to work diligently, live creditably, and act honorably by all men.

5. You agree to hold in veneration the original rules and patrons of Masonry, and their regular successors, supreme and subordinate, according to their stations, and to submit to the awards and resolutions of your brethren when convened, in every case consistent with the constitution of the Order.

6. You agree to avoid private piques and quarrels, and to guard against intemperance and excess.

7. You agree to be cautious in carriage and behavior, cautious to your brethren, and faithful to your Lodge.

8. You promise to respect genuine brethren and discountenance impostors, and all dissenters from the original plan of Masonry.

9. You agree to promote the general good of society, to cultivate the social virtues, and to propagate a knowledge of the arts.

[Pg 76] 10. You promise to pay homage to the Grand Master for the time being, and to his officer when duly installed, strictly to conform to every edict of the Grand Lodge or General Assembly of Masons that is not subversive of the principles and ground work of Masonry.

11. You admit that it is not in the power of any man, or body of men, to make innovations in the body of Masonry.

12. You promise a regular attendance on the committees and communications of the Grand Lodge, on receiving proper notice, and to pay attention to all the duties of Masonry on convenient occasions.

13. You admit that no new Lodge can be formed without permission of the Grand Lodge, and that no countenance be given to any irregular Lodge, or to any person clandestinely initiated therein, being contrary to the ancient charges of the Order.

14. You admit that no person can be regularly made a Mason in, or admitted a member of any regular Lodge, without previous notice, and due inquiry into his character.

15. You agree that no visitors shall be received into your Lodge without due examination, and producing proper vouchers of their having been initiated into a regular Lodge."

The presiding officer then asks the Master-elect (candidate), the following question, which he must answer in the affirmative: Q. "Do you submit to these charges and promise to support these regulations as Masters have done, in all ages, before you?" A. "I do." The presiding officer then addresses him: "Brother A. B., in consequence of your cheerful conformity to the charges and regulations of the Order, you are now to be installed Master of this degree, in full confidence of your care, skill, and capacity, to govern the same. But previous to your investiture, it is necessary you should take upon yourself the solemn oath or obligation appertaining to this degree; if you are willing to take it upon you, you will please to kneel before the altar, when you shall receive the same." [Here Lodges differ very materially, but this is the most prevalent mode of proceeding.] The candidate then kneels on both knees, lays both hands on the Holy Bible, Square and Compass, and takes the following oath or obligation:

"I, A. B., of my own free will and accord, in presence of Almighty God, and this Right Worshipful Lodge of Past Master Masons, do hereby and hereon, most solemnly and sincerely promise and swear, in addition to my former obligations, that I will not give the degree of Past Master Mason, or any of the secrets pertaining thereto, to anyone of an inferior degree, nor to any person in the known world, except it be to a true and lawful brother or brethren Past Master Masons, or within the body of a just and lawfully constituted Lodge of such, and not unto him or unto them whom I shall hear so to be, but unto him and them only whom I shall find so to be, after strict trial and examination, or lawful information. Furthermore, do I promise and swear, that I will obey all regular signs and summons sent, thrown, handed, or given from the hand of a brother of this degree, or from the body of a just and lawfully constituted Lodge of Past Masters, provided it be within the length of my cable-tow. Furthermore, do I promise and swear, that I will support the constitution of the General Grand Royal Arch Chapter of the United States of America, also that of the Grand Chapter of the State of ——, under which this Lodge is held, and conform to all the by-laws, rules and regulations of this or any other Lodge, of which I may at any time hereafter become a member, so far as in my power. Furthermore, do I promise and swear, that I will not assist, or be present at the conferring of this degree upon any person who has not, to the best of my knowledge and belief, regularly received the degrees of Entered Apprentice, Fellow Craft, Master Mason, and Mark Master, or been elected Master of a regular Lodge of Master [Pg 77] Masons. Furthermore, do I promise and swear, that I will aid and assist all poor and indigent Past Master Masons, their widows and orphans, wherever dispersed around the globe, they applying to me as such, and I finding them worthy, so far as in my power, without material injury to myself or family. Furthermore, do I promise and swear, that the secrets of a brother of this degree, delivered to me in charge as such, shall remain as secure and inviolable in my breast as they were in his own, before communicated to me, murder and treason excepted, and those left to my own election. Furthermore, do I promise and swear, that I will not wrong this Lodge, or a brother of this degree, to the value of one cent, knowingly, myself, nor suffer it to be done by others, if in my power to prevent it. Furthermore, do I promise and swear, that I will not govern this Lodge, nor any other over which I may be called to preside, in a haughty, arbitrary, or impious manner; but will at all times use my utmost endeavors to preserve peace and harmony among the brethren. Furthermore, do I promise and swear, that I will never open a Lodge of Master Masons, unless there be present three regular Master Masons, besides the Tyler, nor close the same without giving a Lecture, or some section or part of a Lecture, for the instruction of the Lodge. Furthermore, that I will not, knowingly, set in any Lodge where anyone presides who has not received the degree of Past Master. [This last point is, in many Lodges, entirely omitted. In some, the two last.] All which I do most solemnly and sincerely promise and swear, with a fixed and steady purpose of mind, to keep and perform the same, binding myself under no less penalty than to have my tongue split from tip to root, that I might forever thereafter be unable to pronounce the word, if ever I should prove wilfully guilty of violating any part of this my solemn oath or obligation of a Past Master Mason. So help me God, and make me steadfast to keep and perform the same."

The obligation being administered, the candidate rises, [4] and the Master proceeds to give the sign, word, and grip of this degree, as follows: The sign (sometimes called the due-guard) is given by laying the edge of the thumb of the right hand in a vertical position on the centre of the mouth, high enough to touch the upper lip. The word is given by taking each other by the Master's grip, and pulling the insides of their feet together, when the Master whispers the word, " Giblem ," [5] in the ear of the candidate. Then they clap their left hand on each other's right arm, between the wrist and elbow, disengaging (at the same moment) their right hand from the Master's grip; they each seize the left arm of the other with their right hands, between the wrist and elbow, and (almost at the same instant) yielding their left hand hold on each other's right arm, and moving their left hands with a brisk motion, they clasp each other's right arm with their left hands, above the elbow, pressing their finger nails hard against the arms, as they shift their hands from place to place; and the Master says (in union with these movements), "From grips to spans, and from spans to grips: a twofold cord is strong, but a threefold cord is not easily broken. " The Master then conducts the candidate to the chair, and, as he ascends the steps, the Master says, "Brother, I now have the pleasure of conducting you into the oriental chair of King Solomon;" places a large cocked hat on his head, and comes down to the front of the newly-installed Master, and [Pg 78] addresses him as follows: "Worshipful brother, I now present you with the furniture and various implements of our profession; they are emblematical of our conduct in life, and will now be enumerated and explained as presented. The Holy Writings , that great light in Masonry, will guide you to all truth; it will direct your path to the temple of happiness, and point out to you the whole duty of man. The Square teaches to regulate our actions by rule and line, and to harmonize our conduct by the principles of morality and virtue. The Compass teaches to limit our desires in every station; thus rising to eminence by merit, we may live respected, and die regretted. The Rule directs that we should punctually observe our duty; press forward in the path of virtue, and neither inclining to the right or to the left, in all our actions have ETERNITY in view. The Line teaches the criterion of moral rectitude; to avoid dissimulation in conversation and action, and to direct our steps to the path that leads to IMMORTALITY . The Book of Constitutions you are to search at all times; cause it to be read in your Lodge, that none may pretend ignorance of the excellent precepts it enjoins. Lastly, you receive in charge the by-laws of your Lodge, which you are to see carefully and punctually executed. I will also present you with the mallet; it is an emblem of power. One stroke of the mallet calls to order, and calls up the Junior and Senior Deacons; two strokes call up all the subordinate officers; and three, the whole Lodge." The following charge is then delivered to the newly-installed Master (alias candidate) by the former Master:

"Worshipful Master, being appointed Master of this Lodge, you cannot be insensible of the obligations which devolve on you as their head; nor of your responsibility for the faithful discharge of the important duties annexed to your appointment. The honor, usefulness, and reputation of your Lodge will materially depend on the skill and assiduity with which you manage its concerns; while the happiness of its members will be generally promoted, in proportion to the zeal and ability with which you propagate the genuine principles of our institution. For a pattern of information, consider the luminary of nature, which, rising in the East, regularly diffuses light and lustre to all within its circle. In like manner, it is your province to spread and communicate light and instruction to the brethren of your Lodge. Forcibly impress upon them the dignity and high importance of Masonry, and seriously admonish them never to disgrace it. Charge them to practice out of the Lodge those duties which they have been taught in it; and by amiable, discreet, and virtuous conduct, to convince mankind of the goodness of the institution, so that, when anyone is said to be a member of it, the world may know that he is one to whom the burdened heart may pour out its sorrows—to whom distress may prefer its suit—whose hand is guided by justice, and his heart expanded by benevolence. In short, by a diligent observance of the by-laws of your Lodge, the constitution of Masonry, and, above all, the Holy Scriptures, which are given as a rule and guide of your faith, you will be enabled to acquit yourself with honor and reputation, and lay up a crown of rejoicing which shall continue when time shall be no more." [6]

The Master then says to the newly-installed Master, "I now leave you to the government of your Lodge." He then retires to a seat, and, after a moment or two, rises and addresses the candidate (now in the chair as [Pg 79] Master), "Worshipful Master, in consequence of my resignation, and the election of a new Master, the seats of the Wardens have become vacant. It is necessary you should have Wardens to assist you in the government of your Lodge. The constitution requires us to elect our officers by ballot, but it is common, on occasions of this kind, to dispense with those formalities, and elect by ayes and noes; I move we do so on the present occasion." The question is tried and carried in the affirmative. The Master has a right to nominate one candidate for office, and the brethren one. Here a scene of confusion takes place, which is not easily described. The newly-installed Worshipful is made the butt for every WORTHY brother to exercise his wit upon. Half a dozen are up at a time, soliciting the Master to nominate them for Wardens, urging their several claims, and decrying the merits of others with much zeal, others crying out, "Order, Worshipful, keep order!" Others propose to dance, and request the Master to sing for them; others whistle, or sing, or jump about the room; or scuffle, and knock down chairs or benches. One proposes to call from labor to refreshment; another compliments the Worshipful Master on his dignified appearance, and knocks off his hat, or pulls it down over his face; another informs him that a lady wishes to enter. If the Master calls to order, every one obeys the signal with the utmost promptness, and drops upon the nearest seat; the next instant, before the Master can utter a word, all are on their feet again and as noisy as ever. Finally, a nominal election is effected, and some prudent member, tired of such a ridiculous confusion, moves that the Lodge be closed; which, being done, the poor (and if a stranger) much embarrassed candidate, has his big hat taken from him, and is reduced to the ranks; but, for his consolation, the Worshipful Master informs him that the preceding scene, notwithstanding its apparent confusion, is designed to convey to him, in a striking manner, the important lesson, never to solicit or accept any office or station for which he does not know himself amply qualified.

The Lecture on the fifth, or Past Master's degree, is divided into five sections. The first section treats of the manner of constituting a Lodge of Master Masons. The second treats of the ceremony of installation, including the manner of receiving candidates to this degree, as given above. The third treats of the ceremonies observed at laying the foundation stones of public structures. The fourth section, of the ceremony observed at the dedications of Masonic halls. The fifth, of the ceremony observed at funerals, according to ancient custom, with the service used on the occasion.

The foregoing includes all the ceremonies ever used in conferring the degree of Past Master; but the ceremonies are more frequently shortened by the omission of some part of them; the presenting of the "various implements of the profession," and their explanations, are often dispensed with; and still more often, the charge.

[Pg 80]

MOST EXCELLENT MASTER'S DEGREE.

Ceremonies Used in Opening a Lodge of Most Excellent Masters.

The Lodge being called to order, the Most Excellent Master says, "Brother Junior, are they all Most Excellent Masters in the South?" The Junior Warden replies, "They are, Most Excellent." Most Excellent Master to Senior Warden, "Brother Senior, are they all Most Excellent Masters in the West?" The Senior Warden replies, "They are, Most Excellent." M. E. M.—"They are in the East (gives one rap, which calls up both Deacons); Brother Junior Deacon, the first care of a Mason?" J. D.—"To see the door tyled, Most Excellent." M. E. M.—"Attend to that part of your duty, and inform the Tyler that we are about to open this Lodge of Most Excellent Masters, and direct him to tyle accordingly." Junior Deacon steps to the door and gives six knocks, which the Tyler answers with six more; Junior Deacon gives one more, which the Tyler answers with one; the door is then partly opened, when the Junior Deacon informs the Tyler that a Lodge of Most Excellent Masters is about to be opened, and tells him to tyle accordingly; and then returns to his place in the Lodge and says, "Most Excellent Master, the Lodge is tyled." M. E. M. "By whom?" J. D.—"By a Most Excellent Master

Mason without the door, armed with the proper implements of his office." M. E. M.—"His duty there?" J. D.—"To keep off all cowans and eavesdroppers, and see that none pass and repass without permission from the chair." M. E. M.—"Your place in the Lodge, Brother Junior?" J. D.—"At the right hand of the Senior Warden in the West, Most Excellent." M. E. M.—"Your duty there, Brother Junior?" J. D.—"To wait on the Most Excellent Master and Wardens, act as their proxy in the active duties of the Lodge, and take charge of the door." M. E. M.—"The Senior Deacon's place in the Lodge?" J. D.—"At the right hand of the Most Excellent Master in the East." M. E. M.—"I thank you, brother. Your duty in the East, Brother Senior?" S. D.—"To wait on the Most Excellent Master and Wardens, act as their proxy in the active duties of the Lodge; attend to the preparation and introduction of candidates; and receive and welcome all visiting brethren." M. E. M.—"The Secretary's place in the Lodge, Brother Senior?" S. D.—"At the left hand of the Most Excellent Master in the East." M. E. M.—"I thank you, brother. Your business there, Brother Secretary?" Sec. —"The better to observe the Most Excellent Master's will and pleasure; record the proceedings of the Lodge, and transmit a copy of the same to the Grand Chapter, if required; receive all monies and money-bills from the hands of the brethren; pay them over to the Treasurer, and take his receipt for the same." M. E. M.—"The Treasurer's place in the Lodge?" Sec.—"At your right hand, Most Excellent." M. E. M.—"I thank you, brother. Your duty there, Brother Treasurer?" Treas.—"The better to observe the Most Excellent Master's will and pleasure; receive all monies and money-bills from the hands of the Secretary; keep a just and true account of the same; pay them out by order of the Most Excellent Master, and consent of the brethren." M. E. M.—"The Junior Warden's place in the Lodge?" [Pg 81] Treas.—"In the South, Most Excellent." M. E. M.—"I thank you, brother. Your business in the South, Brother Junior?" J. W.—"As the sun in the South, at high meridian, is the beauty and glory of the day, so stands the Junior Warden in the South, the better to observe the time of high twelve; call the craft from labor to refreshment; superintend them during the hours thereof; see that none convert the hours of refreshment into that of intemperance or excess; call them again in due season; that the Most Excellent Master may have honor, and they profit thereby." M. E. M.—"The Senior Warden's place in the Lodge?" J. W.—"In the West, Most Excellent." M. E. M.—"I thank you, brother. Your duty in the West, Brother Senior?" S. W.—"As the sun sets in the West to close the day, so stands the Senior Warden in the West, to assist the Most Excellent Master in the opening of his Lodge; take care of the jewels and implements; see that none be lost; pay the craft their wages, if any be due, and see that none go away dissatisfied." M. E. M.—"The Most Excellent Master's place in the Lodge?" S. W.—"In the East, Most Excellent." M. E. M.—"His duty in the East, Brother Senior?" S. W.—"As the sun rises in the East to open and adorn the day, so presides the Most Excellent Master in the East to open and adorn his Lodge; to set his craft to work; govern them with good and wholesome laws, or cause the same to be done." [In some Lodges the forgoing ceremonies are omitted.] M. E. M.—"Brother Senior Warden, assemble the brethren around the altar for the purpose of opening this Lodge of Most Excellent Master Masons." S. W.— "Brethren, please to assemble around the altar for the purpose of opening this Lodge of Most Excellent Master Masons." In pursuance of this request, the brethren assemble around the altar and form a circle, and stand in such a position as to touch each other, leaving a space for the Most Excellent Master; they then all kneel on their left knee and join hands, each giving his right hand brother his left hand, and his left hand brother his right hand; their left arms uppermost, and their heads inclining downward; all being thus situated, the Most Excellent Master reads the following portion of Scripture: Psalm xxiv. —"The earth is the Lord's and the fulness thereof; the world and they that dwell therein. For he hath founded it upon the seas, and established it upon the floods. Who shall ascend into the hill of the Lord? and who shall stand in his holy place? He that hath clean hands and a pure heart; who hath not lifted up his soul unto vanity, nor sworn deceitfully. He shall receive the blessing from the Lord, and righteousness from the God of his salvation. This is the generation of them that seek him, that seek thy face, O Jacob. Selah. Lift up your heads, O ye gates; and be ye lifted up, ye everlasting doors; and the King of glory shall come in. Who is this King of glory? The Lord, strong and mighty; the Lord, mighty in battle. Lift up your heads, O ye gates; even lift them up, ye everlasting doors; and the King of glory shall come in. Who is this King of glory? The Lord of hosts; he is the King of glory. Selah." The reading being ended, the Most Excellent Master then kneels, joins hands with the others, which closes the circle; they all lift their hands, as joined together, up and down six times, keeping time with the words as the Most Excellent Master repeats [Pg 82] them—one, two, three; one, two, three. This is masonically called balancing. They then rise, disengage their hands, and lift them up above their heads with a moderate and somewhat graceful motion; cast up their eyes, turning, at the same time, to the right, they extend their arms and then suffer them to fall loose and nerveless against their sides. This sign is said by Masons to represent the sign of astonishment, made by the Queen of Sheba, on first viewing Solomon's Temple. The Most Excellent Master now resumes his seat and says, "Brethren, attend to giving the signs." The Most Excellent Master then gives all the signs from an Entered Apprentice Mason up to the degree of Most Excellent Master; in which they all join and imitate him. M. E. M.—"Brother Senior Warden, you will please to inform Brother Junior, and request him to inform the brethren that it is my will and pleasure that this Lodge of Most Excellent Master Masons be now opened for dispatch of business, strictly forbidding all private committees, or profane language, whereby the harmony of the same may be interrupted, while engaged in their lawful pursuits, under no less penalty than the by-laws enjoin, or a majority of the brethren may see cause to inflict." S. W.—"Brother Junior, it is the will and pleasure of the Most Excellent Master, that this Lodge of Most Excellent Master Masons be now opened for dispatch of business, strictly prohibiting all private committees, or profane language, whereby the harmony of the same may be interrupted, while engaged in their lawful pursuits, under no less penalty than the by-laws enjoin, or a majority of the brethren may see cause to inflict. " J. W.—"Brethren, you have heard the Most Excellent Master's will and pleasure, as communicated to me by Brother Senior—so let it be done."

Ceremonies of Initiation.

The Lodge being now opened and ready for the reception of candidates, the Senior Deacon repairs to the preparation room, where the candidate is in waiting, takes off his coat, puts a cable-tow six times around his body, and in this situation conducts him to the door of the Lodge, against which he gives six distinct knocks, which are answered by the same number by the Junior Deacon from within; the Senior Deacon then gives one knock, and the Junior Deacon answers by giving one more; the door is then partly opened by the Junior Deacon, who says, "Who comes there?" Senior Deacon—"A worthy brother, who has been regularly initiated as an Entered Apprentice Mason; passed to the degree of Fellow Craft; raised to the sublime degree of Master Mason; advanced to the honorary degree of a Mark Master Mason; presided in the chair as Past Master; and now wishes for further light in Masonry by being received and acknowledged as a Most Excellent Master." Junior Deacon—"Is it of his own free will and accord he makes this request?" Senior Deacon—"It is." J. D.—"Is he duly and truly prepared?" S. D.—"He is." J. D.—"Is he worthy and well qualified?" S. D.—"He is." J. D.—"Has he made suitable proficiency in the preceding degrees?" S. D.—"He has." J. D.—"By what further right or benefit does he expect to obtain this favor?" S. D.—"By the benefit of a [Pg 83] pass-word." J. D.—"Has he a pass-word?" S. D.—"He has not, but I have it for him." J. D.—"Will you give it to me?" S. D. whispers in the ear of the Junior Deacon the word, " Rabboni ." [In many Lodges the Past Master's word, " Giblem " is used as a pass-word for this degree, and the word, " Rabboni ," as the real word.] J. D.—"The word is right; since this is the case, you will wait until the Most Excellent Master in the East is made acquainted with your request, and his answer returned." Junior Deacon repairs to the Most Excellent Master in the East and gives six raps, as at the door. M. E. M.—"Who comes here?" J. D.—"A worthy brother, who has been regularly initiated as an Entered Apprentice Mason; passed to the degree of a Fellow Craft; raised to the sublime degree of a Master Mason; advanced to the honorary degree of Mark Master Mason; presided in the chair as Past Master: and now wishes for further light in Masonry by being received and acknowledged as a Most Excellent Master." M. E. M.—"Is it of his own free will and choice he makes this request?" J. D.—"It is." M. E. M.—"Is he duly and truly prepared?" J. D.—"He is." M. E. M.—"Is he worthy and well qualified?" J. D.—"He is." M. E. M.—"Has he made suitable proficiency in the preceding degrees?" J. D.—"He has. " M. E. M.—"By what further right or benefit does he expect to obtain this favor?" J. D.—"By the benefit of a pass-word." M. E. M.—"Has he a pass-word?" J. D.—"He has not, but I have it for him." M. E. M.—"Will you give it to me?" Junior Deacon whispers in the ear of the Most Excellent Master the word, " Rabboni ." M. E. M.—"The pass is right; since he comes endowed with all these necessary qualifications, let him enter this Lodge of Most Excellent Masters in the name of the Lord. " The candidate is then conducted six times around the Lodge by the Senior Deacon, moving with the sun. The first time they pass around the Lodge, when opposite the Junior Warden, he gives one blow with the gavel; when opposite the Senior Warden he does the same; and likewise when opposite the Most Excellent Master. The second time around, each gives two blows; the third, three; and so on, until they arrive to six. During this time, the Most Excellent Master reads the following passage of Scripture:

Psalm cxxii. "I was glad when they said unto me, Let us go into the house of the Lord. Our feet shall stand within Thy gates, O Jerusalem. Jerusalem is builded as a city that is compact together. Whither the tribes go up, the tribes of the Lord, unto the testimony of Israel, to give thanks unto the name of the Lord. For there are set thrones of judgment, the thrones of the house of David. Pray for the peace of Jerusalem; they shall prosper that love thee. Peace be within thy walls, and prosperity within thy palaces. For my brethren and companions' sakes I will now say, Peace be within thee. Because of the house of the Lord, our God, I will seek thy good."

The reading of the foregoing is so timed as not to be fully ended until the Senior Deacon and candidate have performed the sixth revolution. Immediately after this, the Senior Deacon and candidate arrive at the Junior Warden's station in the South, when the same questions are asked and answers returned, as at the door (Who comes here, etc.). The Junior Warden then directs the candidate to pass on to the Senior [Pg 84] Warden in the West for further examination; where the same questions are asked and answers returned, as before. The Senior Warden directs him to be conducted to the Right Worshipful Master in the East for further examination. The Right Worshipful Master asks the same questions, and receives the same answers as before. He then says, "Please to conduct the candidate back to the West from whence he came, and put him in the care of the Senior Warden, and request him to teach the candidate how to approach the East, by advancing upon six upright regular steps to the sixth step, and place him in a proper position to take upon him the solemn oath or obligation of a Most Excellent Master Mason." The candidate is conducted back to the West, and put in care of the Senior Warden, who informs him how to approach the East, as directed by the Most Excellent Master. The candidate kneels on both knees, and places both hands on the leaves of an opened Bible, Square and Compass. The Most Excellent Master now comes forward and says, "Brother, you are now placed in a proper position to take upon you the solemn oath or obligation of a Most Excellent Master Mason; which, I assure you, as before, is neither to affect your religion or politics. If you are willing to take it, repeat your name and say after me." The following obligation is then administered:

"I, A. B., of my own free will and accord, in presence of Almighty God, and this Lodge of Most Excellent Master Masons, do hereby and hereon, in addition to my former obligations, most solemnly and sincerely promise and swear, that I will not give the degree of a Most Excellent Master to any of an inferior degree, nor to any other person or persons in the known world, except it be to a true and lawful brother or brethren of this degree, and within the body of a just and lawfully constituted Lodge of such; and not unto him nor them whom I shall hear so to be, but unto him and them only whom I shall find so to be, after strict trial and due examination, or lawful information. Furthermore, do I promise and swear, that I will obey all regular signs and summons given, handed, sent, or thrown to me from a brother of this degree, or from the body of a just and lawfully constituted Lodge of such, provided it be within the length of my cable-tow, if in my power. Furthermore, do I promise and swear, that I will support the constitution of the General Grand Royal Arch Chapter of the United States of America, also the Grand Royal Arch Chapter of the State of ———, under which this Lodge is held, and conform to all the by-laws, rules and regulations of this or any other Lodge, of which I may at any time hereafter become a member, Furthermore, do I promise and swear, that I will aid and assist all poor and indigent brethren of this degree, their widows and orphans, wheresoever dispersed around the globe, as far as in my power, without injuring myself or family. Furthermore, do I promise and swear, that the secrets of a brother of this degree, given to me in charge as such, and I knowing them to be such, shall remain as secret and inviolable in my breast as in his own, murder and treason excepted, and the same left to my own free will and choice. Furthermore, do I promise and swear, that I will not wrong this Lodge of Most Excellent Master Masons, nor a brother of this degree, to the value of anything, knowingly, myself, nor suffer it to be done by others, if in my power to prevent it; but will give due and timely notice of all approaches of danger, if in my power. Furthermore, do I promise and swear, that I will dispense light and knowledge to all ignorant and uninformed brethren at all times, as far as in my power, without material injury to myself or family. To all which I do most solemnly swear, with a fixed and steady purpose of mind in me, to keep and perform the same binding myself under no less penalty than to have my breast torn [Pg 85] open, and my heart and vitals taken from thence and exposed to rot on the dunghill, if ever I violate any part of this my solemn oath or obligation of a Most Excellent Master Mason. So help me God, and keep me steadfast in the due performance of the same."

"Detach your hands and kiss the book."

The candidate is now requested to rise, and the Most Excellent Master gives him the sign, grip, and word appertaining to this degree. The sign is given by placing your hands, one on each breast, the fingers meeting in the centre of the body, and jerking them apart as though you were trying to tear open your breast; it alludes to the penalty of the obligation. The grip is given by taking each other by the right hand, and clasping them so that each compresses the third finger of the other with his thumb. [If one hand is large and the other small, they cannot both give the grip at the same time.] It is called the grip of all grips, because it is said to cover all the preceding grips. The Most Excellent holds the candidate by the hand, and puts the inside of his right foot to the inside of the candidate's right foot, and whispers in his ear, " Rabboni ." In some Lodges the word is not given in a whisper, but in a low voice. After these ceremonies are over, and the members seated, some noise is intentionally made by shuffling the feet. M. E. M.—"Brother Senior, what is the cause of this confusion?" S. W.—"Is not this the day set apart for the celebration of the copestone, Most Excellent?" M. E. M.—"I will ask Brother Secretary. Brother Secretary, is this the day set apart for the celebration of the copestone?" Secretary (looking in his book)—"It is, Most Excellent." M. E. M.—"Brother Senior Warden, assemble the brethren, and form a procession, for the purpose of celebrating the copestone." The brethren then assemble (the candidate stands aside, not joining in the procession), form a procession double file, and march six times around the Lodge, against the course of the sun, singing the following song, and giving all the signs from an Entered Apprentice to that of Most Excellent Master. When opposite the Most Excellent Master, the first time they march around the Lodge, each member gives the first sign of an Entered Apprentice, and preserves it until he nearly arrives opposite the Most Excellent a second time, then gives the second sign, and continues it in the same manner, and so of all others, up to that of this degree, saying,

All hail to the morning that bids us rejoice,

The Temple's completed, exalt high each voice.

The copestone is finished—our labor is o'er,

The sound of the gavel shall hail us no more.

To the power Almighty, who ever has guided

The tribes of old Israel, exalting their fame;

To Him who hath governed our hearts undivided,
Let's send forth our vows to praise His great name.
Companions, assemble on this joyful day
(The occasion is glorious!) the keystone to lay;
Fulfilled is the promise, by the Ancient of Days,
To bring forth the copestone with shouting and praise.
    The keystone is now produced and laid on the altar.
There is no more occasion for level or plumb-line,
[Pg 86] For trowel or gavel, for compass or square; [7]
Our works are completed, the ark safely seated, [8]
And we shall be greeted as workmen most rare.
Names, those that are worthy our tribes, who have shared,
And proved themselves faithful, shall meet their reward;
Their virtue and knowledge, industry and skill,
Have our approbation—have gained our good will.
We accept and receive them, [9] Most Excellent Masters,
Trusted with honor, and power to preside
Among worthy craftsmen where'er assembled,
The knowledge of Masons to spread far and wide.
Almighty Jehovah, [10] descend now and fill
This Lodge with Thy glory, our hearts with good-will;
Preside at our meeting, assist us to find
True pleasure in teaching good-will to mankind.
Thy wisdom inspired the great institution,
Thy strength shall support it till nature expire;
And when the creation shall fall into ruin,
Its beauty shall rise through the midst of the fire.
[At the time the ark is placed on the altar, there is also placed on it a pot of incense, to which fire is communicated by the Most Excellent Master, just as the last line of the song is sung; this pot to contain incense is sometimes an elegant silver urn; but if the Lodge is too poor to afford that, a common teapot, with spout and handle broken off, answers every purpose; for incense some pieces of paper are dipped in spirits of turpentine.]

The members now all join hands, as in opening; and, while in this attitude, the Most Excellent reads the following passage of Scripture:
2 Chron. vii. 1-4. "Now when Solomon had made an end of praying, the fire came down from heaven and consumed the burnt-offering and the sacrifices; and the glory of the Lord filled the house. And the priests could not enter into the house of the Lord, because the glory of the Lord had filled the Lord's house. And when all the children of Israel saw how the fire came down, and the glory of the Lord upon the house, they bowed themselves with their faces to the ground upon the pavement, and worshipped, and praised the Lord, saying, For He is good ; [11] for His mercy endureth forever ."

The members now balance six times as before; in opening, rise and balance six times more, disengage themselves from each other and take their seats; the Most Excellent Master then delivers the following charge to the candidate:

"Brother, your admittance to this degree of Masonry, is a proof of the good opinion the brethren of this Lodge entertain of your Masonic [Pg 87] abilities. Let this consideration induce you to be careful of forfeiting by misconduct and inattention to our rules, that esteem which has raised you to the rank you now possess.

"It is one of your great duties, as a Most Excellent Master, to dispense light and truth to the uninformed Mason; and I need not remind you of the impossibility of complying with this obligation without possessing an accurate acquaintance with the Lectures of each degree.

"If you are not already completely conversant in all the degrees heretofore conferred on you, remember, that an indulgence, prompted by a belief that you will apply yourself with double diligence to make yourself so, has induced the brethren to accept you.

"Let it, therefore, be your unremitting study to acquire such a degree of knowledge and information as shall enable you to discharge with propriety the various duties incumbent on you, and to preserve unsullied the title now conferred upon you of a Most Excellent Master."

After this a motion is made by some of the members to close the Lodge. This motion being accepted and received, the Most Excellent says, "Brother Junior Warden, you will please assemble the brethren around the altar for the purpose of closing this Lodge of Most Excellent Masters." The brethren immediately assemble around the altar in a circle, and kneel on the right knee, put their left arms over and join hands, as before; while kneeling in this position, the Most Excellent reads the following Psalm: Psalm cxxxiv. "Behold, bless ye the Lord, all ye servants of the Lord, which by night stand in the house of the Lord. Lift up your hands in the sanctuary, and bless the Lord. The Lord that made heaven and earth bless thee out of Zion. " The Most Excellent then closes the circle as in opening, when they balance six times, rise and balance six times more, disengaging their hands, and give all the signs downwards, and declares the Lodge closed.

ROYAL ARCH DEGREE.

All legally constituted bodies of Royal Arch Masons are called Chapters, as regular bodies of Masons of the preceding degrees are called Lodges. All the degrees from Mark Master to Royal Arch are given under the sanction of Royal Arch Chapters. A person making application to a Chapter for admission, is understood as applying for all the degrees, unless he states in his application the particular degree or degrees he wishes to receive. If you ask a Mark Master if he belongs to a Chapter, he will answer yes, but has only been marked. If a person make application for all the degrees, and wishes to receive them all at one time, he is frequently balloted for only on the Mark degree, it being understood that if accepted on that, he is to receive the whole. The members of Chapters who have received all the degrees, style each other companions; if they have not received the Royal Arch degree, brothers. It is a point of the Royal Arch degree "not to assist, or be present at the conferring of this degree upon more or less than three candidates at one time." If there are not three candidates present, one or two companions, as the case may be, volunteer to represent candidates, so as to make the requisite number, or a TEAM, as it is technically styled, and accompany the candidate or candidates through all the stages of exaltation. Every Chapter must consist of a High Priest, King, Scribe, [Pg 88] Captain of the Host, Principal Sojourner, Royal Arch Captain, three Grand Masters of the Veils, Treasurer, Secretary, and as many members as may be found convenient for working to advantage. In the Lodges for conferring the preparatory degrees, the High Priest presides as Master, the King as Senior Warden, the Scribe as Junior Warden, the Captain of the Host as Marshal, or Master of Ceremonies, the Principal Sojourner as Senior Deacon, the Royal Arch Captain as Junior Deacon, the Master of the First, Second, and Third Veils as Junior, Senior, and Master Overseers; the Treasurer, Secretary and Tyler as officers of corresponding rank. The Chapter is authorized to confer the degrees by a charter, or warrant from some Grand Chapter.

The members being assembled, the High Priest calls to order, and demands of the Royal Arch Captain if all present are Royal Arch Masons. The Royal Arch Captain ascertains and answers in the affirmative. The High Priest then directs him to cause the Tyler to be stationed, which, being done, the High Priest says, "Companions, Royal Arch Masons, you will please to clothe, and arrange yourselves for the purpose of opening the Chapter." The furniture of the Chapter is then arranged, the companions clothed with scarlet sashes and aprons, and the officers invested with the proper insignia of their respective offices, and repair to their proper stations. The High Priest then demands whether the Chapter is tyled, and is answered the same as in the Lodge. The stations and duties of the officers are then recited (see Lecture, First Section). After the duties of the officers are recited, the High Priest directs the Captain of the Host to assemble the companions of the altar. The companions form a circle about the altar, all kneeling on the right knee, with their arms crossed, right arm uppermost and hands joined, leaving a space for the High Priest, who reads the following passage of Scripture:

2 Thess. iii. 6-18. "Now, we command you, brethren, that you withdraw yourselves from every brother that walketh disorderly and not after the tradition that ye have received of us, for yourselves know how ye ought to follow us, for we behaved not ourselves disorderly among you, neither did we eat any man's bread for nought, but wrought with labor and travail night and day, that we might not be chargeable to any of you; not because we have not power, but to make ourselves an ensample unto you to follow us. For even when we were with you, this we commanded you, that if any man would not work, neither should he eat. For we hear that there are some, which walk among you disorderly, working not at all, but are busybodies. Now them that are such, we command and exhort, that with quietness they work and eat their own bread. But ye, brethren, be not weary in well doing. And if any man obey not our word, note that man and have no company with him, that he may be ashamed. Yet count him not as an enemy, but admonish him as a brother. Now the Lord of peace Himself, give you peace always. The salutation of Paul, with mine own hand, which is the token, so I write."

[The reader is requested to compare this with Scripture—he will observe that the name of the Savior is intentionally left out.] The High Priest then takes his place in the circle. The whole circle then balance with their arms three times three, that is, they raise their arms and let them fall upon their knees three times in concert, after a short pause three times more, and after another pause three times more. Then all break into squads of three and raise the living arch. This is done by each [Pg 89] companion taking his left wrist in his right hand, and with their left hands the three grasp each other's right wrists, and raise them above their heads. This constitutes the living arch, under which the Grand Omnific Royal Arch word must be given, but it must also be given by three times three. In opening the Chapter, this is done in the following manner: After the three have joined hands they repeat these lines in concert, and at the close of each line raise them above their heads and say, "As we three did agree, the sacred word to keep, and as we three did agree, the sacred word to search, so we three do agree to raise this Royal Arch." At the close of the last line they keep their hands raised, while they incline their heads under them, and the first whispers in the ear of the second the syllable, J A H; the second to the third, B U H, and the third to the first, L U N. The second then commences, and it goes around again in the same manner, then the third, so that each companion pronounces each syllable of the word. [12] They then separate, each repairing to his station, and the High Priest declares the Chapter opened.

The Lecture of the Royal Arch degree is divided into two sections. The first section designates the appellation, number and station of the several officers, and points out the purpose and duties of their respective stations.

Question—Are you a Royal Arch Mason? Answer— I am That, I am .

Q. How shall I know you to be a Royal Arch Mason? A. By three times three.

Q. Where was you made a Royal Arch Mason? A. In a just and lawfully constituted Chapter of Royal Arch Masons, consisting of Most Excellent, High Priest, King and Scribe, Captain of the Host, Principal Sojourner, Royal Arch Captain, and the three Grand Masters of the Veils, assembled in a room or place representing the tabernacle erected by our ancient brethren near the ruins of King Solomon's Temple.

Q. Where is the High Priest stationed, and what are his duties? A. He is stationed in the sanctum sanctorum. His duty, with the King and Scribe, to sit in the Grand Council, to form plans and give directions to the workmen.

Q. The King's station and duty? A. At the right hand of the High Priest, to aid him by his advice and council, and in his absence to preside.

Q. The Scribe's station and duty? A. At the left hand of the High Priest, to assist him and the King in the discharge of their duties, and to preside in their absence.

Q. The Captain of the Host's station and duty? A. At the right hand of the Grand Council, and to receive their orders and see them duly executed.

Q. The Principal Sojourner's station and duty? A. At the left hand of the Grand Council, to bring the blind by a way that they know not, to [Pg 90] lead them in paths they have not known, to make darkness light before them, and crooked things straight.

Q. The Royal Arch Captain's station and duty? A. At the inner veil, or entrance of the sanctum sanctorium, to guard the same, and see that none pass but such as are duly qualified, and have the proper pass-words and signets of truth.

Q. What is the color of his banner? A. White, and is emblematical of that purity of heart and rectitude of conduct, which is essential to obtain admission into the divine sanctum sanctorum above.

Q. The stations and duties of the three Grand Masters of the Veils? A. At the entrance of their respective Veils: to guard the same, and see that none pass but such as are duly qualified and in possession of the proper pass-words and tokens.

Q. What are the colors of their banners? A. That of the third, scarlet, which is emblematical of fervency and zeal, and the appropriate color of the Royal Arch degree. It admonishes us to be fervent in the exercise of our devotions to God, and zealous in our endeavors to promote the happiness of men. Of the second, purple, which being produced by a due mixture of blue and scarlet, the former of which is the characteristic color of the symbolic, or three first degrees, and the latter, that of the Royal Arch degree, is an emblem of union, and is the characteristic color of the intermediate degrees. It teaches us to cultivate and improve that spirit of harmony between the brethren of the symbolic degrees and the companions of the sublime degrees, which should ever distinguish the members of a society founded upon the principles of everlasting truth and universal philanthropy. Of the first, blue, the peculiar color of the three ancient or symbolical degrees. It is an emblem of universal friendship and benevolence, and instructs us that in the mind of a Mason those virtues should be as expansive as the blue arch of heaven itself.

Q. The Treasurer's station and duty? A. At the right hand of the Captain of the Host; his duty to keep a just and regular account of all the property and funds of the Chapter placed in his hands, and exhibit them to the Chapter when called upon for that purpose.

Q. The Secretary's place in the Chapter? A. At the left of the Principal Sojourner; his duty to issue the orders and notifications of his superior officers, record the proceedings of the Chapter proper to be written, to receive all moneys due to the Chapter, and pay them over to the Treasurer.

Q. Tyler's place and duty? A. His station is at the outer avenue of the Chapter, his duty to guard against the approach of cowans and eavesdroppers, and suffer none to pass or repass but such as are duly qualified.

The second section describes the method of exaltation to this sublime degree as follows: "Companion, you informed me, at the commencement of this Lecture, that you was made a Royal Arch Mason in a just and legally constituted Chapter of Royal Arch Masons."

Q. Where was you prepared to be a Royal Arch Mason? A. In a room adjacent to the Chapter.

[Pg 91] Q. How was you prepared? A. In a company of three I was hoodwinked, with a cable-tow seven times around our bodies; in which condition we were conducted to the door of the Chapter and caused to give seven distinct knocks, which were answered by a like number from within, and we were asked "Who comes there?"

Q. Your answer? A. Three brethren, who have been regularly initiated as Entered Apprentices; passed to the degree of Fellow Craft; raised to the sublime degree of Master Mason; advanced to the more honorable degree of Mark Master; presided as Masters in the chair; accepted and received as Most Excellent Masters, and now wish for further light in Masonry by being exalted to the more sublime degree of Royal Arch Masons.

Q. What was then said to you? A. We were asked if we were duly and truly prepared, worthy and well qualified; had made suitable proficiency in the preceding degrees, and were properly avouched for. All of which being answered in the affirmative, we were asked by what further right or benefit we expected to obtain this favor.

Q. Your answer? A. By the benefit of a pass-word.

Q. Had you that pass-word? A. We had not, but our conductor gave it to us.

Q. What was then said to you? A. We were directed to wait with patience till the Grand Council could be informed of our request and their pleasure known.

Q. What answer was returned? A. Let them enter under a living arch, and remember to stoop low, for he that humbleth himself shall be exalted.

Q. Did you pass under a living arch? A. We did.

Q. How were you then disposed of? A. We were conducted to the altar, caused to kneel, and take upon ourselves the solemn oath or obligation of a Royal Arch Mason.

Q. Have you that obligation? A. I have.

Q. Will you give it me? A. "I, A. B., of my own free will and accord, in the presence of Almighty God, and this Chapter of Royal Arch Masons, erected to God, and dedicated to the Holy Order of St. John, do hereby and hereon, most solemnly and sincerely promise and swear, in addition to my former obligations, that I will not give the degree of Royal Arch Mason to to anyone of an inferior degree, nor to any other being in the known world, except it be to a true and lawful companion Royal Arch Mason, or within the body of a just and legally constituted Chapter of such; and not unto him or unto them whom I shall hear so to be, but unto him or them only whom I shall find so to be, after strict trial, due examination, or legal information received. Furthermore, do I promise and swear, that I will not give the Grand Omnific Royal Arch word, which I shall hereafter receive, neither in the Chapter nor out of it, except there be present two companions, Royal Arch Masons, who, with myself, make three, and then by three times three, under a living arch, not above my breath. Furthermore, that I will not reveal the ineffable characters belonging to this degree, or retain the key to them in my possession, but destroy it whenever it comes to my sight. Furthermore, do I promise and swear, that I will not wrong this Chapter, nor a companion of this degree, to the value of anything, knowingly, myself, nor suffer it to be done by others, if in my power to prevent it. Furthermore, do I promise and swear, that I will not be at the [Pg 92] exaltation of a candidate to this degree, at a clandestine Chapter, I knowing it to be such. Furthermore, do I promise and swear, that I will not assist, or be present at the exaltation of a candidate to this degree, who has not regularly received the degrees of Entered Apprentice, Fellow Craft, Master Mason, Mark Master, Past Master, Most Excellent Master, to the best of my knowledge and belief. Furthermore, that I will not assist or see more or less than three candidates exalted at one and the same time. Furthermore, that I will not assist, or be present at the forming or opening of a Royal Arch Chapter, unless there be present nine regular Royal Arch Masons. Furthermore, do I promise and swear, that I will not speak evil of a companion Royal Arch Mason, neither behind his back nor before his face, but will apprise him of approaching danger, if in my power. Furthermore, do I promise and swear, that I will not strike a companion Royal Arch Mason in anger, so as to draw his blood. Furthermore, do I promise and swear, that I will support the constitution of the General Grand Royal Arch Chapter of the United States of America, also the constitution of the Grand Royal Arch Chapter of the State under which this Chapter is held, and conform to all the by-laws, rules and regulations of this or any other Chapter of which I may hereafter become a member. Furthermore, do I promise and swear, that I will obey all regular signs, summons, or tokens given, handed, sent, or thrown to me from the hand of a companion Royal Arch Mason, or from the body of a just and lawfully constituted Chapter of such, provided it be within the length of my cable-tow. Furthermore, do I promise and swear, that I will aid and assist a companion Royal Arch Mason when engaged in any difficulty; and espouse his cause, so far as to extricate him from the same, if in my power, whether he be right or wrong. Also that I will promote a companion Royal Arch Mason's political preferment in preference to another of equal qualifications. [13] Furthermore, do I promise and swear, that a companion Royal Arch Mason's secrets, given to me in charge as such, and I knowing them to be such, shall remain as secure and inviolable in my breast as in his own, MURDER AND TREASON NOT EXCEPTED. [14] Furthermore, do I promise and swear, that I will be aiding and assisting all poor and indigent Royal Arch Masons, their widows and orphans, wherever dispersed around the globe, so far as in my power, without material injury to myself or family. All which, I do most solemnly and sincerely promise and swear, with a firm and steadfast resolution to perform the same, without any equivocation, mental reservation, or self-evasion of mind in me whatever; binding myself under no less penalty than that of having my skull smote off, and my brains exposed to the scorching rays of the sun, should I ever knowingly or wilfully violate or transgress any part of this my solemn oath or obligation of a Royal Arch Mason. So help me God, and keep me steadfast in the performance of the same."

Q. After receiving the obligation, what was said to you? A. We were told that we were now obligated and received as Royal Arch Masons, but as this degree was infinitely more important than any of the preceding, it was necessary for us to pass through many trials, and to travel in rough and rugged ways to prove our fidelity, before we could be entrusted with the more important secrets of this degree. We were further told that, though we could not discover the path we were to travel, we were under the direction of a faithful guide, who would "bring the blind by a way they knew not, and lead them in paths they had not known; who would make darkness light before them, and crooked [Pg 93] things straight; who would do these things, and not forsake them." (See Isa. xlii. 16.)

Q. What followed? A. We were caused to travel three times around the room, when we were again conducted to the altar, caused to kneel, and attend to the following prayer:

Supreme Architect of universal nature, who, by Thine Almighty Word, didst speak into being the stupendous arch of heaven! And for the instruction and pleasure of Thy rational creatures, didst adorn us with greater and lesser lights, thereby magnifying Thy power, and endearing Thy goodness unto the sons of men. We humbly adore and worship Thine unspeakable perfection! We bless Thee, that when man had fallen from his innocence and happiness, Thou didst leave him the powers of reasoning, and capacity of improvement and of pleasure. We thank Thee, that amidst the pains and calamities of our present state, so many means of refreshment and satisfaction are reserved to us while traveling the RUGGED PATH of life: especially would we, at this time, render Thee our thanksgiving and praise for the institution, as members of which we are, at this time, assembled, and for all the pleasures we have derived from it. We thank Thee, that the few here assembled before Thee, have been favored with new inducements, and been laid under new and stronger obligations of virtue and holiness. May these obligations, O Blessed Father! have their full effect upon us. Teach us, we pray Thee, the true reverence of Thy great, mighty, and terrible name. Inspire us with a firm and unshaken resolution in our virtuous pursuits. Give us grace diligently to search Thy word in the book of nature, wherein the duties of our high vocation are inculcated with divine authority. May the solemnity of the ceremonies of our institution be duly impressed on our minds, and have a happy and lasting effect on our lives! O Thou, who didst aforetime appear unto Thy servant Moses IN A FLAME OF FIRE OUT OF THE MIDST OF A BUSH , enkindle, we beseech Thee, in each of our hearts, a flame of devotion to Thee, of love to each other, and of charity to all mankind. May all Thy miracles and mighty works fill us with Thy dread, and Thy goodness impress us with the love of Thy holy name. May holiness to the Lord be engraven upon all our thoughts, words, and actions. May the incense of piety ascend continually unto Thee from the altar of our hearts, and burn day and night, as a sacrifice of sweet-smelling savor, well pleasing unto Thee. And since sin has destroyed within us the first temple of purity and innocence, may Thy heavenly grace guide and assist us in rebuilding a SECOND TEMPLE of reformation, and may the glory of this latter house be greater than the glory of the former! Amen. So mote it be.

Q. After the prayer what followed? A. We were again caused to travel three times around the room, during which the following passage of Scripture was read, and we were shown a representation of the bush that burned and was not consumed:

Exodus iii. 1-6. "Now Moses kept the flock of Jethro, his father-in-law, the priest of Midian; and he led the flock to the back side of the desert, and came to the mountain of God, even to Horeb. And the angel of the Lord appeared unto him in a flame of fire out of the midst of a bush, and he looked, and behold, the bush burned with fire, and the bush was not consumed. And Moses said, I will now turn aside and see this great sight, why the bush is not burned. And when the Lord saw that he turned aside to see, God called unto him out of the midst of the bush and said, Moses, Moses. And he said, Here am I. And He said Draw not nigh hither; put off thy shoes from off thy feet; for the place whereon thou standest is holy ground. Moreover he said, I am the God of thy father, the God of Abraham, the God of Isaac, and the God of Jacob. And Moses hid his face; for he was afraid to look upon God."

Q. What followed? A. We again traveled, while the following passage was read:

2 Chron xxxvi. 11-20. "Zedekiah was one and twenty years old when [Pg 94] he began to reign, and reigned eleven years in Jerusalem. And he did THAT WHICH WAS evil in the sight of the Lord, his God, AND humbled not himself before Jeremiah, the prophet, SPEAKING from the mouth of the Lord. And he also rebelled against King Nebuchadnezzar, and he stiffened his neck and hardened his heart from turning unto the Lord God of Israel. Moreover, all the chiefs of the priests and the people transgressed very much after all the abominations of the heathen: and polluted the house of the Lord which He had hallowed in Jerusalem. And the Lord God of their fathers sent to them by His messengers, rising up betimes and sending; because He had compassion on His people, and on His dwelling place. But they mocked the messengers of God, and despised His words, and misused His prophets, until the wrath of the Lord arose against His people, till THERE WAS no remedy. Therefore he brought upon him the King of the Chaldees, who slew their young men with the sword in the house of their sanctuary, and had no compassion on young men or maidens, old men, or him that stooped for age; he gave them all unto his hand. And all the vessels of the house of God, great and small, and the treasures of the house of the Lord, and treasures of the king, and of his princes; all THESE he brought to Babylon. And they burnt the house of God, and broke down the wall of Jerusalem, and burnt all the palaces thereof with fire, and destroyed all the goodly vessels thereof. And them that had escaped from the sword carried he away to Babylon; where they were servants to him and his sons, until the reign of the kingdom of Persia."

At the close of this there was a representation of the destruction of Jerusalem by Nebuchadnezzar, and the carrying captive of the children of Israel to Babylon. We were seized, bound in chains, and confined in a dungeon.

Q. What followed? A. We heard rejoicing, as of good news; the proclamation of Cyrus, King of Persia, was read in our hearing.

Ezra i. 1-3. "Now in the first year of Cyrus, King of Persia, the Lord stirred up the spirit of Cyrus, King of Persia, that he made a proclamation throughout all his kingdom, and put it also in writing, saying, Thus saith Cyrus, King of Persia, the Lord God of heaven hath given me all the kingdoms of the earth, and He hath charged me to build Him an house at Jerusalem, which is in Judah. Who is there among you of all his people? His God be with him, and let him go up to Jerusalem, which is in Judah, and build the house of the Lord God of Israel, which is in Jerusalem."

Q. What was then said to you? A. We were unbound and requested to go up to Jerusalem to assist in rebuilding the Temple, but objected, as we had no pass by which to make ourselves known to our brethren.

Q. What followed? A. The third chapter of Exodus, 13th and 14th verses, were read to us:

"And Moses said unto God, Behold! when I come unto the children of Israel, and shall say unto them, the God of your fathers hath sent me unto you, and they shall say to me, what is his name? What shall I say to them? And God said unto Moses, I am, that I am . And thus thou shalt say unto the children of Israel, I am hath sent me unto you."

We were directed to use the words, " I am, that I am " as a pass-word.

Q. What followed? A. We arose to go up to Jerusalem, and traveled over hills and valleys, rough and rugged ways, for many days; during which time, as we stopped occasionally, to rest and refresh ourselves, the following passages from the Psalms were read in our hearing for our consolation and encouragement [Psalms cxli, cxlii, cxliii]:

Psalm cxli. "Lord, I cry unto Thee; Make haste unto me; give ear [Pg 95] unto my voice. Let my prayer be set forth before Thee as incense, and the lifting up of hands as the evening sacrifice. Set a watch, O Lord, before my mouth; keep the door of my lips. Incline not my heart to any evil thing, to practice wicked works with men that work iniquity. Let the righteous smite me, it shall be a kindness: and let Him reprove me, it shall be an excellent oil. Mine eyes are unto Thee, O God the Lord; in Thee is my trust; leave not my soul destitute. Keep me from the snare which they have laid for me, and the gins of the workers of iniquity. Let the wicked fall into their own nets, while that I withal escape.

Psalm cxlii. I cried unto the Lord with my voice; with my voice unto the Lord did I make my supplication. I poured out my complaint before him; I showed before him my trouble. When my spirit was overwhelmed within me, then thou knewest my path. In the way wherein I walked, have they privily laid a snare for me. I looked on my right hand, and beheld, but there was no man that would know me; refuge failed me; no man cared for my soul. I cried unto Thee, O Lord; I said, Thou art my refuge and my portion in the land of the living. Attend unto my cry, for I am brought very low: deliver me from my persecutors; for they are stronger than I. Bring my soul out of prison, that I may praise Thy name.

Psalm cxliii. Hear my prayer, O Lord; give ear to my supplications; in Thy faithfulness answer me, and in Thy righteousness. And enter not into judgment with Thy servant; for in Thy sight shall no man living be justified. For the enemy hath persecuted my soul; he hath made me to dwell in darkness. Therefore is my spirit overwhelmed within me; my heart within me is desolate. Hear me speedily, O Lord; my spirit faileth; hide not Thy face from me, lest I be like unto them that go down into the pit. Cause me to hear Thy loving kindness in the morning; for in Thee do I trust; cause me to know the way wherein I should walk, for I lift up my soul unto Thee. Bring my soul out of trouble, and of Thy mercy cut off mine enemies; for I am Thy servant."

At length we arrived at Jerusalem, and presented ourselves at the first Veil of the Tabernacle.

Q. What was there said to you? A. The Master of the first Veil demanded of us, "Who comes there? Who dares approach this outer Veil of our sacred Tabernacle? Who comes here?"

Q. Your answer? A. Three weary travelers from Babylon. They then demanded of us who we were, and what were our intentions.

Q. Your answer? A. We are your own brethren and kindred of the tribe of Benjamin; we are the descendants of those noble families of Giblemites, who wrought so hard at the building of the first temple, were present at its destruction by Nebuchadnezzar, by him carried away captive to Babylon, where we remained servants to him and his sons till the first year of Cyrus, King of Persia, by whose order we were liberated, and are now returned to assist in rebuilding the house of the Lord, without expectation of fee or reward.

Q. What further was demanded, of you? A. The pass-word, "I am, that I am." After giving which, the Master of the Veil, assured of his full confidence in us as worthy brethren, commended us for our zeal and gave us the token and words to enable us to pass the second Veil.

Q. What are they? A. The token is an imitation of that which Moses was commanded to exhibit to the children of Israel, casting his rod upon the ground it became a serpent, and putting forth his hand and taking it again by the tail, it became a rod in his hand. The words are these, " Shem , Ham , and Japheth ."

[Pg 96] Q. What followed? A. We were conducted to the second Veil, where the same questions were asked, and answers returned as before, with the addition of the pass-words and token given at the first Veil.

Q. What followed? A. The Master of the second Veil told us that we must be true and lawful brethren to pass thus far, but further we could not go without his pass and token, which he accordingly gave to us.

Q. What are they? A. The words are Shem , Japheth , and Adoniram ; the token is putting the hand in the bosom, plucking it out again, in imitation of the second sign which Moses was directed to make to the Israelites, when putting his hand into his bosom and taking it out again, it became leprous as snow.

Q. How were you then disposed of? A. We were conducted onwards to the third Veil, when the same questions were asked, and answers returned as before, with the addition of the token and words last received.

Q. What followed? A. The Master of the third Veil then gave us the sign, words, and signet, to enable us to pass the fourth Veil, to the presence of the Grand Council.

Q. What are the words, sign, and signet? A. The words are Japheth , Shem , Noah ; the sign, pouring water upon the ground, in imitation of Moses, who poured water upon the ground and it became blood; the signet is called the signet of truth, and is Zerrubbabel. It alludes to this passage, "In that day I will take thee, O Zerrubbabel, my servant, the son of Shealtiel, and will make thee as a signet; for I have chosen thee." [See Haggai, chap. ii. ver. 23.]

Q. What followed? A. We then passed to the fourth Veil, where, after answering the same questions, and giving the sign, words, and signet last received, we were admitted to the presence of the Grand Council, where the High Priest made the same demands as were made at the Veils, and received the same answers.

Q. What did the High Priest further

demand of you? A. The signs from Entered Apprentice to Most Excellent Master in succession.

Q. What did he then say to you? A. He said we were truly three worthy Most Excellent Masters, commended us for our zeal and disinterestedness, and asked what part of the work we were willing to undertake.

Q. Your answer? A. That we were willing to undertake any service, however servile or dangerous, for the sake of forwarding so great and noble an undertaking.

Q. What followed? A. We were then furnished with a pick-axe, spade and crow, and were directed to repair to the northwest corner of the ruins of the old temple and commence removing the rubbish, to lay the foundation of the new, and to observe and preserve everything of importance and report to the Grand Council. We accordingly repaired to the place, and after laboring several days, we discovered what seemed a rock, but on striking it with the crow, it gave a hollow sound, and upon closer examination, we discovered in it an iron ring, by help of which we succeeded in removing it from its place, when we found it [Pg 97] to be the keystone of an arch, and through the aperture there appeared to be an immense vault curiously arched. We then took the stone and repaired to the Grand Council, and presented it for their inspection.

Q. What did the Grand Council then say to you? A. They told us that the stone contained the mark of our ancient Grand Master, Hiram Abiff; that it was truly a fortunate discovery, and that without doubt the vault contained things of the utmost consequence to the craft. They then directed us to repair again to the place and continue our researches.

Q. What followed? A. We returned again to the place and agreed that one of our number should descend by means of a rope, the middle of which was fixed firmly around his body, and if he wished to descend, he was to pull the rope in his right hand, if to ascend, that in his left. He accordingly descended, and in groping about, he found what appeared to be some ancient jewels, but the air becoming offensive, he pulled the rope in his left hand, and was immediately drawn out. We then repaired to the Grand Council, made our report, and presented the articles found, which they pronounced the jewels of our three ancient Grand Masters, Solomon, Hiram, and Hiram Abiff. They commended us highly for our zeal and fidelity, assured us that it was a fortunate discovery, that it would probably lead to still more important ones, and that our disinterested perseverance should not go unrewarded. They directed us to repair again to the place, and make what further discoveries lay in our power.

Q. What followed? A. We again returned to the place, and let down one of our companions as before. The sun having now reached its meridian height, darted its rays to the inmost recesses of the vault, and enabled him to discover a small chest or box, curiously wrought; but the air becoming exceedingly offensive, he gave the sign, and was immediately drawn out. We immediately repaired to the Grand Council and presented our discovery. On examination, the Grand Council pronounced it to be the ARK OF THE COVENANT , which was deposited in the vault by our ancient Grand Master for safe keeping. On inspecting it more closely, they found a key with which they opened it. The High Priest then took from it a book, which he opened, and read as follows:

Gen. i. 1-3. "In the beginning God created the heavens and the earth. And the earth was without form, and void; and darkness was upon the face of the deep; and the Spirit of God moved upon the face of the waters. And God said, Let there be light, and there was light."

Deut. xxxi. 24-26. "And it came to pass when Moses had made an end of writing the words of this law in a book, until they were finished, that Moses commanded the Levites, which bare the ark of the covenant of the Lord, saying, Take this book of the law and put it in the side of the ark of the covenant of the Lord your God, that it may be there for a witness against thee."

Ex. xxv. 21. "And thou shalt put the mercy-seat above, upon the ark, and in the ark thou shalt put the testimony that I shall give thee."

He then declared it to be the book of the law upon which the Grand Council, in an ecstasy of joy, exclaimed three times, "Long lost, now found, holiness to the Lord;" at the same time drawing their hands across their foreheads.

[Pg 98] Q. What further was found in the ark? A. A small vessel containing a substance, which, after the Council had examined, and the High Priest again read from the book of the law, Ex. xvi. 32-34, he pronounced to be manna:

"And Moses said, This is the thing which the Lord commanded; fill an omer of the manna to be kept for your generations, that they may see the bread wherewith I have fed you in the wilderness, when I brought you forth from the land of Egypt. And Moses said unto Aaron, Take a pot and put an omer full of manna therein, and lay it up before the Lord to be kept for your generations. As the Lord commanded Moses, so Aaron laid it up before the testimony, to be kept for a token."

The High Priest then took a rod from the ark, which, after he had read the following passage,

Numb. xvii. 10. "And the Lord said unto Moses, Bring Aaron's rod again before the testimony to be kept for a token."

He pronounced to be Aaron's rod, which budded and blossomed as the rose.

Q. Was there anything further found in the ark? A. There was a key to the ineffable characters belonging to this degree, as follows

⊐ ⊐ ⊏ ⊏ X

beginning at top of this diagram at the left hand angle. The upper left angle without a dot is A, the same with a dot is B, etc.

A B C D E F G H I J K L M
⌐ ⌐˙ ⊔ ⊔˙ ⊔ ⊔˙ ⊏˙ ⊐ ⊐˙ ⊐⊏ ⊏˙ ⊏

N O P Q R S T U V W X Y Z
⊓ ⊓˙ ⊓ ⊓˙ ⌐ ⌐˙ V V˙ < <˙ ∧ ∧˙ >

Q. What further was said to you? A. The High Priest read the following passage: Exodus vi. 2, 3. "And God spake unto

Moses, and said unto him, I am the Lord, and I appealed unto Abraham, unto Isaac, and unto Jacob, by the name of God Almighty, but by my name Jehovah was I not known to them."

He then informed us that the name of Deity, the divine Logos, or word, to which reference is made in John i. 1-5.

"In the beginning was the word, and the word was with God, and the word was God, the same was in the beginning with God, all things were made by Him, and without Him was not anything made that was made. In Him was life, and the life was the light of men. And the light shineth in darkness, and the darkness comprehendeth it not."

That this Logos or word was anciently written only in these sacred characters, and thus preserved from one generation to another. That this was the true Masonic word, which was lost in the death of Hiram Abiff, and was restored at the rebuilding of the temple, in the manner we had at that time assisted to represent.

Q. What followed? A. We were reminded of the manner in which we were sworn to give the Royal Arch word, were instructed in the manner, and finally invested with the all important word in due form.

Q. What is the Grand Royal Arch word? A. JAH BUH LUN.

Q. How is it to be given? A. Under a living arch by three times three, in low breath (see description of opening a Chapter).

[Pg 99] Q. What followed? A. We were presented with the signs belonging to this degree.

Q. Will you give me those signs? Answered by giving the signs thus: Raise the right hand to the forehead, the hand and arm horizontal; thumb towards the forehead, draw it briskly across the forehead, and drop it perpendicularly by the side. This constitutes the due-guard of this degree, and refers to the penalty of the obligation. The grand sign is made by locking the fingers of both hands together, and carrying them to the top of the head, the palms upward, alluding to the manner in which the brother who descended into the vault and found the ark, found his hands involuntarily placed to protect his head from the potent rays of the meridian sun.

Q. What followed. A. The High Priest then placed crowns upon our heads, and told us that we were now invested with all the important secrets of this degree, and crowned and received as worthy companions, Royal Arch Masons. He then gives the charge.

The second section of the Lecture on this degree states minutely the ceremonies and forms of exaltation (as the conferring of this degree is styled), but there seems to be some parts which require explanation. The Principal Sojourner conducts the candidate, and is considered as representing Moses conducting the children of Israel through the wilderness. He is usually dressed to represent an old man, bowed with age, with a mask on his face, and long beard hanging down upon his breast; is introduced to the candidate in the preparation room by the name of Moses. On entering the Chapter, the candidates are received under a "living arch;" that is, the companions arrange themselves in a line on each side of the door, and each joins hands with the one opposite to himself. The candidates entering, the conductor says, "Stoop low, brothers! we are about to enter the arches; remember that he that humbleth himself shall be exalted; stoop low, brothers, stoop low!" The candidates seldom pass the first pair of hands, or, in other words, the first arch, without being so far humbled as to be very glad to support themselves on all fours. Their progress may be imagined to be very slow; for, in addition to their humble posture, they are obliged to support on their backs the whole weight of the living arches above. The conductor, to encourage them, calls out occasionally, "Stoop low, brothers, stoop low!" If they go too slow to suit the companions, it is not unusual for some one to apply a sharp point to their bodies to urge them on; the points of the pasteboard crown answer quite well for this purpose. After they have endured this humiliating exercise as long as suits the convenience of the companions, they pass from under the living arches. The candidates next receive the obligation, travel the room, attend the prayer, travel again, and are shown a representation of the Lord appearing to Moses from the burning bush. This last is done in various ways. Sometimes an earthen pot is filled with earth, and green bushes set around the edge of it, and a candle in the centre; and sometimes a stool is provided with holes about the edge, in which bushes are placed, and a bundle of rags or tow, saturated with oil of turpentine, placed in the centre, to which fire is communicated. Sometimes a [Pg 100] large bush is suspended from the ceiling, around the stem of which tow is wound wet with oil of turpentine. In whatever way the bush is prepared, when the words are read, "He looked, and behold, the bush burned with fire," etc., the bandage is removed from the eyes of the candidates, and they see the fire in the bush, [15] and, at the words, "Draw not nigh hither; put off thy shoes," etc., the shoes of the candidates are taken off, and they remain in the same situation while the rest of the passage is read to the words, "And Moses hid his face; for he was afraid to look upon God." The bandage is then replaced, and the candidates again travel about the room, while the next passage of Scripture is read. [See Lecture.] At the words, "And break down the walls of Jerusalem," the companions make a tremendous crashing and noise, by firing pistols, overturning chairs, benches, and whatever is at hand; rolling cannon balls across the floor, stamping, etc., etc., and in the midst of the uproar the candidates are seized, a chain thrown about them, and they are hurried away to the preparation room. This is the representation of the destruction of Jerusalem, and carrying captive the children of Israel to Babylon. After a short time the proclamation of Cyrus is read, the candidates are unbound, and start to go to Jerusalem, to assist in rebuilding the temple. The candidates, still hoodwinked, are brought into the Chapter, and commence their journey over the rugged and rough paths. They are literally rough paths, sticks of timber framed across the path the candidate must travel, some inches from the floor, make no comfortable traveling for a person blindfolded. But this is not always the way it is prepared; billets of wood singly, or in heaps, ladders, nets of cord, etc., etc., are all put in requisition to form the rough and rugged paths, which are intended as a trial of the FIDELITY of the candidates. If they escape with nothing more than bruised shins they do well. They have been known to faint away under the severity of the discipline, and occasion the WORTHY companions much alarm. After traveling the rugged paths till all are satisfied, they arrive at the first Veil of the Tabernacle, give the pass-word, and pass on to the second, give the pass-words, and present the sign. This, it will be recollected, is in imitation of the sign which Moses was directed to make to the children of Israel. He threw his rod upon the ground and it became a serpent; he put forth his hand and took it by the tail, and it became a rod in his hand. The conductor is provided with a rod, made in the form of a snake, and painted to resemble one. This he drops upon the floor, and takes it up again. They then pass on to the next Veil, give the pass-word and make the sign (put the right hand in the bosom and pluck it out again); pass on to the next, give the pass-words and make the sign (pour water upon the ground), and are [Pg 101] ushered into the presence of the Grand Council . The Veils are four in number, and of the same color as the banners of the three Grand Masters of the Veils, and that of the Royal Arch Captain, blue, purple, scarlet and white, and have the same references and explanations. [See Lecture.] The Grand Council consists of the Most Excellent High Priest, King and Scribe. The High Priest is dressed in a white robe, with a breastplate of cut-glass, consisting of twelve pieces, to represent the twelve tribes of Israel; an apron, and a mitre. The King wears a scarlet robe, apron, and crown. The mitre and crown are generally made of pasteboard: sometimes they have them of the most splendid materials, gold and silk velvet; but these are kept for public occasions. The mitre has the words, " Holiness to the Lord " in gold letters across the forehead. The Scribe wears a purple robe, apron, and turban. After having satisfied the Grand Council that they are true brethren, and stated their object in coming to Jerusalem, the candidates are directed to commence the labor of removing the rubbish of the old temple preparatory to laying the foundation of the new. For the purpose of performing this part of the ceremony, there is in or near the Chapter a narrow kind of closet, the only entrance to which is through a scuttle at the top; there is placed over this scuttle whatever rubbish is at hand, bits of board, brick bats, etc., and among them the keystone. After the candidates are furnished with the tools (pick-axe, spade, and crow), they are directed to this place, and remove the rubbish till they discover the keystone. This they convey to the Grand Council, as stated in the Lecture. After the Grand Council have examined it, they pronounce it to be the work of the Grand Master, Hiram Abiff, and direct them to return and prosecute their researches, not doubting that they will make many important discoveries. The candidates return and let down one of their number by a rope; he finds three squares, is drawn out, and all proceed with them to the Grand Council. The Grand Council inspect them, and pronounce them to be the three ancient jewels that belonged to the three ancient Grand Masters, Solomon, Hiram and Hiram Abiff. The candidates then return to the vault and let down another of their number. Here, let it be remarked, some Chapters, for the purpose of lightening the labor of the candidates, call in the aid of machinery. A pulley is suspended over the vault, and the candidate is EXALTED from the bottom at the tail of a snatch block; the one last let down find at the bottom a small chest or box, upon which he gives the signal to be drawn out; he no sooner discovers the box than the air in the vault, in the language of the Lecture, "becomes exceedingly offensive." This is strictly true; for at the moment he takes up the box and is preparing to ascend, fire is communicated to a quantity of gunpowder at his feet, so that by the time he arrives at the top, he is so completely suffocated with the fumes of the powder, that he is almost deprived of the power of respiration or motion. The box is carried to the Grand Council and pronounced to be the ark of the covenant. It is opened, and a Bible taken out, and some passages read from it. [See Lecture.] One word respecting the representation of the ark. It ought to be a splendid box covered with gold, and some of them are really elegant; but the Chapter must [Pg 102] have such as it can afford; if it is too poor to procure splendid furniture, cheap articles are made to answer; for an ark, if the funds are low, a plain cherry or pine box will answer, and sometimes a cigar box is made the humble representation of the splendid ark, made by divine command, of shittim wood, and overlaid with pure gold. The High Priest takes then from the ark a vessel containing something to represent manna. This vessel is of various forms and materials, from an elegant silver urn to a broken earthen mug; and the substance contained is as various as the vessels in which it is deposited; such as a bit of sugar, a piece of cracker, or a few kernels of wheat. Whichever is used, the High Priest takes it out and gravely asks the King and Scribe their opinion of it; they say they think it is manna. The High Priest then looks at it intently and says, "It looks like manna;" smells it and says, "It smells like manna;" and then tastes it and says, "It is manna." The High Priest then takes from the ark a bit of an apple tree sprout, a few inches long, with some withered buds upon it, or a stick of a similar length, with some artificial buds upon it, which, after consulting with the King and Scribe, he pronounces Aaron's rod. He then takes out the key to the ineffable characters and explains it. This key is kept in the ark on four distinct pieces of paper. The key is marked on a square piece of paper, and the paper is then divided into four equal parts, thus:

The outside lines represent the dimensions of the paper; the inside ones are the key, and the dotted ones, the section that is made of the whole for the pur-

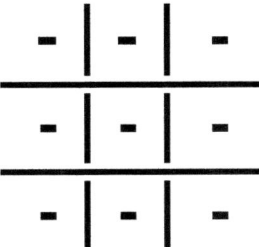

pose of keeping it secret, should any GRACELESS COWAN ever get possession of the sacred ark, and attempt to rummage its contents. The other part of the key x is made on the back of the same piece of paper, so that on putting them together, it shows equally plain. It is said that these characters were used by Aaron Burr, in carrying on his treasonable practices, and by that means made public; since which time they have been written and read from left to right. After the ceremonies are ended, the High Priest informs the candidates, in many or few words, according to his ability, that this degree owes its origin to Zerrubbabel and his associates, who rebuilt the temple by order of Cyrus, King of Persia. He informs them that the discovery of the secret vault and the inestimable treasures, with the long lost WORD, actually took place in the manner represented in conferring this degree, and that it is the circumstance upon which the degree is principally founded. The ceremony of closing a Chapter is precisely the same as at opening, to the raising of the living arch. The companions join hands by threes, in the same manner, and say in concert, "As we three did agree the sacred word to keep, as we three did agree the sacred word to search, so we three do agree to close this royal arch." They then break without giving the word, as the High Priest reads the following prayer:

"By the wisdom of the Supreme High Priest may we be directed, by His strength may we be enabled, and by the beauty of virtue may we be incited to perform the obligations here enjoined upon us; to keep inviolable the mysteries here unfolded to us, and invariably to practice all [Pg 103] those duties out of the Chapter, which are inculcated in it. (Response.) So mote it be. Amen." The High Priest then declares the Chapter closed in due form.

KNIGHTS OF THE RED CROSS.

At the sound of the trumpet the line is formed. Master of Calvary to the Sir Knight Warden, "When a Council of Knights of the Red Cross is about to be formed and opened, what is the first care?" Warden—"To see the Council chamber duly guarded." M. C.—"Please to attend to that part of your duty, see that the sentinels are at their respective posts, and inform the Captain of the Guards that we are about to open a Council of Knights of the Red Cross for the dispatch of business." W.—"The sentinels are at their respective posts, and the Council chamber duly guarded." M. C.—"Are all present Knights of the Red Cross?" W.—"They are." M. C.—"Attention, Sir Knights, count yourselves from right to left—right files handle sword—draw sword—carry sword—right files to the left double—second division forward, march, halt—right about face!" Sir Knight Master of Infantry, accompanied by the sword-bearer and Warden—"Please inform the Sovereign Master that the lines are formed waiting his pleasure." At the approach of the Council the trumpet sounds. M. C.—"Form avenue (the Council pass); the Sovereign Master passes uncovered; recover arms, poise arms!" Sovereign Master—"Attention, Sir Knights; give your attention to the several signs of Masonry; as I do, so do you." [The Sir Knights give the signs from the first to the seventh degree.] S. M.—"Draw swords, and take care to advance and give the Jewish countersign—recover arms; take care to advance and give the Persian countersign—recover arms." S.M. to Sir Knight Master of the Palace—"Advance and give me the word of a Knight of the Red Cross; the word is right—receive it on your left." The word is then passed around; when it arrives at the Chancellor he says, "Sovereign Master of the Red Cross, word has arrived." S. M.—"Pass it on to me [he gives it to the Sovereign Master]. Sir Knight, the word is right." S. M. to Sir Knight Chancellor—"Advance and give me the grand sign, grip, and word of a Knight of the Red Cross; it is right—receive it on your left." The word passes around as before, as will hereafter be explained, and when arrived at the Master of the Palace, he says, "Sovereign Master, the grand sign, grip and word have arrived. " S. M.—"Pass them on to me; Sir Knight, they are right. Left face—deposit helmets—centre face—reverse arms—to your devotions [the Sir Knights all kneel and repeat the Lord's prayer]—recover arms—left face—recover helmets—centre face—right about face—to your posts—march!"

First Section.

Question—Are you a Knight of the Red Cross? Answer—That is my profession.

Q. By what test will you be tried? A. By the test of truth.

[Pg 104] Q. Why by the test of truth? A. Because none but the good and true are entitled to the honors and privileges of this illustrious order.

Q. Where did you receive the honors of this illustrious order? A. In a just and regular Council of Knights of the Red Cross.

Q. What number compose a Council? A. There is an indispensable number and a constitutional number.

Q. What is the indispensable number? A. Three.

Q. Under what circumstances are they authorized to form and open a Council of Knights of the Red Cross? A. Three Knights of the Red Cross, being also Knight Templars, and hailing from three different commanderies, may, under the sanction of a legal warrant from some regular Grand Encampment, form and open a Council of Knights of the Red Cross for the dispatch of business.

Q. What is a constitutional number? A. Five, seven, nine, eleven, or more.

Q. When composed of five, seven, nine, eleven, of whom does it consist? A. Sovereign Master, Chancellor, Master of the Palace, Prelate, Master of

Cavalry, Master of Infantry, Master of Finance, Master of Dispatches, Standard-Bearer, Sword-Bearer, and Warder.

Q. Warder's station in the Council? A. On the left of the Standard-Bearer in the West.

Q. His duty? A. To announce the approach of the Sovereign Master; to see that the sentinels are at their respective posts, and the Council chambers duly guarded.

Q. Sword-Bearer's station in the Council? A. On the right of the Standard-Bearer in the West.

Q. His duty? A. To assist in the protection of the banner of our Order; to watch all signals from the Sovereign Master, and see his orders duly executed.

Q. Standard-Bearer's station? A. In the West.

Q. His duty? A. To display, support, and protect the banners of our Order.

Q. Why is the Standard-Bearer's station in the West? A. That the brilliant rays of the rising sun, shedding their lustre upon the banners of our Order, may encourage and animate all true and courteous Knights, and dismay and confound their enemies.

Q. Station of Master of Dispatches? A. In front of the Master of the Palace.

Q. His duty? A. To observe with attention the transactions of the Council; to keep a just and regular record thereof, collect the revenue, and pay the same over to the Master of Finance.

Q. Station of the Master of Finance? A. In front of the Chancellor.

Q. His duty? A. To receive in charge the funds and property of the Council, pay all orders drawn upon the Treasurer, and render a just and regular account when called for.

Q. Station of the Master of Infantry? A. On the right of the second division when separately formed: on the left of the whole when formed in line.

[Pg 105] Q. His duty? A. To command the second division or line of infantry, teach them their duty and exercise; also to prepare all candidates, attend them on their journey, answer all questions for them, and finally introduce them into the Council chamber.

Q. Station of the Master of Cavalry? A. On the right of the first division when separately formed, and on the right of the whole when formed in line.

Q. His duty? A. To command the first division or line of cavalry, teach them their duty and exercise; to form the avenue at the approach of the Sovereign Master, and prepare the lines for inspection and review.

Q. Prelate's station? A. On the right of the Chancellor.

Q. His duty? A. To preside in the Royal Arch Council; administer at the altar; to offer up prayers and adoration to Deity.

Q. Station of Master of the Palace? A. On the left of the Sovereign Master in the East.

Q. His duty? A. To see that the proper officers make all due preparations for the several meetings of the Council; to take special care that the Council chamber is in suitable array for the reception of candidates and the dispatch of business; to receive and communicate all orders issued by the Sovereign Master through the officers of the line.

Q. Chancellor's station? A. On the right of the Sovereign Master.

Q. His duty? A. To receive and communicate all orders and petitions; to assist the Sovereign Master in the discharge of his various duties, and in his absence to preside in the Council.

Q. Sovereign Master's station? A. In the East.

Q. His duty? A. To preside in the Council; confer this order of knighthood upon those whom his Council may approve; to preserve inviolable the laws and constitution of our Order; to dispense justice, reward merit, encourage truth, and diffuse the sublime principles of universal benevolence.

S. M.—"Sir Knight Chancellor, it is my will and pleasure that a Council of Knights of the Red Cross be now opened, and to stand open for the dispatch of such business as may regularly come before it at this time, requiring all Sir Knights now assembled, or who may come at this time, to govern themselves according to the sublime principles of our Order. You will communicate this to the Sir Knight Master of the Palace, that the Sir Knights present may have due notice thereof, and govern themselves accordingly." [The Sir Knight Chancellor communicates it to the Sir Knight Master of the Palace, and he to the Knights.] S. M.—"Return arms—right about face—to your posts—march—center face—Sir Knights, this Council is now open for the dispatch of business."

Second Section.

Question—What were the preparatory circumstances attending your reception to this illustrious Order? Answer—A Council of Royal Arch Masons being assembled in a room adjacent to the Council chamber, I was conducted to the door, where a regular demand was made by two, three, and two.

[Pg 106] Q. What was said to you from within? A. Who comes there?

Q. Your answer? A. Companion A. B., who has regularly received the several degrees of Entered Apprentice, Fellow Craft, Master Mason, Mark Master, Past Master, Most Excellent Master, and Royal Arch, and now solicits the honor of being regularly constituted a Knight of the Red Cross.

Q. What was then said to you? A. I was asked if it was of my own free will and accord that I made this request; if I was worthy and well qualified; if I had made suitable proficiency in the foregoing degrees, and was properly vouched for; all of which being answered in the affirmative, I was asked by what further right or benefit I expected to gain admittance.

Q. Your answer? A. By the benefit of a pass-word.

Q. Did you give that pass-word? A. I did, with the assistance of my companions. [Here the Royal Arch word is given as described in the Royal Arch degree.]

Q. What was then said to you? A. I was then directed to wait with patience till the Most Excellent Prelate should be informed of my request, and his answer returned.

Q. What was his answer? A. Let him be admitted.

Q. What was you then informed? A. The Most Excellent Prelate observed that the Council there assembled represented the Grand Council convened at Jerusalem, in the second year of the reign of Darius, King of Persia, to deliberate on the unhappy state of the fraternity during the reigns of Artaxerxes and Ahasuerus, and to devise some means to obtain favor of the new Sovereign, and to gain his consent to proceed in rebuilding their new city and temple.

Q. What followed? A. The Most Excellent Prelate then informed me if I was desirous of attending the deliberations of the Council at this time, it was necessary that I should assume the name and character of Zerrubbabel, a prince of the house of Judah, whose hands laid the foundation of the second temple, and whose hands the Lord has promised should complete it.

Q. What followed? A. The Most Excellent Prelate then read a lesson from the records of the Fathers, stating the impediments with which they were troubled by their adversaries on the other side of the river, and the grievous accusations which were brought against them before the King.

Q. What followed? A. My conductor then addressed the Most Excellent Prelate thus: Most Excellent Prelate, our Sovereign Lord, Darius the King, having now ascended the throne of Persia, new hopes are inspired of protection and support in the noble and glorious undertaking which has been so long and so often interrupted by our adversaries on the other side of the river; for while yet a private man, he made a vow to God that should he ever ascend the throne of Persia, he would send all the holy vessels remaining at Babylon back to Jerusalem. Our Most Excellent and faithful companion, Zerrubbabel, who was formerly honored with the favorable notice and friendship of the Sovereign, now offers his services to encounter the hazardous enterprise of traversing [Pg 107] the Persian dominions, and seeking admission to the presence of the Sovereign, where the first favorable moment will be seized to remind the King of his vow, and impress on his mind the almighty force and importance of truth; and from his known piety no doubt can be entertained of gaining his consent, that our enemies be removed far hence, and that we be no longer hindered or impeded in our noble and glorious undertaking.

Q. What was the Most Excellent Prelate's reply? A. Excellent Zerrubbabel, the Council accept with gratification and joy your noble and generous offer, and will invest you with the necessary passports, by means of which you will be enabled to make yourself known to the favor of one Council wherever you may meet them; but in an undertaking of so much importance, it is necessary that you enter into a solemn obligation to be faithful to the trust reposed in you.

Q. What followed? A. The Most Excellent Prelate then invested me with a sword, to enable me to defend myself against my enemies, and said he was ready to administer the obligation.

Q. Did you consent to that obligation? A. I did, in due form.

Q. What was that due form? A. Kneeling on my left knee, my right foot forming a square, my body erect, my right hand grasping the hilt of my sword, my left hand covering the Holy Bible, Square, and Compass, with two cross-swords thereon, in which due form I took upon me the solemn oath and obligation of Knight of the Red Cross.

Q. Repeat the obligation. "I, A. B., of my own free will and accord, in the presence of the Supreme Architect of the Universe, and these witnesses, do hereby and hereon most solemnly and sincerely promise and swear, that I will always hail, forever conceal, and never reveal, any of the secret arts, parts, or points of the mysteries appertaining to this Order of Knight of the Red Cross, unless it be to a true and lawful companion Sir Knight of the Order, or within the body of a just and lawful Council of such; and not unto him or them, until by due trial, strict examination, or lawful information, I find him or them lawfully entitled to receive the same. I furthermore promise and swear, that I will answer and obey all due signs and regular summons, which shall be sent to me from a regular Council of Knights of the Red Cross, or given to me from the hands of a companion Sir Knight of the Red Cross, if within the distance of forty miles; natural infirmities and unavoidable accidents only excusing me. I furthermore promise and swear, that I will not be present at the conferring of this Order of Knighthood upon any person, unless he shall have previously regularly received the several degrees of Entered Apprentice, Fellow Craft, Master Mason, Mark Master, Past Master, Most Excellent Master, and Royal Arch degree, to the best of my knowledge and belief. I furthermore promise and swear, that I will not assist or be present at the forming and opening of a Council of Knights of the Red Cross, unless there be present at least five regular Knights of the Order, or the representatives of three different Encampments, acting under the sanction of a legal warrant. I furthermore promise and swear, that I will vindicate the character of a courteous Sir Knight of the Red Cross when wrongfully traduced; that I will help him on a lawful occasion in preference to any brother of an inferior degree, and so far as truth, honor, and justice may warrant. I furthermore promise and swear, that I will support and maintain the by-laws of the Council, of which I may hereafter become a member, the laws and regulations of the Grand Encampment, under which the same may be holden, together with the constitution and ordinances of the General Grand Encampment of the United States of America, so far as the same shall come to my [Pg 108] knowledge. To all which I do most solemnly promise and swear, binding myself under no less penalty than of having my house torn down, the timbers thereof set up, and I hanged thereon; and when the last trump shall blow, that I be forever excluded from the society of all true and courteous Knights, should I ever wilfully or knowingly violate any part of this solemn obligation of Knight of the Red

Cross; so help me God, and keep me steadfast to keep and perform the same." [16]

Q. What followed? A. The Most Excellent Prelate then directed me to rise and be invested with a countersign, which he informed me would enable me to make myself known to the friends of our cause wherever I should meet them, and would insure me from them succor, aid, and protection. [Here the Master of Infantry, who is the conductor, gives the candidate the Jewish countersign; it is given under the arch of steel; that is, their swords elevated above their heads, forming a cross, each placing his left hand upon the other's right shoulder, and whispering alternately in each other's ear the names of Judah and Benjamin.]

Q. What followed? A. The Most Excellent Prelate then invested me with a green sash, as a mark of our particular friendship and esteem; you will wear it as a constant memorial to stimulate you to the faithful performance of every duty, being assured that the memory of him, who falls in a just and virtuous cause, shall forever flourish like the green bay tree.

Q. What followed? A. I then commenced my journey, and was frequently accosted by guards, all of which, by means of the countersign I had received, I was enabled to pass in friendship, until I arrived at the bridge, which was represented to be in the Persian dominions; on attempting to pass this bridge, which I found strongly guarded, the Persian countersign was demanded, and being unable to give it, I was attacked, overpowered, and made prisoner.

Q. What followed? A. After remonstrating in vain against their violations, I told them I was a prince of the house of Judah, and demanded an audience with their sovereign.

Q. What was the answer? A. You are a prisoner, and can obtain an audience with the sovereign only in the garb of a captive and slave.

Q. Did you consent to this? A. I did; being firmly persuaded that could I by any means gain access to the presence of the sovereign, I should be able to accomplish the object of my mission.

Q. What followed? A. They then deprived me of my outward apparel, sash and sword, and having confined my hands and feet in chains, the links thereof were of a triangular form, they put sackcloth and ashes on my head.

Q. Why were the links of the captive's chain of a triangular form? A. The Assyrians having learned that among the Jews the triangle was an emblem of the Eternal, caused the links of their chain to be made of a triangular form, thinking thereby to add to the miseries of their captives.

[Pg 109] Q. What followed? A. I was conducted to the door of the Council chamber, where the alarm being given by 4 × 2, the Warder appeared and demanded, "Who comes there?"

Q. What answer was returned? A. A detachment of his majesty's guards, having made prisoner of one, who reports himself to be prince of the house of Judah.

Q. What was then said to you? A. I was asked from whence I came.

Q. Your answer? A. From Jerusalem.

Q. What was then demanded of you? A. Who are you?

Q. Your answer? A. The first among my equals, a Mason, and free by rank, but a captive and slave by misfortune.

Q. What was you then asked? A. My name.

Q. Your answer? A. Zerrubbabel.

Q. What were you then asked? A. What are your demands?

Q. Your answer? A. To see the sovereign, if possible.

Q. What was then said to you? A. I was then directed to wait with patience until the Sovereign Master should be informed of my request, and his answer returned.

Q. What was that answer? A. That the necessary caution should be taken that I was not armed with any hostile weapons, and that I should then be admitted.

Q. How were you then received? A. The guard being drawn up on the right and left of the throne, swords drawn, two of them placed at the door with swords crossed, under which I was permitted to enter, my face covered with my hands.

Q. How were you then disposed of? A. I was conducted in front of the Sovereign Master, who received me with kindness and attention, and listened with patience to my request.

Q. What did the Sovereign Master then observe to the Council? A. That this Zerrubbabel was the friend of his youth, that he could neither be an enemy nor a spy.

Q. What followed? A. The Sovereign Master thus addressed me: "Zerrubbabel, having now gained admittance into our presence, we demand that you immediately declare the particular motives which induced you, without our permission, and with force and arms, to pass the lines of our dominions?"

Q. Your answer? A. Sovereign Master, the tears and complaints of my companions at Jerusalem, who have been so long and so often impeded in the noble and glorious undertaking in which they were permitted to engage by our late sovereign, Lord Cyrus, the King; but our enemies having made that great work to cease by force and power, I have now come up to implore your majesty's clemency, that you would be pleased to restore me to favor, and grant me employment among the servants of your household.

Q. What was the Sovereign's reply? A. Zerrubbabel, I have often reflected with much pleasure upon our early intimacy and friendship, and I have frequently heard, with great satisfaction, of your fame as a wise and accomplished Mason, and having myself a profound veneration for that ancient and honorable institution, and having a sincere desire to [Pg 110] become a member of the same, I will this moment grant your request, on condition that you will reveal to me the secrets of Freemasonry.

Q. Did you consent to that? A. I did not.

Q. What was your reply? A. Sovereign Master, when our Grand Master Solomon, King of Israel, first instituted the fraternity of Free and Accepted Masons, he taught us that truth was a divine attribute, and the foundation of every virtue; to be good and true is the first lesson we are taught in Masonry. My engagements are sacred and inviolable: I cannot reveal our secrets. If I can obtain your majesty's favor only at the expense of my integrity, I humbly beg leave to decline your royal protection, and will cheerfully submit to any honorable exile.

Q. What was the Sovereign's reply? A. Zerrubbabel, your virtue and integrity are truly commendable, and your fidelity to your engagements is worthy of imitation; from this moment you are free—my guards will divest you of those chains and that garb of slavery, and clothe you in suitable habiliments to attend me at the banquet hall. Zerrubbabel, you are free; guards, strike off those chains; and may those emblems of slavery never again disgrace the hands of a Mason, more particularly a prince of the house of Judah; Zerrubbabel, we assign you a seat of rank and honor among the princes and rulers of our assembly.

Q. What followed? A. The guards being drawn up in the court yard, the Warder informed the Sovereign Master that the guards were in readiness, waiting his pleasure.

Q. What followed? A. He then ordered the guards to attend him to the banquet hall.

Q. What occurred there? A. After having participated in a liberal entertainment, the Sovereign Master not being inclined to sleep, and many of the guard having retired, he amused himself by entering into conversation with some of his principal officers and friends, proposing certain questions to them, and offering a princely reward to such as should give the most reasonable and satisfactory answer.

Q. What questions were proposed? A. Among others, "Which was the strongest, wine, the King, or woman?" [17]

Q. What answers were returned? A. The Chancellor said wine was the strongest; the Master of the Palace said the King was the strongest; but I, being firmly persuaded that the time had arrived in which I could remind the King of his vow, and request the fulfilment of it, replied that women were stronger than either of the former, but, above all things, truth beareth the victory.

Q. What followed? A. The King being deeply struck with the addition I made to the question, ordered us to be prepared with proper arguments in support of our respective propositions on the day following.

Q. What followed? A. On the day following, the Council being convened at the sound of the trumpet, the Chancellor was called upon for his answer, and thus replied: (See Templar's Chart of Freemasonry.)

Q. What followed? A. The Master of the Palace thus replied: (See Templar's Chart of Freemasonry.)

[Pg 111] Q. What followed? A. I then being called upon for my defence, answered as follows: (See Templar's Chart of Freemasonry.)

Q. What followed? A. The King being deeply struck with the force of the arguments I had used, involuntarily exclaimed, "Great is truth, and mighty above all things; ask what thou wilt, Zerrubbabel, and it shall be granted thee, for thou art found wisest among thy companions."

Q. Your answer? (See Templar's Chart of Freemasonry.)

Q. What followed? A. The Sovereign Master then addressed me: "Zerrubbabel, I will punctually fulfil my vow; letters and passports shall be immediately issued to my officers throughout the realm, and they shall give you, and those who accompany you, safe conveyance to Jerusalem, and you shall be no longer hindered or impeded in rebuilding your city and temple, until they shall be completed."

Q. What followed? A. The Sovereign Master then invested me with a green sash, and thus addressed me, "This green sash, of which you were deprived by my guards, I now with pleasure restore to you, and will make it one of the insignia of a new Order, calculated to perpetuate the remembrance of the event which caused the renewal of our friendship; its color will remind you that truth is a divine attribute and shall prevail, and shall forever flourish in immortal green. I will now confer on you the highest honor in our power at this time to bestow, and will create you the first Knight of an Order, instituted for the express purpose of inculcating the almighty force and importance of truth.

Q. What followed? A. The Sovereign Master then directed me to kneel, and said, By virtue of the high power in me vested, as the successor and representative of Darius, King of Persia, I now constitute you a Knight of the illustrious Order of the Red Cross (at the same time laying the blade of his sword first upon the right shoulder, then upon the head, and then upon the left shoulder of the candidate).

Q. What followed? A. The Sovereign Master then directed me to arise, and presenting me with a sword, thus addressed me: "This sword, of which you were deprived by my guards, I now restore in your hands, as a true and courteous Knight; it will be endowed with three most excellent properties—its hilt be faith, its blade be hope, its point be charity; it should teach us this important lesson, that when we draw our swords in a just and virtuous cause, having faith in God, we may reasonably hope for victory, ever remembering to extend the hand of charity to the fallen foe; sheathe it, and sooner may it rust in its scabbard than be drawn in the cause of injustice or oppression."

Q. What followed? A. The Sovereign Master then invested me with the Persian countersign.

Q. Give it? A. This countersign is given like the Jewish, excepting this variation, it is given over instead of under the arch of steel. The words are Tatnai Shethar-boznai, Enavdai.

Q. Who were they? A. They were governors of Persian provinces, and enemies of the Jews.

Q. What followed? A. The Sovereign Master then invested me with the Red Cross word.

[Pg 112] Q. Give it? A. (Each placing his left hand upon the other's right shoulder, at the same time bringing the point of the swords to each other's left side, in which position the word Libertas is given.)

Q. What followed? A. The Sovereign Master then invested me with the grand sign, grip, and word of Knight of the Red Cross.

Q. Give them. A. The grand sign is given by bringing the thumb and finger of the left hand to the mouth, and carrying it off in an oblique direction; the grip is given by interlacing the fingers of the left hand; the word is Veritas. The sign, grip, and word are given under the arch of steel.

Q. How do you translate the word? A. Truth.

Q. To what does the sign allude? A. To the blowing of the trumpet upon the walls and watch towers of the Council, but more particularly to the obligation, "that when the last trump shall sound, I shall be forever excluded from the society of all true and faithful Sir Knights."

Q. What is the motto of our Order? A. "Magna est veritas et prevalebit." [Great is truth, and will prevail.]

KNIGHT TEMPLAR, AND KNIGHT OF MALTA.

First Section.

Question—Are you a Knight Templar? Answer—That is my title.

Q. Where were you created a Knight Templar? A. In a just and lawful Encampment of Knight Templars.

Q. What number composes a just and lawful Encampment of Knight Templars? A. There is an indispensable number and a constitutional number.

Q. What is an indispensable number? A. Three.

Q. Under what circumstances are they authorized to form and open an Encampment of Knight Templars? A. Three Knight Templars, hailing from three different commanderies, may, under the sanction of a charter or warrant from some regular Grand Encampment, form and open an Encampment for the dispatch of business.

Q. What is a constitutional number? A. Seven, nine, eleven, or more.

Q. When composed of eleven, of whom does it consist? A. Warden, Sword-Bearer, Standard-Bearer, Recorder, Treasurer, Junior Warden, Senior Warden, Prelate, Captain-General, Generalissimo, and Grand Commander.

Q. Warden's station? A. On the left of the Standard-Bearer in the West, and on the left of the third division.

Q. His duty? A. To observe the orders and directions of the Grand Commander; to see that the sentinels are at their respective posts, and that the Encampment is duly guarded.

Q. Sword-Bearer's station? A. On the right of the Standard-Bearer in the West, and on the right of the third division.

Q. His duty? A. To assist in the protection of the banners of our Order; to watch all signals from the Grand Commander, and see his orders duly executed.

[Pg 113] Q. Standard-Bearer's station in the Encampment? A. In the West, and in the centre of the third division.

Q. His duty? A. To display, support, and protect the banners of our Order.

Q. Why is the Standard-Bearer's station in the West? A. That the brilliant rays of the rising sun, shedding their lustre upon the banners of our Order, may encourage and animate all true and courteous Knights, and dismay and confound their enemies.

Q. Recorder's station in the Encampment? A. In front of the Captain-General.

Q. His duty? A. To observe with attention the order of the Encampment; keep a just and regular record of the same; collect the revenue, and pay the same over to the Treasurer.

Q. Treasurer's station in the Encampment? A. In front of the Generalissimo.

Q. His duty? A. To receive in charge all funds and property of the Encampment; pay all orders drawn upon him, and render a just and faithful account when required.

Q. Station of the Junior Warden in the Encampment? A. At the southwest angle of the triangle, and on the left of the first division.

Q. His duty? A. To attend to all poor and weary pilgrims traveling from afar; to accompany them on the journey; answer all questions for them, and finally introduce them into the asylum.

Q. Senior Warden's station in the Encampment? A. At the northwest angle of the triangle, and on the right of the second division.

Q. His duty there? A. To attend on pilgrim warriors traveling from afar; to comfort and support pilgrims penitent, and after due trial, to recommend them to the hospitality of the Generalissimo.

Q. Prelate's station in the Encampment? A. On the right of the Generalissimo.

Q. His duty there? A. To administer at the altar, and offer up prayers and adorations to the Deity.

Q. Captain-General's station? A. On the left of the Grand Commander.

Q. His duty? A. To see that the proper officers make all suitable preparations for the several meetings of the Encampment, and take special care that the asylum is in a suitable array for the introduction of candidates and dispatch of business; also to receive and communicate all orders from the Grand Commander to officers of the line.

Q. Generalissimo's station? A. On the right of the Grand Commander.

Q. His duty? A. To receive and communicate all orders, signals, and petitions, and assist the Grand Commander in the discharge of his various duties, and in his absence to govern the Encampment.

Q. Grand Commander's station? A. In the East.

Q. His duty? A. To distribute alms, and protect weary pilgrims traveling from afar; to encourage pilgrim warriors; to sustain pilgrims penitent; feed the hungry, clothe the naked, bind up the wounds of the afflicted; to inculcate hospitality, and govern his Encampment with justice and moderation.

[Pg 114]

Second Section.

Question—What were the preparatory circumstances attending your reception into this illustrious Order? Answer—I was conducted to the chamber of reflection, where I was left in silence and solitude, to reflect upon three questions, which were left with me in writing.

Q. What were your answers? A. They were satisfactory to the Grand Commander; but as a trial of my patience and perseverance, he enjoined upon me the performance of seven years' pilgrimage, clothed in pilgrim's weeds.

Q. What followed? A. I was then invested with sandals, staff, and scrip, and commenced my tour of pilgrimage, but was soon accosted by the guard, who demanded of me, "Who comes there?"

Q. Your answer? A. A poor and weary pilgrim, traveling from afar, to join with those who oft have gone before, and offer his devotions at the holy shrine.

Q. What said the guard? A. Pilgrim, I greet thee; gold and silver have I none, but such as I have give I unto thee.

Q. What followed? A. After having participated in the refreshments (which is a glass of water and a cracker), the guard took me by the hand and thus addressed me, "Pilgrim, harken to a lesson to cheer thee on thy way, and insure thee of success."

Q. What followed? Lesson read. (See Templar's chart.) The guard then took me by the hand and said, "Fare thee well! God speed thee on thy way."

Q. What followed? A. I still pursued my pilgrimage, but was often accosted by guards, from whom I received the same friendly treatment as from the first.

Q. Where did your term of pilgrimage end? A. At the door of the asylum, where after giving the alarm by 3 × 3, the Warder appeared and demanded, "Who comes there?"

Q. Your answer? A. A poor and weary pilgrim, traveling from afar, who, having passed full three long years of pilgrimage, now craves permission, if it shall please the Grand Commander, forthwith to dedicate the remaining four years to deeds of more exalted usefulness, and if found worthy, his strong desire is now to be admitted to those valiant Knights, whose well-earned fame has spread both far and near for deeds of charity and pure beneficence.

Q. What were you then asked? A. What surety can you offer that you are no impostor?

Q. Your answer? A. The commendations of a true and courteous Knight, the Junior Warden, who recommends to the Grand Commander the remission of four remaining years of pilgrimage.

Q. What followed? A. The Grand Commander then addressed the Most Excellent Prelate: "This being true, Sir Knight, our Prelate, you will conduct this weary pilgrim to the altar, where having taken an obligation always to be faithful to his vow, cause him forthwith to be invested with a sword and buckler, that as a pilgrim warrior he may perform seven years' warfare as a trial of his courage and constancy."

[Pg 115] Q. What followed? A. The Senior Warden then detached a party of Knights to escort me to the altar, where, in due form, I took upon me the obligation of a Knight Templar.

Q. What was that due form? A. Kneeling on both knees upon two cross swords, my body erect, my naked hands covering the Holy Bible, Square, and Compass, with two cross swords lying thereon, in which due form I received the solemn obligation of Knight Templar.

Q. Repeat the obligation.

"I, A. B., of my own free will and accord, in the presence of Almighty God and this Encampment of Knight Templars, do hereby and hereon most solemnly promise and swear, that I will always hail, forever conceal, and never reveal, any of the secret arts, parts, or points appertaining to the mysteries of this Order of Knight Templars, unless it be to a true and lawful companion Knight Templar, or within the body of a just and lawful Encampment of such; and not unto him or them, until by due trial, strict examination, or lawful information, I find him or them lawfully entitled to receive the same. Furthermore do I promise and swear, that I will answer and obey all due signs and regular summons, which shall be given or sent to me from regular Encampments of Knight Templars, if within the distance of forty miles, natural infirmities and unavoidable accidents only excusing me. Furthermore do I promise and swear, that I will help, aid, and assist with my council, my purse, and my sword, all poor and indigent Knight Templars, their widows and orphans, they making application to me as such, and I finding them worthy, so far as I can do it without material injury to myself, and so far as truth, honor, and justice may warrant. Furthermore do I promise and swear, that I will not assist or be present at the forming and opening of an Encampment of Knight Templars, unless there be present seven Knights of the Order, or the representatives of three different Encampments, acting under the sanction of a legal warrant. Furthermore do I promise and swear, that I will go the distance of forty miles, even barefoot and on frosty ground, to save the life and relieve the distresses of a worthy Knight, should I know that his distresses required it, and my abilities permit. Furthermore do I promise and swear, that I will wield my sword in defence of innocent virgins, destitute widows, helpless orphans, and the Christian religion. Furthermore do I promise and swear, that I will support and maintain the by-laws of the Encampment, of which I may hereafter become a member, the edicts and regulations of the Grand Encampment, under which the same may be holden, together with the laws and constitution of the General Grand Encampment of the United States of America, so far as the same shall come to my knowledge. To all this I most solemnly and sincerely promise and swear, with a firm and steady resolution to perform and keep the same, without any hesitation, equivocation, mental reservation, or self-evasion of mind in me whatever, binding myself under no less penalty than to have my head struck off and placed on the highest spire in Christendom, should I knowingly or wilfully violate any part of this my solemn obligation of a Knight Templar; so help me God, and keep me steadfast to perform and keep the same."

Q. What followed? A. The Most Excellent Prelate directed me to arise, and thus addressed me: "Pilgrim, thou hast craved permission to pass through our solemn ceremonies, and enter the asylum of our Encampment; by thy sandals, scrip, and staff, I judge thee to be a child of humility; charity and hospitality are the grand characteristics of this magnanimous Order; in the characters of Knight Templars, you are bound to give alms to poor and weary pilgrims, traveling from afar; to succor the needy, feed the hungry, clothe the naked, and bind up the wounds of the afflicted. We here wage war against the enemies of innocent virgins, destitute widows, helpless [Pg 116] orphans, and the Christian religion. If thou art desirous of enlisting in this noble and glorious warfare, lay aside thy staff and take up the sword, fighting manfully thy way, and with valor running thy course; and may the Almighty, who is a strong tower and defence to all those who put their trust and confidence in him, be now and ever thy defence and thy salvation."

Q. What followed? A. Having laid aside my staff and taken up the sword, the Most Excellent Prelate continued: "Having now taken up the sword, we expect you will make a public declaration of the cause in which you will wield it."

Q. Your answer? A. I wield my sword in defence of innocent virgins, destitute widows, helpless orphans, and the Christian religion.

Q. What was the Prelate's reply? A. With confidence in this profession, our Senior Warden will invest you with the warrior's pass, and under his direction, as a trial of your courage and constancy, we must now assign you seven years of warfare—success and victory attend you. (The pass-word is Mahershalalhashbaz, and is given under the arch of steel, as has been described.)

Q. What followed? A. I then commenced my tour of warfare, and made professions of the cause in which I would wield my sword.

Q. Where did your tour of warfare end? A. At the door of the asylum, where, on giving the alarm by 3 × 4, the Warder appeared and demanded, "Who comes there?"

Q. Your reply? A. A pilgrim warrior, traveling from afar, who, having passed full three long years of warfare, is most desirous now, if it should please the Grand Commander, to be admitted to the honors and rewards that await a valiant Templar.

Q. What was then demanded of you? A. What surety can you give that you are no impostor?

Q. Your answer? A. The commendation of a true and courteous Knight, the Senior Warden, who recommends to the Grand Commander the remission of the four remaining years of warfare.

Q. What was then demanded? A. By what further right or benefit do you expect to gain admittance to the asylum?

Q. Your answer? A. By the benefit of a pass-word.

Q. Give it. (Here the warrior's pass is given, as before described.)

Q. What was then said to you? A. I was directed to wait with courage and constancy, and soon an answer would be returned to my request.

Q. What answer was returned? A. Let him be admitted.

Q. What did the Grand Commander then observe? A. Pilgrim, having gained admittance to our asylum, what profession have you now to make in testimony of your fitness to be received a Knight among our number.

Q. Your answer? A. Most Eminent, I now declare, in truth and soberness, that I hold no enmity or hatred against a being on earth, that I would not freely reconcile, should I find him in a corresponding disposition.

Q. What was the Grand Commander's reply? A. Pilgrim, the sentiments you utter are worthy of the cause in which you are engaged; but [Pg 117] still we must require some stronger proofs of your faithfulness; the proofs we demand are, that you participate with us in five libations; this being accomplished, we will receive you a Knight among our number.

Q. What were the ingredients of the libations? A. Four of them were taken in wine and water, and the fifth in pure wine.

Q. What was the first libation? A. To the memory of Solomon, King of Israel.

Q. What was the second libation? A. To the memory of Hiram, King of Tyre.

Q. What was the third? A. To the memory of Hiram, the widow's son, who lost his life in defence of his integrity.

Q. What followed? A. The Grand Commander then addressed me: "Pilgrim, the Order to which you seek to unite yourself is founded on the Christian religion; let us, then, attend to a lesson from the holy evangelist."

Q. What followed? A. The Most Excellent Prelate then read a lesson relative to the apostasy of Judas Iscariot. (See Templar's Chart.)

Q. What followed? A. The Grand Commander then addressed me: "Pilgrim, the twelve tapers you see around the triangle, correspond in number with the disciples of our Saviour while on earth, one of whom fell by transgression, and betrayed his Lord and Master; and as a constant admonition to you always to persevere in the paths of honor, integrity, and truth, and as a perpetual memorial of the apostasy of Judas Iscariot, you are required by the rules of our Order to extinguish one of those tapers; and let it ever remind you that he who can basely violate his vow and betray his secret, is worthy of no better fate than Judas Iscariot." (The candidate extinguishes one of the tapers; the triangle is placed in the centre of the room, on which are twelve burning candles; between each candle stick a glass of wine; in the centre of the triangle is placed a coffin, on which are the Bible, skull and cross-bones.)

Q. What followed? A. The relics were then uncovered, and the Grand Commander thus addressed me: "Pilgrim, you here behold an emblem of mortality resting on divinity—a human skull resting on the Holy Scriptures; it is to teach us that among all the trials and vicissitudes which we are destined to endure while passing through the pilgrimage of this life, a firm reliance on divine protection can alone afford us the consolation and satisfaction which the world can neither give nor take away."

Q. What followed? A. The Most Excellent Prelate then read a lesson to me with respect to the bitter cup.

Q. What followed? A. The Grand Commander took the skull in his hand, and pronounced the following soliloquy: "How striking is this emblem of mortality, once animated, like us, but now it ceases to act or think; its vital energies are extinct, and all the powers of life have ceased their operations; and such, my brethren, is the state to which we are all hastening; let us, therefore, gratefully improve the remaining space of life, that when our weak and frail bodies, like this memento, shall become cold and inanimate and [Pg 118] mouldering in sepulchral dust and ruins, our disembodied spirits may soar aloft to the blessed regions, where dwell light and life eternal."

Q. What followed? A. The Most Excellent Prelate then read a lesson relative to the crucifixion. (See Templar's Chart.)

Q. What was the fourth libation? A. To the memory of Simon of Cyrene, the early friend and disciple of our Saviour, who was compelled to bear his cross, and fell a martyr to his fate.

Q. What followed? A. The Grand Commander then addressed me: "Pilgrim, before you can be permitted to participate in the fifth libation, we must enjoin on you one year's penance as a trial of your faith and humility, which you will perform under the direction of the Junior and Senior Wardens, with the skull in one hand, and a lighted taper in the other; which is to teach you that with faith and humility you should cause your light so to shine before men, that they, seeing your good works, may glorify our Father, which is in heaven."

Q. What followed? A. I then commenced my tour of penance, and passed in an humble posture through the sepulchre, where the fifth lesson was read by the Senior Warden relative to the resurrection. (Here the ascension of the Saviour is represented on canvas, which the candidate is directed to look at: at the same time the Sir Knights sing a hymn.) After the hymn, the Prelate speaks as follows:

"I am the resurrection and the life, saith the Lord; he that believeth on me, though he were dead, yet shall he be made alive; and whosoever liveth and believeth on me shall never die. Pilgrim, the scene before you represents the splendid conclusion of the hallowed sacrifice offered by the Redeemer of the world, to propitiate the anger of an offended Deity. This sacred volume informs us that our Saviour, after having suffered the pains of death, descended into the place of departed spirits, and that on the third day he burst the bands of death, triumphed over the grave, and, in due time, ascended with transcendent majesty to heaven, where he now sits on the right hand of our Heavenly Father, a mediator and intercessor for all those who have faith in Him. I now invest you with an emblem of that faith (at the same time suspends from his neck a black cross): it is also an emblem of our Order, which you will wear as a constant memorial, for you to imitate the virtues of the immaculate Jesus, who died that you might live. Pilgrim, the ceremonies in which you are now engaged are calculated deeply to impress your mind, and I trust will have a happy and lasting effect upon your character. You were first, as a trial of your faith and humility, enjoined to perform seven years of pilgrimage; it represents the great pilgrimage of life, through which we are all passing; we are all weary pilgrims, anxiously looking forward to that asylum, where we shall rest from our labors, and be at rest forever. You were then directed, as a trial of your courage and constancy, to perform seven years' warfare; it represents to you the constant warfare with the lying vanities and deceits of this world, in which it is necessary for us always to be engaged. You are now performing a penance as a trial of your humility. Of this our Lord and Saviour has left us a bright example. For though he was the Eternal Son of God, he humbled himself to be born of a woman, to endure the pains and afflictions incident to human nature, and finally to suffer a cruel and ignominious death upon the cross; it is also a trial of that faith which will conduct you safely over the dark gulf of everlasting death, and land your enfranchised spirit in the peaceful abodes of the blessed. Pilgrim, keep ever in your memory this awful truth; you know not how soon you may be called upon to render an account to that Supreme Judge, from whom not even the most minute action of your life is hidden; for although you now stand erect in all the strength [Pg 119] of manhood and pride of beauty, in a few short moments you may become a pale and lifeless corpse. This moment, even while I yet speak, the angel of death may receive the fatal mandate to strike you from the role of existence; and the friends who now surround you may be called upon to perform the last sad duty of laying you in the earth, a banquet for worms, and this fair body become as the relic you now hold in your hand. Man that is born of a woman is of few days and full of sorrow; he cometh up and is cut down like a flower; he fleeth as a shadow and continueth not; in the midst of life we are in death; of whom may we seek for succor but of Thee, O Lord, who for our sins are justly displeased. Yet, O God most holy, thou God most mighty, O holy and most merciful Saviour, deliver us from the pains of eternal death. I heard a voice from heaven saying unto me, write from henceforth, blessed are the dead that die in the Lord; even so, saith the spirit, for they rest from their labors; be ye also ready, and rest assured that a firm faith in the truths here revealed will afford you consolation in the gloomy hour of dissolution, and insure you ineffable and eternal happiness in the world to come. Amen and amen."

Q. Where did your tour of penance end? A. It has not yet ended; neither can it end until this mortal shall put on immortality; for all men err, and all error need repentance.

Q. Were you then permitted to participate in the fifth libation? A. I was.

Q. Where? A. Within the asylum.

Q. How gained you admittance there? A. After having passed my year of penance, I returned to the door of the asylum, where, on giving the alarm, the Warden appeared and demanded, "Who comes there?"

Q. Your answer? A. Pilgrim penitent, traveling from afar, who begs your permission here to rest, and at the shrine of our departed Lord to offer up his prayers and meditations.

Q. What was then demanded of you? A. What surety can he offer that he is no impostor?

Q. Your answer? A. The commendation of two true and courteous Knights, the Junior and Senior Wardens.

Q. What was then demanded of you? A. By what further right or benefit I expected to gain admittance.

Q. Your answer? A. By the benefit of a pass-word.

Q. Did you give that pass-word? A. I did not; my conductor gave it for me.

Q. Give it? A. Golgotha. (It is given as before described.)

Q. What was then said to you? A. Wait with faith and humility, and soon an answer shall be returned to your request.

Q. What was the answer of the Grand Commander? A. That I should be admitted.

Q. What did the Grand Commander then demand? A. Who have you there in charge, Sir Knight?

Q. What answer was returned? A. A pilgrim penitent, traveling from afar, who, having passed his term of penance, seeks now to participate in the fifth libation, thereby to seal his fate.

Q. What did the Grand Commander then observe? A. Pilgrim, in granting your request and receiving you a Knight among our number, I can only offer you a rough habit, coarse diet, and severe duties; if, on [Pg 120] these conditions, you are still desirous of enlisting under our banners, you will advance and kneel at the base of the triangle.

Q. What did the Grand Commander then observe? A. Pilgrim, the fifth libation is taken in the most solemn and impressive manner; we cannot be too often reminded that we are born to die; and the fifth libation is an emblem of that bitter cup of death, of which we must all sooner or later partake, and from which even the Saviour of the world, notwithstanding his ardent prayers and solicitations, was not exempt.

Q. What was then said to you? A. The Grand Commander asked me if I had any repugnance to participate in the fifth libation.

Q. Your answer? A. I am willing to conform to the requirements of the Order.

Q. What followed? A. I then took the cup (the upper part of the human skull) in my hand, and repeated after the Grand Commander the following obligation:

"This pure wine I now take in testimony of my belief in the mortality of the body and the immortality of the soul, and may this libation appear as a witness against me, both here and hereafter, and as the sins of the world were laid upon the head of the Saviour, so may all the sins committed by the person whose scull this was be heaped upon my head, in addition to my own, should I ever knowingly or wilfully violate or transgress any obligation that I have heretofore taken, take at this time, or shall at any future period take, in relation to any degree of Masonry, or Order of Knighthood. So help me God."

Q. What was this obligation called? A. The sealed obligation.

Q. Why so? A. Because any obligation entered into, or promise made in reference to this obligation, is considered by Knight Templars as more binding and serious than any other special obligation could be.

Q. What followed? A. The Most Excellent Prelate then read the sixth lesson, relative to the election of Matthias. (See Chart.)

Q. What followed? A. The Generalissimo thus addressed the Grand Commander: "Most Eminent, by the extinguished taper on the triangle, I perceive there is a vacancy in our Encampment, which I propose should be filled by a choice from among those valiant Knights who have sustained the trials and performed the ceremonies required by our Order." [18]

Q. What followed? A. The Grand Commander then ordered the lots to be given forth, which being done, I was elected, and the Grand Commander thus addressed me: "In testimony of your election as a companion among us, and of your acceptance of that honor, you will relight that extinguished taper; and may the Almighty lift upon you the light of His countenance, and preserve you from falling."

Q. What followed? A. The Grand Commander then directed me to kneel, and said by virtue of the high power in me vested, as the successor and representative of Hugh De Paganis, and Geoffrey, of St. Omers, I now dub and create you Knight Templar, Knight of Malta, of the Holy Order of St. John of Jerusalem. [This is repeated three times, at the same time laying the blade of the sword first upon the right shoulder, [Pg 121] then upon the head, and then upon the left shoulder of the candidate.]

Q. What followed? A. The Grand Commander then presented me a sword, and thus addressed me: "This sword in your hand, as a true and courteous Knight, will be endowed with three most excellent qualities; its hilt be justice impartial, its blade be fortitude undaunted, and its point be mercy; and let it teach us this important lesson, that we should ever be assured of the justice of the cause in which we draw our swords, and being thus assured, we should persevere with the most undaunted fortitude, and finally, having subdued our enemies, we should consider them no longer such, but extend to them the most glorious attribute of God's mercy."

Q. What followed? A. The Grand Commander then communicated to me the due-guard, the penitent's pass, and the grand sign, grip and word of Knight Templars.

Q. Give the due-guard? [The sign is given by placing the end of the right thumb under the chin.]

Q. To what does it allude? A. To the penalty of my obligation; to have my head struck off and placed upon the highest spire in Christendom.

Q. Give the penitent's pass? A. It is given as before described; the word is Golgotha.

Q. Give the grand sign. [This sign is given by placing yourself in a situation representing the crucifixion of Christ.]

Q. To what does this sign allude? A. To the manner in which the Saviour expired upon the cross, and expiated the sins of the world.

Q. Give the grip and word. [This grip is given by interlacing the fingers of the right and left hands of the candidate, which forms a cross.]

Q. What is the word? A. Immanuel. [The word is given at the time of giving the grip, and is the name of the grip.]

Q. What does the grip teach us? A. That as our fingers are thus strongly interlaced, so should the hearts of Knight Templars be firmly interlaced in friendship and brotherly love.

Q. What is the motto of our Order? A. Rex regum, et Dominus dominorum.

Q. How do you translate it? A. King of kings, and Lord of Lords.

KNIGHTS OF THE CHRISTIAN MARK, AND GUARDS OF THE CONCLAVE.

This Conclave is governed by an Invincible Knight of the Order of St. John of Jerusalem, a Senior and Junior Knight, six Grand Ministers, Recorder, Treasurer, Conductor, and Guard.

Opening. —"Sir Junior Knight, are all convened in a secret place, and secured from the prying eye of the profane?"

"We are, Invincible."

"Sir Senior Knight, instruct the Sir Knights to assemble in form for the purpose of opening this Invincible Order."

The members kneel on both knees in a circle, each with his right hand on his heart, his left on his forehead.

Prayer. —"Eternal source of life, of light, and [Pg 122] perfection, Supreme God and Governor of all things, liberal dispenser of every blessing! We adore and magnify Thy holy name for the many blessings we have received from Thy hands, and acknowledge our unworthiness to appear before Thee; but for the sake, and in the name of Thy atoning Son, we approach Thee as lost and undone children of wrath; but through the blood of sprinkling, and the sanctification of the Holy Ghost, we come imploring a continuation of Thy favors, for thou hast said, that he who cometh to Thee through faith in the Son of Thy love, Thou wilt in no wise cast out; therefore, at the foot of the cross we come, supplicating pardon for our past offences, that they may be blotted out from the book of Thy remembrance and be seen no more, and that the remainder of our days may be spent as becometh the followers of the Holy One of Israel; and graciously grant that love, harmony, peace, and unity may reign in this Council; that one spirit may animate us—one God reign over us—and one heaven receive us, there to dwell in Thine adorable presence forever and ever. Amen."

The Invincible Knight takes the Bible and waves it four times over his head, saying, "Rex regnantium, et Dominus dominantium;" [that is, King of kings, and Lord of Lords;] kisses it and passes it on his right; it goes around until it comes again to the Invincible Knight, who opens and reads, Matthew v. 3-12, 16.

Always interlace the fingers of the left hand, draw your sword and present it to the heart, and say, "Tammuz Touliumeth, I pronounce this Convention opened in ample form. Let us repair to our several stations, and strictly observe silence."

Preparation. —The candidate is shown into the anti-chamber by the conductor, who clothes him in a gown of brown stuff, and leads him to the door of the Council chamber, where he knocks twice, six, and two—2, 6, and 2.

Junior Knight—"Some one knocks for admission, Invincible Knight." Invincible—"See who it is and make report." J. K. (goes to the door and reports)—"One that is faithful in good works wishes admission here." Inv.—"What good works hath he performed?" J. K.—"He hath given food to the hungry, drink to the thirsty, and clothed the naked with a garment." Inv.—"Thus far he hath done well; but there is still much for him to do. To be faithful in my house, saith the Lord, he should be filled with love for my people. If so, let him enter under the penalties of his symbolic obligation." He enters, makes signs until he arrives at the altar, there kneels.

Vow. —"I, A. B., do promise and vow, with this same volume clasped in my hands, that I will keep secret the words, signs, tokens, and grips of this Order of Knighthood from all but those Knights of St. John of Jerusalem, who have shown a Christian disposition to their fellow-men, are professors of the Christian faith, and have passed through the degrees of symbolic Masonry; and that I will protect and support, as far as in me lies, the followers of the Lord Jesus Christ; feed them, if hungry; give them drink, if thirsty; if naked, clothe them with garments; teach them, if ignorant; and advise them for their good and their advantage. All this I promise in the name of the Father, of the Son, and of the Holy Ghost; and if I perform it not, LET ME BE ANATHEMA MARANATHA! ANATHEMA MARANATHA! " [i.e., accursed at the coming of the Lord.]

The Invincible Knight interlaces the fingers of his left hand with those of the candidate, who lays his right hand on his heart. The Invincible Knight draws his sword; the Senior Knight does the same; they cross [Pg 123] them on the back of the candidate's neck, and the Invincible Knight says, "By virtue of the high power in me vested, by a bull of His Holiness, Pope Sylvester , I dub you a Knight of the Christian Mark, member of the Grand Council, and Guard of the Grand Conclave." The Invincible Knight then whispers in his ear, "Tammuz Touliumeth." The Knights come to order; the Senior Knight takes his seat; the candidate continues standing; the conductor brings a white robe; the Senior Knight says:

"Thus saith the Lord, he that believeth and endureth to the end shall overcome, and I will cause his iniquities to pass from him, and he shall dwell in my presence forever and ever. Take away his filthy garments from him, and clothe him with a change of raiment. For he that overcometh the same shall be clothed in white raiment, and his name shall be written in the Book of Life, and I will confess his name before my Father and his holy angels. He that hath an ear to hear, let him hear what the Spirit saith unto the true believer. Set ye a fair mitre upon his head, place a palm in his hand, for he shall go in and out and minister before me, saith the Lord of hosts; and he shall be a disciple of that rod taken from a branch of the stem of Jesse. For a branch has grown out of his root, and the spirit of the Lord hath rested upon it; the spirit of his wisdom, and might, and righteousness is the girdle of his loins and faithfulness the girdle of his vine, and he stands as an insignia to the people, and him shall the Gentiles seek, and his rest shall be glorious. Cause them that have charge over the city to draw near, every one with the destroying weapon in his hand."

The six Grand Ministers came forward from the north with swords and shields. The first is clothed in white, and has an ink-horn by his side, and stands before the Invincible Knight, who says:

"Go through the city: run in the midst thereof and smite: let not thine eye spare, neither have pity; for they have not executed my judgments with clean hands, saith the Lord or Hosts."

The candidate is instructed to exclaim:

"Woe is me, for I am a man of unclean lips, and my dwelling has been In the tents of Kedar, and among the children of Meshec."

Then he that has the ink-horn by his side, takes a live branch with the tongs from the altar, and touches the lips of the candidate, and says:

"If ye believe, thine iniquities shall be taken away, thy sins shall be purged. I will that these be clean with the branch that shall be given up before me. All thy sins are removed, and thine iniquities blotted out. For I have trodden the wine-press alone, and with me was none of my people. For behold, I come with dyed garments from Bozrah, mighty to save. Refuse not, therefore, to hearken; draw not away thy shoulders; shut not thine ear, that thou shouldest not hear."

The six Ministers now proceed as if they were about to commence the slaughter, when the Senior Knight says to him with the ink-horn:

"Stay thine hand; proceed no further until thou hast set a mark on those that are faithful in the house of the Lord, and trust in the power of his might. Take ye the signet, and set a mark on the forehead of my people that have passed through great tribulation, and have washed their robes, and have made them white in the blood of the Lamb, which was slain from the foundation of the world."

The Minister takes the signet and presses it on the candidate's forehead. He leaves the mark in red letters, " King of Kings, and Lord of Lords ." The Minister opens the scroll and says, "Sir Invincible Knight, the number of the sealed are one hundred and forty and four thousand." [Pg 124] The Invincible Knight strikes four, and all the Knights stand before him. He says, "Salvation belongeth to our God, which sitteth upon the throne, and unto the Lamb." All the members fall on their faces, and say "Amen. Blessing, honor, glory, wisdom, thanksgiving, and power, might, majesty, and dominion, be unto our God forever and ever. Amen." They all cast down crowns and palm branches, and rise up and say, "Great and numberless are thy works, thou King of saints. Behold the star which I laid before Joshua, on which is engraved seven eyes, as the engraving of a signet, shall be set as a seal on thine arm—as a seal on thine heart; for love is stronger than death: many waters cannot quench it. If a man would give all the treasures of his house for love, he cannot obtain it; it is the gift of God through Jesus Christ, our Lord."

Charge. —"Invincible Knight, I congratulate you on your having been found worthy to be promoted to this honorable Order of Knighthood. It is highly honorable to all those worthy Knights, who with good faith and diligence, perform its many important duties. The honorable situation to which you are now advanced, and the illustrious office which you now fill is one that was much desired by the first noblemen of Italy, but ambition and jealousy caused his highness, Pope Alexander, to call on his ancient friend, the Grand Master of the Knights of St. John of Jerusalem, to guard his person and the Holy See, as those Knights were known to be well grounded in the faith, and zealous followers of the Lord. The members of the guard were chosen BY THEIR COUNTENANCES , for it is believed that a plain countenance is an indication of the heart; and that no stranger should gain admission and discover the secrets of this august assembly, this Order of the Christian Mark was conferred on those who went about doing good, and following the example of their illustrious Master, Jesus Christ. Go thou and do likewise.

Motto. —"Christus regnat, vincit, triumphat;" [i.e., Christ rules, conquers, triumphs.] Rex regnantium, et Dominus dominantium.

Israel on the left breast, a triangular plate of gold, seven eyes engraved on one side, on the other the letter G in the five points.

KNIGHTS OF THE HOLY SEPULCHRE.

History. —St. Helena, daughter of Caylus, King of Britain, consort of Constantine, and mother of Constantine the Great, in the year 296, made a journey to the Holy Land in search of the cross of Jesus Christ. After leveling the hillocks and destroying the temple of Venus, three crosses were discovered. It was now difficult to discover which of the three was the one sought for by her. By order of his Holiness, Pope Marcellinus, they were borne to the bed of a woman who had long been visited by sickness, and lay at the point of death; she placed her hands upon the second cross first, which rendered her no service; but when she laid her hand upon the third, she was restored to her former health. She instantly arose, giving glory to God, saying, He was wounded for our transgressions, he was bruised for our iniquities, the chastisement of sin was upon him, and with his stripes we are healed. On the spot where the crosses were found, St. Helena erected a stately church, one hundred paces long and sixty wide; the east end takes in the place where the crosses stood, and the west of the sepulchre. By leveling the hills, the sepulchre is above the floor of the church, like a grotto, which is twenty feet from the floor to the top of the rock. There is a superb cupola over the sepulchre, and in the aisles are the tombs of Godfrey and Baldwin, kings of Jerusalem. In 302, St. Helena instituted the Order of Knights of the Holy Sepulchre of our Lord and Saviour, Jesus Christ. This Order was confirmed in 304 by his Holiness, Pope Marcellinus; they were bound by a sacred vow to guard the Holy Sepulchre, protect pilgrims, and fight infidels and enemies of the cross of [Pg 125] Christ. The city of Jerusalem was rebuilt and ornamented by Ælius Adrian, Emperor of Rome, and given to the Christians in 120. The Persians took it from them in 637, and in 1008 it fell into the hands of the Turks, under whose oppressions it long groaned, until Peter the Holy steered the western princes to release the distressed church, and in 1096 Godfrey and Baldwin unfurled the banner of the cross and expelled the Turks. He was invested with a crown of laurel, and suffered himself to be called the King of Palestine.

Description, Etc. —The Council must represent a Cathedral Church, the altar covered with black, upon which must be placed three large candles, a cross, and in the centre a skull and cross-bones. The Principal stands on the right side of the altar, with a Bible in one hand, and a staff in the other; soft music plays, and the veil is drawn up, and discovers the altar; the choir say:
Hush, hush, the heavenly choir,
They cleave the air in bright attire;
See, see, the lute each angel brings,
And hark divinely thus they sing.
To the power divine,
All glory be given,
By man upon earth,
And angels in heaven.
The priest steps before the altar and says, "Kyrie Elieson; Christe Elieson; Kyrie Elieson; [that is, O Lord, have mercy; O Christ, have mercy; O Lord, have mercy.] Amen. Gloria Sibi Domino! [i.e., Glory to the Lord himself.] I declare this Grand Council opened and ready to proceed to business." The Priests and Ministers take their several stations and observe order. The candidates being prepared, he alarms at the door by seven raps, and the Prelate says to Verger, "See the cause of that alarm and report." Verger goes to the door and reports, "Right Reverend Prelate, there are seven brethren who solicit admission to this Grand Council." Prelate says, "On what is their desire founded?" Verger—"On a true Christian principle, to serve the church and its members by performing the seven corporeal works of mercy, and to protect and guard the Holy Sepulchre from the destroying hands of our enemies." Prelate—"Admit them, that we may know them, if you please." They are then admitted. Prelate says to them, "Are you followers of the Captain of our salvation?" Verger says, "We are, Right Reverend Prelate." P.—"Attend, then, to the sayings of our Master, Jesus Christ." Thou shalt love the Lord thy God with all thy heart, with all thy mind, with all thy soul, and with all thy might. This is the first great commandment, and the second is like unto it; thou shalt love thy neighbor as thyself; on these two commandments hang all the law and the prophets. The Verger and Beadle hold the Bible, on which the candidates place their right hands.

Vow. —"I, A. B., in the name of the high and undivided Trinity, do promise and vow to keep and conceal the high mysteries of this noble and Invincible Order of Knights of the Holy Sepulchre, from all but such as are ready and willing to serve the church of Christ by acts of valor and charity, and its members by performing all the corporeal works of mercy, and that, as far as in me lies, I will defend the church of the Holy Sepulchre from pillage and violence, and guard and protect pilgrims on their way to and from the Holy Land; and if I perform not this, my vow, to the best of my abilities, let me become INANIMATUS [dead].

Interlace your fingers with the candidate, cross your arms, and say, "De mortuis, nil nisi bonum; [i.e., concerning the dead, say nothing but [Pg 126] good.] Prelate says, "Take the sword and travel onward—guard the Holy Sepulchre—defeat our enemies—unfurl the banner of our cross—protect the Roman Eagle—return to us with victory and safety." The candidates depart, go to the south, where they meet a band of Turks—a desperate conflict ensues—the Knights are victorious; they seize the crescent, and return to the cathedral in triumph, and place the banner, eagle, and crescent before the altar, and take their seats. (22d chapter St. John read by Prelate.) Then the choir sing:
"Creator of the radiant light,
Dividing day from sable night;
Who with the light bright origin,
The world's creation didst begin."
Prelate then says, "Let our prayer come before Thee, and let our exercise be acceptable in thy sight." The seven candidates kneel at the foot of the altar. The Prelate takes the bread, and says, "Brethren, eat ye all of this bread in love, that ye may learn to support each other." He then takes the cup, and says, "Drink ye all of this cup to ratify the vow that ye have made, and learn to sustain one another." The Prelate then raises them up by the grip (interlace the fingers), and says, "1st, Sir, I greet thee a Knight of the Holy Sepulchre; go feed the hungry; 2d, Give drink to the thirsty; 3d, Clothe the naked with a garment; 4th, Visit and ransom the captives; 5th, Harbor the harborless, give the orphan and widow where to lay their heads; 6th, Visit and relieve the sick; 7th, Go and bury the dead." All make crosses and say, "In nomini patria filio et spiritus sancto. Amen." Prelate says, "Brethren, let us recommend to each other the practice of the four cardinal virtues—prudence, justice, temperance, fortitude."

Closing. —The Knights all rise, stand in circle, interlace their fingers, and say, "Sepulchrum." Prelate then says, "Gloria patri, et filio, et spiritus sancto;" [i.e., Glory to the Father, Son, and Holy Spirit.] Brethren answer, "Sicut erat in principio, et nunc, et semper et in secula seculorum; [i.e., As it was in the beginning, is now, and shall be, world without end.] Amen."

Benediction. —"Blessed be thou, O Lord, our God! Great first cause and

Governor of all things; thou createst the world with thy bountiful hand, and sustained it by thy wisdom, by thy goodness, and by thy mercy! It cometh to pass that seed time and harvest never fall! It is Thou that givest every good and perfect gift! Blessed be thy name forever and ever!"

To examine a Knight of the Holy Sepulchre; he holds up the first finger of the right hand, Knight holds up the second; you then hold up the third, and he shuts up his first; this signifies three persons in one God.

THE HOLY AND THRICE ILLUSTRIOUS ORDER OF THE CROSS, CALLED A COUNCIL.

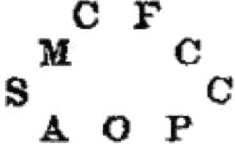

Diploma of a Comp. of the Ancient Council of the Trinity, Anno Cr. seu Covt. 896.—The Ancient Council of the Trinity, by Their Successors in the United States of America.

St. Albert, to every Knight Companion of the Holy and Thrice Illustrious Order of the Cross: Be it known unto you, that with regard [Pg 127] to unquestionable vouchers, we have confirmed the Induction of the Knight Templar Mason into the Councils of the said Order of Knighthood, and herein do warrant him as a worthy and Illustrious Companion, thereof; and hoping and confiding that he will ever so demean himself as to conduct to the glory of I. H. S., the Most Holy and Almighty God, and to the honor of his Mark, we do recommend and submit him to the confidence of all those throughout the world, who can truly and deservedly say, "I am a Christian;" and that no unwarrantable benefits shall arise from this Diploma, and we charge all concerned cautiously and prudently to mark the bearer on the mystic letters therein contained, and to regard only the result, in its application and privileges.

Done out of Council, at ——, in the county of ——, and State of ——, on this —— day of ——.

Sir ——
Sovereign Prefect.
Sir ——
Acting Pref.
Commendations,
Sir Knights Comp'ns.

The officers and council all in their places. The Most Illustrious Prefect addresses the Most Worthy Provost thus: "Most Worshipful Provost, what is the o'clock?" Most Worshipful Provost says, rising and facing the east, at the same time raising his mark in his right hand, "Most Illustrious Prefect, it is now the first hour of the day, the time when our Lord suffered and the veil of the temple was rent asunder, when darkness and consternation was spread over the earth, when the confusion of the old covenant was made light in the new in the temple of the cross. It is, Most Illustrious Prefect, the third watch, when the implements of Masonry were broken—when the flame, which led the wise men of the east, reappeared—when the cubic stone was broken, and the word was given." Most Illustrious Prefect says to Worthy Herald, "It is my will that this house of God be closed, and the remembrance of those solemn and sacred events, be here commemorated: make this; Worthy Herald, known to the Most Worshipful Provost, in due and ancient form." The Worthy Herald bows and approaches the Most Worshipful Provost, where he bows thrice, faces about and gives a blast with his horn, and after the Knights have filed out by threes without the door, except the worthy Senior Inductor, he does his errand, viz.:—"Most Worshipful Provost, it is the sovereign will of Count Albertus, of Pergamus, that this house of God be closed, and that those solemn and sacred events in the new covenant be here commemorated: you will observe this." The Worthy Herald bows, and the Most Worshipful Provost rises and addresses the Worthy Senior Inductor thus: "It is the will of the Most Illustrious Prefect that here now be opened a Council of Knights of the Cross: what therein becomes your duty?" Worthy Senior Inductor says, "To receive the commands of my superiors in the order, and pay obedience thereto—to conduct and instruct my ignorant pass-brethren; and to revere, and inculcate reverence in others, for the Most Holy and Almighty God." The Most Worshipful Provost rises fiercely and says, "By what right do you claim this duty?" Worthy S. Inductor says, "By the right of a sign, and the mark of a sign." Most Worshipful Provost says, "Will you give me a sign?" Worthy Sen. "I could if I should. " [Pg 128] The Most Worshipful Provost then partly extends both arms, pointing downwards to an angle of 39°, with the palms open, and upwards, to show they are not sullied with iniquity and oppression, and says, "Worthy Sen. Inductor, you may give it." The Worthy Sen. Inductor then looks him full in the face, and with his forefinger touches his right temple, and lets fall his hand, and says, "This is a sign." Most Worshipful Provost says, "A sign of what?" Worthy Senior Inductor says, "Aye, a sign of what?" Most Worshipful Provost says, "A penal sign." Worthy Senior Inductor says, "Your sign is ——." Most Worshipf. Pro. says, "The last sign of my induction. But you have the mark of a sign." Worthy S. Inductor says, "The sign whereof my mark is a mark, I hope is in the Council above." Most Worshipf. Pro. says, "But the mark ——." Worthy S. Inductor says, "Is in my bosom." Thereupon he produces his mark in his left hand, and with the forefinger of his right on the letter S, on the cross, asks, "What's that?" Most Wor. Pro. says, "Lisha." Wor. Pro. puts his finger on the letter H, and asks, "What is this?" Worthy S. Inductor says, "Sha." Worthy S. Inductor then puts his finger on the letter I, and asks, "What is this?" Most Worshipf. Pro. says, "Baal." "What, then, is your mark?" Worthy S. Inductor says, "Baal, Sha-Lisha; ['Lord of the three'] I am the Lord." The Most Worshipful Provost then says, "You are my brother, and the duty is yours of ancient right; please announce the Council open." The Worthy Senior Inductor steps to the door and gives three raps, and is answered by some Knight from without, who is then admitted, and the Worthy S. Inductor gives the CONDITIONAL sign (which is by partly extending both arms, as before described), the Knight answering by putting his finger to his right temple, as before. The Worthy S. Inductor then addresses the chair, thus:—"Most Illustrious Prefect, a professing brother is within the Council by virtue of a sign." Most Illustrious Prefect says to Worthy Herald, "Go to this professing brother, and see him marked before the chair of the Most Worshipful Provost; conduct him thither, Worthy Herald." The Worthy Herald says to the Knight, "Worthy Sir, know you the sacred cross of our Council?" Knight says, "I am a Christian." The Worthy Herald then says, "Follow me." When arrived before the Most Wor. Pro. the Worthy Herald says, "Most Worthy Provost, by order of the Most Illustrious Prefect, I here bring you to be marked a professing brother of the cross." The Most Worthy Provost says, "Worthy Sir, know you the cross of our Council; and can you, without fear or favor, support and bear that cross?" Knight says, "I am a Christian." The Most Worthy Provost says. "Worthy Sir, know you the cross of our Council; and can you, without fear or favor, support and bear that cross?" Knight says, "I am a Christian." The Most Worthy Provost says, "No more."

THE OBLIGATIONS OF THRICE ILLUSTRIOUS KNIGHTS OF THE CROSS.

First Obligation. —You, Mr. ——, do now, by your honor, and in view of the power and union of the Thrice Illustrious Order of the Cross, now first made known to you, and in the dread presence of the Most Holy and [Pg 129] Almighty God, solemnly and sincerely swear and declare, that, to the end of your life, you will not, either in consideration of gain, interest, or honor, nor with good or bad design, ever take any, the least, step or measure, or be instrumental in any such object, to betray or communicate to any person, or being, or number of the same, in the known world, not thereto of cross and craft entitled, any secret or secrets, or ceremony or ceremonies, or any part thereof appertaining to the order and degree known among Masons as the Thrice Illustrious Order of the Cross. That you will not, at any time or times whatever, either now or hereafter, directly or indirectly, by letter, figure, or character, however or by whoever made, ever communicate any of the information and secret mysteries heretofore alluded to. That you will never speak on or upon, or breathe high or low, any ceremony or secret appertaining thereto, out of Council, where there shall not be two or more Knights companions of the order present, besides yourself, and that in a safe and sure place, whereby any opinion, even of the nature and general principles of the institution, can be formed by any other person, be he Mason or otherwise, than a true Knight companion of the cross; nothing herein going to interfere with the prudent practice of the duties enjoined by the order, or arrangement for their enforcement.

2.—You further swear, that, should you know another to violate any essential part of this obligation, you will use your most decided endeavors, by the blessing of God, to bring such person to the strictest and most condign punishment, agreeably to the rules and usages of our ancient fraternity; and this by pointing him out to the world as an unworthy vagabond; by opposing his interest, by deranging his business, by transferring his character after him wherever he may go, and by exposing him to the contempt of the whole fraternity and the world, but of our illustrious order more especially, during his whole natural life: nothing herein going to prevent yourself, or any other, when elected to the dignity of Thrice Illustrious, from retaining the ritual of the order, if prudence and caution appear to be the governing principle in so retaining it, such dignity authorizing the elected to be governed by no rule but the dictates of his own judgment, in regard to what will best conduce to the interest of the order; but that he be responsible for the character of those whom he may induct, and for the concealment of the said ritual.

3.—Should any Thrice Illustrious Knight or acting officer of any council which may have them in hand, ever require your aid in any emergency in defence of the recovery of his said charge, you swear cheerfully to exercise all assistance in his favor, which the nature of the time and place will admit, even to the sacrifice of life, liberty, and property. To all, and every part thereof, we then bind you, and by ancient usage you bind yourself, under the no less infamous penalty than dying the death of a traitor, by having a spear, or other sharp instrument, like as our divine Master, thrust in your left side, bearing testimony, even in death, of the power and justice of the mark of the holy cross.

Second Obligation. —Mr. ——, before you can be admitted to the light and benefit of this Thrice Illustrious order, it becomes my duty, by ancient usage, to propose to you certain questions, not a thing vainly ceremonial; but the companions will expect true answers: they will concern your past life, and resolutions for the future. Have you given me without evasion or addition, your baptismal and family names, and those of your parents, your true age as far as within your knowledge; where you were educated; where you were born, and also where was your last place of residence? or have you not? "I have." It is well.

2d.—Were your parents free and not slaves? had they right and title in the soil of the earth? were they devoted to the religion of the cross, and did they so educate their family? have you searched the spiritual claims of that religion on your gratitude and your affections? and have you continued steadfast in that faith from choice and a conviction of your duty to heaven, or from education? "From duty and choice." This also is right.

3d.—Have you ever up to this time lived according to the principles of that religion, by acting upon the square of virtue with all men, nor [Pg 130] defrauding any, nor defamed the good name of any, nor indulged sensual appetites unreasonably, but more especially to the dishonor of the matrimonial tie, nor extorted on, or oppressed the poor. "I have not been guilty of these things. " You have then entitled yourself to our highest confidence, by obeying the injunctions of our Thrice Illustrious Prefect in Heaven, "of doing to all men even as you would that they should do unto you." Mr. ——, can you so continue to act, that yearly on the anniversary of St. Albert, you can solemnly swear for the past season you have not been guilty of the crimes enumerated in these questions? "By the help of God I can. " Be it so, then, that annually, on the anniversary of St. Albert you swear to these great questions; and the confidence of the Knights Companions of the order in you, rests on your being able so to do.

4th.—For the future, then, you promise to be a good man, and to be governed by the moral laws of God and the rules of the order, in always dealing openly, honorably, and above deceit, especially with the Knights companions of the order? "I do."

5th.—You promise so to act with all mankind, but especially with the fraternity, as that you shall never be justly called a bad paymaster, ungrateful, a liar, a rake, or a libertine, a man careless in the business of your vocation, a drunkard, or a tyrant? "I do."

6th.—You promise to lead a life so upright and just in relation to all mankind as you are capable of, but in matters of difference to preserve the interest of a companion of the order; of a companion's friend for whom he pleads, to any mere man of the word? "I do."

7th.—You promise never to engage in mean party strife, nor conspiracies against the government or religion of your country, whereby your reputation may suffer, nor ever to associate with dishonorable men even for a moment, except it be to secure the interest of such person, his family or friends, to a companion, whose necessities require this degradation at your hands? "I do."

8th.—You promise to act honorably in all matters of office or vocation, even to the value of the one-third part of a Roman penny, and never to take any advantage therein unworthy the best countenance of your companions, and this, that they shall not, by your unworthiness, be brought into disrepute? "I do."

Third Obligation. —I do now, by the hopes and power of the mark of the Holy and Illustrious Order of the Cross, which I do now hold to Heaven in my right hand as the earnest of my faith, and in the dread presence of the most holy and Almighty God, solemnly swear and declare that I do hereby accept of, and forever will consider the cross and mark of this order as my only hope: that I will make it the test of faith and fellowship; and that I will effect its objects and defend its mysteries to the end of my days, with my life and with my property—and first, that in the state of collision and misunderstanding impiously existing among the princes and pilgrims, defenders and champions of the Holy Cross of Jesus our Lord, now assembled in the land and city of their peace, and considering that the glory of the Most High requires the greatest and strictest unanimity of measures and arms, the most sacred union of sentiment and brotherly love in the soldiers who there thus devote themselves to his cause and banner, I swear strictly to dedicate myself, my life, and my property forever hereafter to his holy name and the purposes of our mark, and to the best interest of all those who thus with me become Knights of the Cross: I swear forever to give myself to this holy and illustrious order, confiding fully and unreservedly in the purity of their morals and the ardor of their pious enthusiasm, for the recovery of the land of their fathers, and the blessed clime of our Lord's sufferings, and never to renounce the mark of the order nor the claims and welfare of my brethren.

2d.—And that the holy and pious enthusiasm of my brethren may not have slander or disgrace at my hands, or the order be injured by my unworthiness, I swear forever to renounce tyranny and oppression in my own person and place, whatever it may be, and to stand forth against it in others, whether public or private; to become the champion of the [Pg 131] cross, to observe the common good; be the protector of the poor and unfortunate; and ever to observe the common rights of human nature without encroachment, or permitting encroachment thereon, if in my power to prevent or lessen it. I will, moreover, act in subordination to the laws of my country, and never countenance any change in the government under which I live, without good and answerable reasons for so doing, that ancient usages and immemorial customs be not overturned.

3d.—I swear to venerate the mark as the wisdom and decree of Heaven, to unite our hands and hearts in the work of the holy crusade, and as an encouragement to act with zeal and efficacy; and I swear to consider its testimonies as the true and only proper test of an illustrious brother of the cross.

4th.—I swear to wear the mark of this order, without any the least addition, except what I shall be legally entitled to by INDUCTION , forever, if not without the physical means of doing so, or it being contrary to propriety; and even then, if possible, to wear the holy cross; and I swear to put a chief dependence for the said worthy and pious objects therein.

5th.—I swear to put confidence unlimited in every illustrious brother of the cross, as a true and worthy follower of the blessed Jesus, who has sought this land, not for private good, but pity, and the glory of the religion of the Most High and Holy God.

6th.—I swear never to permit my political principles nor personal interest to come counter to his, if forbearance and brotherly kindness can operate to prevent it; and never to meet him if I know it, in war or in peace, under such circumstances that I may not, in justice to myself, my cross, and my country wish him unqualified success; and if perchance it should happen without my knowledge, on being informed thereof, that I will use my best endeavors to satisfy him, even to the relinquishing my arms and purpose. I will never shed a brother's blood nor thwart his good fortune, knowing him to be such, nor see it done by others if in my power to prevent it.

7th.—I swear to advance my brother's best interest, by always supporting his military fame and political preferment in opposition to another; and by employing his arms or his aid in his vocation, under all circumstances where I shall not suffer more by so doing, than he, by my neglecting to do so, but this never to the sacrifice of any vital interest in our holy religion, or in the welfare of my country.

8th.—I swear to look on his enemies as my enemies, his friends as my friends, and stand forth to mete out tender kindness or vengeance accordingly; but never to intrude on his social or domestic relations to his hurt or dishonor, by claiming his privileges, or by debauching or defaming his female relations or friends.

9th.—I swear never to see calmly nor without earnest desires and decided measures to prevent the ill-treatment, slander, or defamation, of any brother knight, nor ever to view danger or the least shadow of injury about to fall on his head, without well and truly informing him thereof; and, if in my power to prevent it, never to fail, by my sword or counsel, to defend his welfare and good name.

10th.—I do swear never to prosecute a brother before those who know not our order, till the remonstrance of a council shall be inadequate to do me justice.

11th.—I swear to keep sacred my brother's secrets, both when delivered to me as such, and when the nature of the information is such as to require secrecy for his welfare.

12th.—I swear to hold myself bound to him, especially in affliction and adversity, to contribute to his necessities my prayers, my influence, and my purse.

13th.—I swear to be under the control of my council, or, if belonging to none, to that which is nearest to me, and never to demur to, or complain at, any decree concerning me, which my brethren, as a council, shall conceive me to deserve, and enforce on my head, to my hurt and dishonor.

14th.—I swear to obey all summons sent from any council to me, or from any Most Illustrious Knight, whether Illustrious Counsellor for the time being, or by INDUCTION , and to be governed by the constitution, usages, and customs of the order without variation or change.

[Pg 132] 15th.—I swear never to see nor permit more than two candidates, who, with the Senior Inductor, will make three, to be advanced, at the same time, in any council where I shall be; nor shall any candidate, by suffrage, be inducted without a unanimous vote of the illustrious brethren in council; nor shall any council advance any member, there not being three illustrious Knights, or one Most Illustrious and four Illustrious Knights of the Cross present, which latter may be substituted by Most Illustrious Induction; nor yet where there shall not be a full and proper mark of the order, such as usage has adopted to our altar, of metal, or other durable and worthy material, contained within the apartment of council, as also the Holy Bible; nor will I ever see a council opened for business, without the ceremony of testing the mark, exercised on the character of every brother, prayers, and the reading of the 35th Psalm of David; nor will I ever see, consent to, or countenance, more than two persons of the same business or calling in life, to belong to, or be inducted and advanced in any one council of which I am a member, at the same time; nothing therein going to exclude members from other parts of the country, or from foreign parts, from joining us, if they consent formally and truly to stand in deference and defence, first, of their special BAR-BRETHREN in the council, nor to prevent advancements to fill vacancies, occasioned by death or removal. To all this, and every part thereof, I do now, as before, by the honor and power of the mark, as by an honorable and awful oath, which confirmeth all things in the dread presence of the Most Holy and Almighty God, solemnly and in truth, bind and obligate my soul; and in the earthly penalties, to wit, that, for the violation of the least matter or particle of any of the here taken obligations, I become the silent and mute subject of the displeasure of the Illustrious Order, and have their power and wrath turned on my head, to my destruction and dishonor, which, like the nail of Jael , may be the sure end of an unworthy wretch, by piercing my temples with a true sense of my ingratitude—and for a breach of silence in case of such an unhappy event, that I shall die the infamous death of a traitor, by having a spear, or other sharp weapon, like as my Lord, thrust in my left side—bearing testimony, even in death, of the power of the mark of the Holy and Illustrious Cross, before I. H. S., our thrice Illustrious Counsellor in Heaven, the Grand Council of the good. To this I swear.

THE LODGE OF PERFECTION: COMPRISING THE ELEVEN INEFFABLE DEGREES OF MASONRY.

In these several degrees some name of God is used, as the distinguishing word. Each name, however, is only a mode of pronouncing the Hebrew word Jehovah. The later Jews have a superstitious fear of pronouncing that name. Whenever it occurs in the Hebrew Text, they substitute the word Adonai in its place. To those who read the original language of the Old Testament, it is known, that while the consonants of the Hebrew word remain, the vowel points may be so changed as to afford several different pronunciations. In the different degrees of Ineffable Masonry, the four consonants (Jod, He, Vau, He) of the name Jehovah are differently pointed, so as to furnish a word for each degree. In the degree of Perfection, the candidate is sworn not to pronounce the word but once during his life, hence it is termed INEFFABLE , or unutterable. The ordinary mode of giving it in that degree consists in simply repeating the names of its letters, "Jod, He, Vau, He." On receiving that degree, the candidate is told that he is to become acquainted with the true pronunciation of the ineffable name of God, as it was revealed to Enoch. He is then taught to pronounce the word "Ya-ho"—sounding the *a* like *a* in wall. When written in Masonic manuscripts, this word is spelled "Ja-hoh."

SECRET MASTER.
Opening. —The Master strikes five. At this signal the Grand Marshal rises, and the Master addresses him: Master. Your place in the Lodge? Answer: In the North, Most Powerful.

[Pg 133] M. Your business there? A. To see that the Sanctum Sanctorum is duly guarded.

M. Please to attend to your duty, and inform the guards that we are about to open a Lodge of Secret Masters by the MYSTERIOUS NUMBER . A. It is done.

M. How are we guarded? A. By seven Secret Masters stationed before the veil of the Sanctum Sanctorum.

The Master strikes six. The Inspector rises. Master. Brother Adoniram, are you a Secret Master? Inspector. I have passed from the square to the compass.

M. What is the hour? I. The dawn of day has driven away darkness, and the great light begins to shine in this Lodge.

The Master strikes seven. The brethren rise. Master. If the great light is the token of the dawn of day, and we are all Secret Masters, it is time to begin our labors; give notice that I am about to open a Lodge of Secret Masters by the mysterious number. The Inspector obeys. The signs of the degrees from Entered Apprentice to Royal Arch, inclusive, are given with that of silence, which belongs to this degree. The Master places the two forefingers of his right hand on his lips. This is answered by the brethren with the two forefingers of the left. All clap hands seven times.

M. I declare this Lodge of Secret Masters open, and in order for business. Brother Grand Marshal, please to inform the guards.

Second Section. —Question—What did you see in the Sanctum Sanctorum when the thick veil was removed? Answer—I saw the great circle, in which was enclosed the blazing star, which filled me with awe and reverence.

Q. What do the Hebrew characters in the triangle signify? A. Something above my knowledge, which I cannot pronounce.

Q. What word did those Hebrew characters compose? A. The ineffable name of the Great Architect of the Universe.

Q. To whom was that name revealed? A. To Moses; he received the pronunciation thereof from the Almighty on the mount, when he appeared to him, and by a law of Moses it was forbidden ever to be pronounced unless in a certain manner, so that in process of time the true pronunciation was lost.

Q. What more did you perceive? A. Nine other words.

Q. Where were they placed? A. In the nine beams of the blazing luminary.

Q. What did they signify? A. The nine names which God gave himself when speaking to Moses on Mount Sinai, and the promise that his posterity should one day discover his real name.

Q. Give them to me, with their significations? A. "Eloah," The Strong. "Hayah," He is. "Shaddai," The Almighty. "Elyon," The Most High. "Adonai," The Lord. "Ahad Kodesh," The Holy One. "Riba," The Mighty. "Mahar," Merciful. "Eloham," Merciful God.

Q. What doth the circle which surrounds the delta signify? A. The eternity of the power of God, which hath neither beginning nor end.

[Pg 134] Q. What doth the blazing star denote? A. That light which should guide us to the Divine Providence.

Q. What is signified by the letter G in the centre of the blazing star? A. Glory, Grandeur and Gomez, or Gibber Hodihu.

Q. What is meant by these? A. By Glory is meant God, by Grandeur, man who may be great by perfection; and Gibber Hodihu, is a Hebrew word signifying thanks to God. It is said to have been the first word spoken by the first man.

Q. What else did you see in the Sanctum Sanctorum? A. The ark of alliance or covenant.

Q. Where was the ark of alliance placed? A. In the west end of the Sanctum Sanctorum, under the blazing star.

Q. What did the ark with the blazing star represent? A. As the ark was the emblem of the alliance which God had made with his people, so is the circle which surrounds the delta in the blazing star, the emblem of the alliance of Brother Masons.

Q. Of what form was the ark? A. A solid oblong square.

Q. Of what was it made? A. Of shittim wood covered within and without with pure gold, surmounted with a golden crown and two cherubims of gold.

Q. What was the covering of the ark called? A. Propitiatory.

Q. Why so? A. Because God's anger was there appeased.

Q. What did the ark contain? A. The tables of the law which God gave to Moses.

Q. Of what were they made? A. Of white marble.

Q. Who constructed the ark? A. Bezeleel of the Tribe of Judah, and Aholiab of the Tribe of Dan, who were filled with the spirit of God in wisdom and understanding, and in knowledge and in all manner of workmanship.

Q. What was the name of the Sanctum Sanctorum in Hebrew? A. "Dabir."

Q. What does the word signify? A. Speech.

Q. Why was it so called? A. Because the Divinity resided there in a peculiar manner, and delivered his oracles.

Q. How many doors were there in the Sanctum Sanctorum? A. Only one on the east side called "Zizon," or Balustrade. It was covered with hangings of purple, scarlet, blue, and fine twined linen of cunning work, embroidered with cherubims, and suspended from four columns.

Q. What did these columns represent? A. The four cardinal points.

Q. Your duty as a Secret Mason? A. To guard the Sanctum Sanctorum, and sacred furniture of the holy place.

Q. What was that furniture? A. The altar of incense, the two tables of shewbread, and the golden candlesticks.

Q. How were they placed? A. The altar of incense stood nearest the Sanctum Sanctorum, and the tables and candlesticks were placed five on the north and five on the south side of the holy place.

Q. What is meant by the EYE in our Lodge? A. That Secret Masters should keep a careful watch over the conduct of the craft in general.

Q. What is your age? A. Three times 27, and accomplished 81.

[Pg 135] Closing a Lodge of Secret Masters. —The Master strikes five.— The Grand Marshal rises.

Master. Brother Grand Marshal, what is the last as well as the first care of a Lodge of Secret Masters? Answer. To see that the Sanctum Sanctorum is duly guarded.

Master. Please attend to your duty, and inform the guards that we are about to close this Lodge of Secret Masters by the mysterious number. The Grand Marshal obeys, and repeats, "It is done, Most Powerful." Master strikes six.— Adoniram rises.

Master. Brother Adoniram, what is the hour? Answer. The end of day.

Master. What remains to do? Adoniram—To practice virtue, fly from vice, and remain in silence.

Master. Since there remains nothing to do but to practice virtue and fly vice, let us enter again into silence, that the will of God may be accomplished. The signs are given, and seven blows struck as at opening.

Master. I declare this Lodge duly closed.

DEGREE OF PERFECT MASTER.

Opening. —Right Worshipful and Respectable Master strikes two, upon which Grand Marshal rises, and Master says, "Brother Grand Marshal, are we all Perfect Masters?" Answer—We are, Right Worshipful and Respectable.

Q. Your place in the Lodge? A. In the North, Right Worshipful and Respectable.

Q. Your business there? A. To see that the Lodge is duly tyled.

Q. Please to attend to your duty and inform the Tyler that we are about to open a Lodge of Perfect Masters. (Grand Marshal reports.) Right Worshipful and Respectable Master knocks three, upon which the Warden and the Master of Ceremonies in the South rise. Master says, "Brother Stokin, are you a Perfect Master?" Answer—I have seen the tomb of our respectable Master, Hiram Abiff, and have in company with my brethren shed tears at the same.

Q. What is the hour? A. It is four.

Master then knocks four, upon which all the brethren rise. Master says, "If it is four, it is time to set the workmen to labor. Give notice that I am going to open a Lodge of Perfect Masters by four times four." (Senior Warden reports to brethren.) Signs given of former degrees, together with those of this degree. Master knocks four, Stokin four, Master of Ceremonies four, and Grand Marshal four—then all the brethren strike four times four with their hands. Then Master declares the Lodge open, and orders the Marshal to inform the Tyler.

Reception. —The candidate has a green cord put 'round his neck and is led by the Master of Ceremonies to the door, who knocks four, which is repeated by the Warden and answered by the Master. The Senior Warden says, "While the craft are engaged in lamenting the death of our Grand Master, Hiram Abiff," an alarm is heard at the inner door of the Lodge.

[Pg 136] Lecture. —Question—Are you a Perfect Master? Answer—I have seen the tomb of Hiram Abiff, and have in company with my brethren, shed tears at the same.

Q. How were you prepared to be a Perfect Master? Answer—A sprig of cassia was placed in my left hand, and a green cord about my neck.

Q. Why was the sprig of cassia placed in the left hand? A. That I might deposit it in the grave of Hiram Abiff.

Q. Why was a rope of green color put 'round your neck? A. Because the body of Hiram Abiff was lowered into the grave by the brethren, at his second interment, by a rope of that color. There is another reason, to signify thereby that a Perfect Master by flourishing in virtue, might hope for immortality.

Q. How did you gain admission? A. By four distinct knocks.

Q. What did they denote? A. Life, virtue, death, and immortality.

Q. How were they answered? A. By four from within.

Q. What was then said to you? A. Who comes there?

Q. Your answer? A. A Secret Master who is well qualified, etc.

Q. What was then said to you? A. I was then asked by what further right, etc.

Q. Your answer? A. By the right, etc.

Q. What was then said to you? A. Wait until the Right Worshipful and Respectable Master has been informed of your request and his answer returned.

Q. What was his answer? A. Introduce him in due and ancient form.

Q. What was that form? A. I was conducted to the West by the Master of Ceremonies and interrogated by the Master, "What is your request?"

Q. Your answer? A. To receive the degree of Perfect Master.

Q. What was then said to you by the Master? A. Before you can be admitted to this privilege, it will be necessary for you to join the funeral procession of Hiram Abiff.

Q. What followed? A. I joined in the procession, which moved four times 'round the Lodge, the brethren singing a funeral ode; when we arrived at the grave, the procession moved in an inverted order—the coffin was lowered with a green rope, and the sprigs of cassia thrown into the grave.

Q. What followed? A. The Master resumed his station, and the procession moved to the east.

Q. What followed? A. When he directed the Grand Marshal to inform King Solomon that the tomb of Hiram Abiff was completed, and request him to examine the same.

Q. What followed? A. Solomon entered and proceeded with the procession to the tomb of Hiram Abiff, and having examined the same and read the inscription J. M. B., he made a sign of admiration, and said in the joy of his heart, "It is accomplished and complete;" the brethren all making the same sign.

Q. What followed? A. The brethren resumed their places, and the Master directed the Master of Ceremonies to cause me to approach the east by four times four steps from the compass extended from an angle [Pg 137] of seven to that of sixty degrees, and take the obligation of a Perfect Master.

Q. Repeat that obligation. A. Obligation.—"1st point, Secrecy. 2d. Obey orders and decrees of Council of Princes of Jerusalem, under penalty of all the former degrees; also, under penalty of being smitten on the right temple with a common gavel or setting maul. So help," etc.

Q. What did the Master then communicate to you? A. He said, "It is my desire to draw you," etc., and then gave me the signs, words, tokens and history of this degree.

Q. Give me the signs. A. 1st sign—Place the palm of the right hand on the right temple, at the same time stepping back with the right foot, then bring up the right foot to its first position and let the right arm fall perpendicularly on the right side (alluding to the penalty). Second sign is that of admiration.—Raise the hands and eyes to heaven, let the arms fall crossed upon the belly, looking downwards.

Q. Give me the pass-word. A. (Accassia.)

Q. To what does the word allude, etc. Give me the token and mysterious word. A. Token is that of the Mark Master, given on the five points of fellowship; the mysterious word Jeva (pronounced Je-vau).

Q. What was then done? A. The Master invested me with the jewel and apron of this degree, and informed me that my jewel was designed to remind me, that, as a perfect Master, I should measure my conduct by the exact rule of equity.

Q. Give me the history of this degree. A. After the body of Hiram Abiff had been found, Solomon, pleased with having an opportunity of paying a tribute of respect to the memory of so great and good a man, ordered the noble Adoniram, his Grand Inspector, to make the suitable arrangements for his interment; the brethren were ordered to attend with white aprons and gloves, and he forbade that the marks of blood which had been spilled in the temple, should be effaced until the assassins had been punished. In the meantime, Adoniram furnished a plan for a superb tomb and obelisk of white and black marble, which were finished in nine days. The tomb was entered by passing between two pillars, supporting a square stone surrounded by three circles; on the stone was engraved the letter J. On the tomb, was a device representing a virgin, etc. (as in third degree). The heart of Hiram Abiff was enclosed in a golden urn, which was pierced with a sword to denote the desire of the brethren to punish the assassins. A triangular stone was affixed to the side of the urn, and on it were the letters J. M. B., surrounded by a wreath of cassia. This urn was placed on the top of the obelisk which was erected on the tomb. Three days after the interment, Solomon repaired with his court to the temple, and all the brethren being arranged as at the funeral, he directed his prayer to heaven, examined the tomb and the inscription on the urn: struck with admiration, he raised his hands and eyes to heaven, and said in the joy of his heart, "It is accomplished and complete."

Q. Where was this monument situated? A. Near the west end of the temple.

[Pg 138] Q. What is meant by the letter J. on the square stone? A. Jeva. The ineffable name as known by us.

Q. What is meant by the letters J. M. B. on the triangular stone? A. They are the initials of the three Hebrew words, Joshagn, Mawkoms, Bawheer—signifying "the elect sleeps in his place."

Q. What is signified by the pyramids in the Lodge? A. Pyramids were used by our Egyptian brethren, for Masonic purposes. Being built on rocks, they shadow forth the durability of Masonry. Their bases were four-cornered, their external surfaces equilateral triangles, pointing to the four cardinal points. The pyramidical form is also intended to remind us of our mortality. Its broad base represents the commencement, and its termination in a point, the end of human life.

Closing.—Master strikes two.—Marshal rises. Master says, "The last as well as the first care," etc., as in opening.

INTIMATE SECRETARY.

Opening.—Most Illustrious Master knocks nine.—Marshal rises.

Master says, "Are we all Intimate Secretaries?" Answer—We are, Most Illustrious.

Q. Your place? A. In the anti-chamber at the head of the guards.

Q. Your business there? A. To see that the hall of audience is duly guarded.

Q. How are we guarded? A. By Perfect Masters.

The Most Illustrious says, "I appoint Brother ———, Lieutenant of the Guards, to aid you in the execution of your duty. Repair to your station and see that none approach without permission." The guards then fall on their right knees, cross their hands in such a manner that their thumbs touch their temples, and repeat in a low voice, Jeva (pron. Jevau), thrice, and then retire. Solomon then strikes twice nine, upon which Hiram rises; they make signs of former degrees with twenty signs of this degree. Most Illustrious strikes three times nine and declares Lodge open. A triple triangle is placed on a Bible.

Lecture.—Question—Are you an intimate Secretary? Answer—I am.

Q. How were you received? A. By curiosity.

Q. Explain that. A. Being placed among the guards in the anti-chamber, a brother, representing the King of Tyre, hastily made his way through the guards, with a countenance expressive of anger, and entered the hall of audience, leaving the door partly open; curiosity led me to the door to observe what passed within.

Q. Was you perceived by them? A. I was. Hiram, King of Tyre, hearing the noise I made, suddenly turned his head and discovered me. He exclaimed to Solomon, "My brother, there is a listener." Solomon replied, "It is impossible, since the guards are without."

Q. What followed? A. Hiram, without replying, rushed to the door, and dragging me into the Lodge, exclaimed, "Here he is." Solomon inquired, "What shall we do with him?" Hiram laid his hand on his sword, and answered, "Let him be delivered into the custody of the guards, that we may determine what punishment we shall inflict upon [Pg 139] him, for this offence." Solomon then struck on the table which stood before him, whereupon the guards entered, and saluting the Lodge, received this order from him: "Take this prisoner, secure him, and let him be forthcoming when called for."

Q. Were those Guards Intimate Secretaries or Perfect Masters? A. Of that I was then ignorant, but I am now convinced that I was the first that was made an Intimate Secretary.

Q. What followed? A. I was conducted out of the hall of audience, and detained in the custody of the guards, until a second alarm from within caused them to return with me into the hall; when, the guards taking their seats around me, I was thus addressed by Solomon: "I have, by my entreaties, prevailed upon my worthy ally, Hiram, King of Tyre, whom your vain curiosity had offended, to pardon you, and receive you into favor, etc.; are you willing to take an obligation to that effect?" which question I answered in the affirmative, and then received at the altar the obligation of this degree.

Q. Repeat the obligation (same as Perfect Master). A. Under penalty of having my body quartered. So help me, etc.

Q. What did the Master then communicate to you? A. He addressed me thus: "My brother, I receive you an Intimate Secretary, on your having promised to be faithful," etc., and then gave me the signs, words, and tokens of this degree.

Q. Give me the signs? A. The first alludes to the penalty made by clenching the right hand, and drawing it from the left shoulder to the right hip. The second is the one made at opening by guards.

Q. Give me the token? A. Made by joining right hands, and turning them downwards thrice, saying, the first time, Berith—the second time, Nedir—and the third time, Shelemoth.

Q. Give me the pass-words? A. Joabert, response Terbel. The first is the name of the listener; the second, of the captain of the guards.

Q. Give me the mysterious word? A. Jeva (pronounced Je-vau).

Q. What was then done to you? A. I was invested with the jewel and apron of this degree, and was thus addressed by the Master: "The color of your ribbon is intended to remind you of the blood of Hiram Abiff, the last drop of which he chose to spill, rather than betray his trust; may you be equally faithful. The triple triangle is emblematical of the three theological virtues, faith, hope and charity; it is also emblematical of the three masons who were present at the opening of the first lodge of Intimate Secretaries, to wit: Solomon, King of Israel; Hiram, King of Tyre, and Joabert, a favorite of King Solomon."

Q. What then followed? A. I was ordered to salute the King of Tyre as an Intimate Secretary, and attend to the instruction of this degree.

Q. To what does the three times nine allude in this degree? A. To the twenty-seven lamps with which the hall of audience was enlightened.

Q. What is signified by the letter J which you perceive in the clouds? A. It is the initial of the ineffable name as known by us.

Q. What is represented by the door? A. The door by which they entered from the palace.

Q. Why was the hall of audience furnished with black hangings [Pg 140] strewed with tears? A. To represent the grief of Solomon, for the unhappy fate of Hiram Abiff.

Q. What is meant by the A and the two P's in the triangle? A. Alliance, promise and perfection.

Q. Give me the history of this degree. A. Hiram gave Solomon cedar trees, and fir trees, etc.

Closing. —Master knocks nine (Marshal rises) and says, "Brother Grand Marshal, the last as well as the first care of an Intimate Secretary? To see that the hall of audience is duly guarded. Your place, etc. How are we guarded, etc. Brother Captain of the guards, we are about to close this Lodge of Intimate Secretaries, repair to your station," etc. (Upon this, guards all make sign as at opening, and leave the room.) Then Solomon strikes twice nine, and Hiram rises—signs reversed. Solomon knocks three times nine, and declares Lodge closed.

PROVOST AND JUDGE.

Opening. —Thrice Illustrious knocks three. Marshal rises. Thrice Illustrious says, "Brother Grand Marshal, are we all Provosts and Judges?" Marshal. We are.

Thrice Illustrious. Your place? M. In the North.

T. I. Your business there? M. To see that the middle chamber is duly tyled.

Thrice Illustrious says, "Attend to your duty, and inform the Tyler that we are about to open this Lodge of Provost and Judge." (Grand Marshal obeys.) Thrice Illustrious strikes four. Wardens rise. "Brother Junior Warden, where is the Master placed?" Answer.—Everywhere.

Q. Why so? A. To superintend the workmen, direct the work, and render justice to every man.

Q. What is the hour? A. Break of day, eight, two and seven. Thrice Illustrious strikes five.—Brethren rise. Thrice Illustrious says, "It is then time to begin our labors; give notice that I am going to open a Lodge of Provost and Judge, by four and one." (Signs given, Master strikes four and one—Senior Warden, four and one—Junior Warden, four and one, and Marshal, four and one; the brethren all strike four and one, with their hands, and the Master declares the Lodge open.)

Reception. —Master of Ceremonies conducts candidate to the door, and knocks four and one, which is answered from within by Senior Warden, and

Thrice Illustrious and Senior Warden says, "While the Provosts and Judges are engaged in right, an alarm is heard at the inner door of the Lodge," etc. A golden key is placed on the Bible.

Lecture. —Question—Are you a Provost and Judge? A. I am, and render justice to all men without distinction.

Q. Where were you received? A. In the middle chamber.

Q. How did you gain admission there? A. By four and one distinct knocks.

Q. To what do they allude? A. To the qualifications of a Provost and Judge, to wit: impartiality, justice, prudence, discretion and mercy; of which the five lights in the middle chamber are also emblematical.

[Pg 141] Q. How were these knocks answered? A. By four and one from within.

Q. What was then said to you? A. I was asked by what further right, etc.

Q. Your answer? A. By the right of a pass.

Q. What was then said to you? A. Wait until the Thrice Illustrious is informed of your request, and his answer returned.

Q. What was his answer? A. Introduce him in due and ancient form.

Q. What was that form? A. I was conducted by the Master of Ceremonies to the south-west corner of the middle chamber, between the Wardens, and caused to kneel on my right knee and say Beroke.

Q. What answer was given to that? A. The Thrice Illustrious said Kumi.

Q. What do these words signify? A. The first signifies to kneel, the last, to rise.

Q. What followed? A. I was conducted three times 'round the Lodge, giving the signs of the ineffable degrees, and led to the altar, and caused to kneel and take the obligation of this degree.

Q. Repeat that obligation. A. Same as Perfect Master, with the addition, that I will justly and impartially decide all matters of difference between brethren of this degree, if in my power so to do, under penalty of being punished as an unjust Judge, by having my nose severed from my face. So help me, etc.

Q. What followed? A. The Thrice Illustrious gave me the signs, tokens and words of this degree.

Q. Give me the signs? A. (Put the two first fingers of your right hand to the right side of your nose, the thumb under the chin, forming a square.)

Q. Give me the token? A. (Clench the three first fingers of the right hand over the thumb, and join hands by interlacing the little fingers.)

Q. Give me the pass-word? A. Jev (pronounced Jo).

Q. What was then done to you? A. I was invested with the jewel, apron and gloves of this degree, and was thus addressed:—"Respectable Brother, it gives me joy that I am now about to recompense, etc. This key opens a small ebony box, in which are contained the plans for the building of the temple, and this key opens a small ivory box containing all the keys of the temple. I clothe you with a white apron, lined with red, having a pocket in its centre, and in which you are intended to carry the plans for the building of the temple, that they may be laid out on the tressel board for the use of the workmen when wanted. I also give you a balance in equilibrio, as a badge of your office. Let it remind you of that equity of judgment which should characterize your decisions."

Q. What was next done? A. He made me a Provost and Judge.

Q. In what manner? A. He gave me a blow on each shoulder, and said, "By the power with which I am invested, I constitute you Provost and Judge over all the works and workmen of the temple. Be impartial, just, prudent, discreet and merciful. Go salute the Junior and Senior Wardens as a Provost and Judge, and return to the Lodge for further instruction.

[Pg 142] Second Section. —Question—What did you perceive in the middle chamber? Answer—A curtain, behind which was suspended a small ebony box containing the plans for the construction of the temple.

Q. What else did you see? A. A triangle enclosing the letters G. A.

Q. What is their meaning and use? A. Grand Architect, and are designed to make us remember him in all our decisions and actions.

Q. Did you perceive anything more? A. I saw the letters I. H. S. with the sprig of cassia.

Q. What is meant thereby? A. Imitate Hiram's Silence, and Justice, Humanity and Secrecy, which are designed to teach Provost and Judge, that while their decisions are just, they should be tempered with humanity, or mercy, and that all differences which may arise among the craft, should be kept secret from the world.

Q. What was the intention of Solomon in instituting this degree? A. To strengthen the means of preserving order among such a vast number of workmen; the duty of Provosts and Judges being, to decide all differences that might arise among the brethren.

Q. Who was the first that was made Provost and Judge? A. Joabert being honored with the intimate confidence of King Solomon, received this new mark of distinction. Solomon first created Tito, Adoniram, and Abda, his father, Provosts and Judges, and gave them orders to initiate Joabert into the mysteries of this degree, and to give him all the keys of the temple, which were inclosed in a small ivory box suspended in the Sanctum Sanctorum, under a rich canopy. When Joabert was first admitted into this sacred place, he was struck with awe, and involuntarily found himself in a kneeling posture, and said, Beroke; Solomon observing him, said Kumi, which signifies to rise.

Q. Whence came you as a Provost and Judge? A. I came and am going everywhere.

Closing. —Thrice Illustrious Master knocks three (Marshal rises) and says, "Brother Grand Marshal, the last as well as the first care of Provost and Judge?" Answer—To see that the middle chamber is duly tyled.—"Attend to your duty, and inform the Tyler that we are about to close this Lodge of Provosts and Judges by four and one." Marshal reports. Thrice Illustrious strikes four. Wardens rise, and Master says, "Brother

Senior Warden, what is the hour?" Ans. —Break of day, 8, 2 and 7.

Q. Brother Junior Warden, how so? A. Because Provosts and Judges should be ready at all times to render Justice. Thrice Illustrious knocks four and one, and brethren all rise. Signs reversed given. Thrice Illustrious strikes four and one, Marshal four and one, Junior Warden four and one, and Senior Warden four and one, and then all the brethren strike four & one with their hands, and Thrice Illustrious declares Lodge duly closed.

INTENDANT OF THE BUILDINGS (OR I. B.).

Opening. —Most Puissant knocks three (Marshal rises) and says, "Brother Grand Marshal, are we all I. B.?" Answer—We are, Most Puissant.

[Pg 143] Q. Your place? A. In the north.

Q. Your business there? A. To see that the Lodge is duly tyled.—"Attend to your duty, and inform the Lodge that we are about to open a Lodge of I. B. by the number five." Marshal obeys. Most Puissant knocks four, and Wardens rise. —Q. Brother Senior Warden, what is the hour? A. Break of day.—Most Puissant knocks five, and brethren all rise. Most Puissant says, "If it is break of day, it is time to begin our labors; give notice that I am going to open a Lodge of I. B." Senior Warden obeys. All make signs. Most Puissant knocks five, Senior Warden five, Junior Warden five, and brethren five, with their hands; and Most Puissant declares the Lodge open.

Reception. —Most Puissant knocks seven, and Senior Warden rises. Most Puissant says, "My excellent brother, how shall we repair the loss of our worthy Hiram Abiff, he is now removed from us, and we are thereby deprived of his counsel and services; can you give me any advice in this important matter?" Senior Warden answers, "The method I would propose, would be to select a chief from the five orders of architecture upon whom we may confer the degree of I. B., and by his assistance fill the secret chamber of the third story. " Most Puissant says, "I approve of your advice, and to convince you of my readiness to follow it, I appoint you and brothers Adoniram and Abda to carry the same into execution. Excellent Brothers, let Adoniram go into the middle chamber and see if he can find a chief of the five orders of architecture. " Junior Warden goes out of the Lodge into the ante-chamber, and finding the candidate, addresses him as in the Lecture.

Note. —When the alarm of five is given Senior Warden rises and says, "Most Puissant, we are disturbed in our deliberations by an alarm at the inner door of the secret chamber." Most Puissant says, "Brother Senior Warden, see the cause of that alarm."

Lecture. —Question—Are you an Intendant of the Buildings? A. I have made the five steps of exactness; I have penetrated the inmost parts of the temple, and have seen the great light, in which were three mysterious characters, J. J. J.

Q. How were you received? A. Being in the middle chamber, in company with the Master of Ceremonies, Adoniram entered and inquired, "Is there here a chief of the five orders of architecture?"

Q. Your answer? A. I am one.

Q. What followed? A. I was then asked, "My dear brother, have you zeal to apply yourself with attention to that which the Most Puissant shall request of you?"

Q. Your answer? A. I have, and will comply with the request of the Most Puissant, and raise this edifice to his honor and glory.

Q. What followed? Ans. Adoniram demanded of me the signs, words, and tokens of my former degrees, which being given, the Master of Ceremonies conducted me to the door of the Lodge, where he gave me five distinct knocks.

Q. To what did they allude? A. To the five orders of architecture.

Q. How were they answered? A. By five from within.

Q. What was then said to you. A. I was asked, "Who comes there?"

[Pg 144] Q. Your answer? A. A chief of the five orders of architecture, who is to be employed in the works of the secret chamber.

Q. What was then said to you? A. I was then asked by what further right, etc.

Q. Your answer? A. By the right of a pass-word.

Q. Give me that pass-word? A. Bonahim (pronounced Bo-nau-heem).

Q. What was then said to you? A. Wait until the Most Puissant is informed, etc.

Q. What was his answer? A. Let him be introduced in due form.

Q. What followed? A. I was conducted to the altar and caused to recede five steps, and then to advance to the altar by five steps of regular exactness.

Q. What is meant thereby? A. That I should recede from vice, and advance to virtue, before I was qualified to supply the place of so good a man as the lamented Hiram Abiff.

Q. What followed? A. I was laid prostrate before the altar, with a sprig of cassia in my right hand, and my left upon the first great light of Masonry, in which posture I took the obligation of this degree.

Q. Repeat that obligation. A. (Same as Perfect Master) under penalty of being deprived of my sight. So help, etc.

Q. What followed? A. I was thus addressed by the Most Puissant: "Your present posture is that of a dead man, and is designed to remind you of the fate of our worthy Hiram Abiff. I shall now raise you in the same manner he was raised, under the sprig of cassia." I was then raised by the Master's grip, and further addressed, "By your being raised, our hope is signified, that in some measure you will repair his loss, by imitating his bright example."

Q. What followed? A. I received the signs, tokens and words of this degree.

Q. Give me the signs. A. (Interlace the fingers, and place the hands over the eyes, alluding to penalty; second sign is that of grief, made like Fellow Craft's, with left hand on the left hip.)

Q. Give me the token? A. (Take hold of each other by the right wrists with the right hand.)

Q. Give me the pass-word. A. Bonahim.

Q. What does that word signify? A. Builders.

Q. Give me the words. A. Achard, jenok (pronounced yo-kayn).

Q. Give me the mysterious word. A. Jah (pronounced yaw).

Q. What was next done? A. I was invested with the apron, gloves and jewels of this degree, and was thus addressed: "I decorate you with a red ribbon, to be worn crossing the breast from the right shoulder to the left hip, to which is suspended a triangle fastened with a green ribbon. I also present you with a white apron, lined with red, and bordered with green. The red is emblematical of that zeal which should characterize you as an I. of B., and the green, of the hope we entertain that you will supply the place of our lamented Hiram Abiff.

Q. What is meant by the letters B. A. J. in the triangle which you wear? A. They are the initials of the pass-word and words of this degree.

Q. What followed? A. I was directed to salute the Senior Warden as an Intendant of the Buildings, and return to the east for further instruction.

Second Section.—Question—What did you see in the Lodge? Answer—A triangle enclosing a circle, having on its circumference the letters J. A. I. N., and in its centre the letters J. J. J.

Q. What is signified by the circle in the triangle? A. The eternity of the powers of God, which hath neither beginning nor end.

Q. What is signified by the letters J. A. I. N.? A. They are the initials of the four Hebrew words, Jad, Ail, Jotsare, and Nogah, which are expressive of four attributes of the Deity; power, omnipresence, creation and splendor.

Q. What is signified by the letters J. J. J? A. Jah, Jokayn and Jireh, signifying "The Lord, the Creator seeth."

Q. What else did you see? A. A blazing star with five beams, in the centre of which appeared the letter J.

Q. What is signified by the five beams? A. The five equal lights of Masonry, the Bible, the square, the compass, the key, and the triangle.

Q. What is signified by the letter J.? A. It is the initial of the ineffable name, as known by us.

Q. Are you in darkness? A. No, the blazing star is my guide.

Q. What is your age? A. 27, or 5, 7 and 15.

Q. To what do those three numbers allude? A. To the five chiefs of the five orders of architecture, to seven cubits, which was the breadth of the golden candlestick with seven branches, and the fifteen Fellow Crafts, who conspired against the life of our Grand Master, Hiram Abiff.

Closing.—Most Puissant knocks three (Grand Marshal rises) and says, "Brother Grand Marshal, the last as well as the first care of I. of B.?" Answer. To see that the Lodge is duly tyled. "Attend to your duty," etc. Most Puissant knocks four, and Warden rises; "Brother Senior Warden, what is the hour?" A. Seven at night. Most Puissant strikes five—all brethren rise. Most Puissant says, "As it is seven at night, it is time to retire: Brother Junior Warden, give notice that I am going to close this Lodge of Intendants of the Building." Signs reversed, Most Puissant knocks five, Junior Warden seven, and Senior Warden fifteen, then the brethren five, seven and fifteen, with their hands, and the Most Puissant declares the Lodge closed.

ELECTED KNIGHTS OF NINE.

Opening.—The brethren sit cross-legged, and lean their heads on their right hands. Most Potent knocks seven (Grand Marshal rises), "Brother Grand Marshal, are we all Elected Knights of Nine?" Ans. We are.

Q. Your place? A. In the north, Most Potent.

Q. Your business there? A. To see that the Chapter is duly guarded.—"Please attend to your duty, and inform the Sentinel that we are about to open this Chapter of E. K. and charge him," etc. Marshal obeys. Most Potent knocks eight, and Warden rises, and Master says, "Brother Stokin, are you an E. K.?" A. One cavern received me, one lamp gave me light, and one fountain refreshed me. Q. What is the hour? A. Break of day. Most Potent knocks eight quick and one slow strokes, and companies all arise. Most Potent says, "If it is break of day, it is time to open a Chapter of E. K's. Inform the companies," etc. Warden obeys. Signs given. Most Potent knocks eight and one, and Warden eight and one, and companies eight and one, with their hands; and Most Potent declares the Chapter open.

Lecture.—Question—Are you an E. K.? A. One cavern received me, one lamp gave me light, and one fountain refreshed me.

Q. Where were you received? A. In the audience chamber of Solomon.

Q. How were you received? A. I was hoodwinked and conducted by the Master of Ceremonies to the door of the Chapter, where he gave eight and one distinct knocks.

Q. To what do those knocks allude? A. To the number of the nine elect.

Q. How were those knocks answered? A. By eight and one from within.

Q. What followed? A. I was asked, "Who comes there?"

Q. Your answer? A. A companion, to whose lot it has fallen to accompany the stranger in search of the assassins of Hiram Abiff.

Q. What followed? A. I was conducted by the hand to the west, and asked by the Most Potent, what I wanted.

Q. Your answer? A. To be made an Elected Knight.

Q. What then followed? A. I was asked if I had courage to go in pursuit of the assassins of Hiram Abiff, which question I answered in the affirmative, and was addressed by the Most Potent in the following manner:—"If you have, you shall be shown the place where one of his murderers lies concealed; a stranger has discovered it to me, and if you have resolution, follow this stranger."

Q. What was then done to you? A. The Master of Ceremonies led me out of the Chapter, by intricate roads, and at last seated me on a stone, and thus addressed me:—"I am going to leave you, but be of good cheer, I shall not be long absent; when I am gone, you must take the bandage off your eyes, and drink some water from the fountain beside you, that you may be refreshed after so fatiguing a journey."

Q. What followed? A. I removed the bandage and found myself alone in a cavern, in which was a lamp, a fountain, and a head just severed from the body. In a short time the Master of Ceremonies returned, and directed me to take a poniard in my right hand, and the head in my left, and then conducted me to the door of the Chapter, where I knocked eight and one with my foot, which was answered from within, and I was asked, "What do you want?"

Q. Your answer? A. To enter this Chapter of Elected Knights.

Q. What followed? A. I was asked by what right I claimed this privilege.

Q. Your answer? A. I Have performed a feat for the honor of the craft, which I hope will entitle me to this degree.

Q. What followed? A. I was admitted, and directed to approach the altar by eight quick and one slow steps, still holding the head in my left hand, and the poniard in my right, as if in the act of striking; the ninth step brought me to the altar, where the Most Potent addressed me in an [Pg 147] angry tone: "Wretch, what have you done, do you not know that by this rash act you have deprived me of an opportunity of inflicting condign punishment on the assassin?"

Q. What followed? A. The companies made earnest intercession for me, observing that my offence had doubtless arisen from the wrath of my zeal, and not from any bad intention. Upon this the Most Potent was reconciled, and he administered to me the obligation of this degree, the companies all standing 'round me with their poniards as if going to stab me.

Q. Repeat that obligation? A. (Same as in Perfect Master.) Under penalty of being stabbed in my head and in my heart. So help, etc.

Q. What followed? A. The Most Potent gave me the sign, token and words of this degree.

Q. Give me the sign? A. (Clap your right hand first to your head and then to your heart.)

Q. Give me the token? A. (Grasp the thumb of your brother's right hand, both clenching the fingers and extending the thumb of the hand that is uppermost.)

Q. To what does that token allude? A. The eight fingers and extended thumb allude to the eight and one elect; the one to Joabert, who left his eight companions, and went alone in search of, etc.

Q. Give me the pass-words? A. Rawkam and Akirop.

Q. What is the word? A. Bugelkal, who was chief of the tabernacle.

Q. Give me the mysterious word? A. Jeva (pronounced Je-vau).

Q. What was then done to you? A. I was invested with the apron, gloves and jewels of this degree, and ordered to salute the Warden, and to return to the east for further instructions.

Second Section. —Question—Give me the history of this degree? Ans. After the death of Hiram Abiff, the three ruffians who had been apprehended having made their escape, a great assembly of Masters had sat, etc., he had only time to pronounce Naukam, which signifies, "vengeance is taken," and expired. Joabert being extremely fatigued, refreshed himself at the spring which he found in the cavern, and then slept until he was awakened by the other eight, who arrived shortly after. On beholding what Joabert had done, they all exclaimed Naukam. Joabert then severed the head from the body, divided the body into 4 quarters, which were burnt to ashes, and the ashes scattered to the four winds of heaven. Joabert then taking the head, etc., again reconciled. Solomon then ordered the head to be placed on the east pinnacle of the temple.

Q. What was the name of the assassin? A. Jubelum Akirop.

Q. From what number were the nine elect chosen? A. Ninety-nine.

Q. Where was the assassin found? A. In a cavern, near the coast of Joppa.

Q. How did the nine elect travel? A. By dark and intricate roads, which often obliged them to cross their legs, and this is the reason why the nine elect sit in this manner in the Chapter.

Q. What is meant by the dog you saw on the carpet, in the Lodge? A. [Pg 148] The dog of the stranger, through whose sagacity Akirop was discovered.

Q. What does the color, black, denote in this degree? A. Grief.

Q. What is your age? A. Eight and one, accomplished.

Closing.—Most Potent knocks seven (Grand Marshal rises) and says, "The last as well as the first care of a Chapter of E. K.?" Ans. To see that the Chapter is duly guarded.—Please attend to your duty and inform the Sentinel, etc. Most Potent knocks eight, and Warden rises. Q. What is the hour? A. Evening. Most Potent knocks eight and one. Companies all rise. Companion Stokin gives notice, etc. Most Potent knocks eight and one, Warden eight and one, Companions eight and one, and the Chapter is declared duly closed.

MASTERS ELECTED OF FIFTEEN.

Opening. —Most Potent knocks five (Grand Marshal rises) and says, "Brother Grand Marshal, are we all Masters Elected of Fifteen?" A. We are, Most Potent. Q. Your place, etc.? Your business, etc.? Please inform the Tyler that we are about to open a Lodge of Masters Elected of Fifteen. Most Potent knocks twice five—Senior Warden rises. Most Potent knocks three times five. Brethren rise. Most Potent says, "Brother Inspector, give notice that I am going to open a Lodge of Masters Elected of Fifteen, by three times five." Inspector obeys. Most Potent knocks three times five, Senior Warden three times five, Junior Warden three times five, and the brethren the same, and the lodge is declared open.

Lecture. —Question—Are you a Master Elected of Fifteen? Answer—My zeal and works have prepared me that honor.

Q. How were you prepared? A. A head was placed in my hand, and I was conducted to the door of the Lodge by the Master of Ceremonies who knocked three times five.

Q. How were those knocks answered? A. By three times five from within.

Q. To what do they allude? A. The fifteen elected Masters.

Q. What followed? A. I was asked, "Who comes there?"

Q. Your answer? A. An Elected Knight who is desirous of joining the other Knights, for the purpose of discovering the other assassins.

Q. What was then said to you? A. I was told to wait until the Most Potent had been informed of my request, and his answer returned.

Q. What was his answer? A. Let him be introduced in due form.

Q. What was that due form? A. I was conducted to the altar, and caused to make fifteen steps in a triangular form, which brought me again to the altar, when the Most Potent ordered me to kneel, and thus addressed me: "My brother, the Elected Masters here present, wish me to admit you to this degree; will you take the obligation appertaining to the same?" which being answered in the affirmative, I took the obligation.

Q. Repeat that obligation? A. (Same as Perfect Master.) Under penalty of having my body cut open perpendicularly, and my head cut off and placed on the highest pinnacle in the world. So help me, etc.

[Pg 149] Q. What did the Most Potent then communicate to you? A. He gave me the signs, words, and token of this degree.

Q. Give me the signs? A. (Hold the thumb of the right hand at the bottom of the belly, and move it perpendicularly upwards.) The second sign (that of the Entered Apprentice, with the fingers clenched.)

Q. Give me the token? A. (Join hands.)

Q. Give me the pass-word? A. Eleham.

Q. Give me the mysterious word? A. Jevah (pronounced Je-vau).

Q. What then followed? A. I was invested with the apron, gloves and jewels of this degree, and directed to salute the Senior Warden as a Master Elected of Fifteen, and return to the east for further instruction.

Second Section. —Question—Give me the history of this degree? A. Not long after the execution, they were discovered cutting stone, in a quarry. They were immediately seized and carried to Jerusalem, and imprisoned in the tower of Achizer, and at ten o'clock on the ensuing morning, they were brought forth for execution. They were bound neck and middle, to posts, with their arms extended, and their bellies were cut open by the executioner, lengthways and across, and thus they remained until six in the evening, their entrails exposed to flies and other insects; their tongues and entrails were afterwards taken out for the beasts of the field and the birds of the air to prey upon, and their heads were cut off and placed upon spikes, like that of Akirop, on the west and south pinnacles of the temple. Thus we see that although corruption, perjury and treason assisted our ancient Knights, their quarters were discovered by the unerring eye of justice, and they were doomed to suffer penalty tantamount to their crimes.

Q. What were the names of the two assassins? A. Jubela Kurmavel, and Jubelo Gravolet.

Q. At what hour did the assassins expire? A. At six in the evening.

Closing. —Most Potent knocks five. Grand Marshal rises. Most Potent says, "Brother Grand Marshal, the last as well as the first care of a Lodge of Masters Elected of Fifteen?" A. To see that the Lodge is duly tyled.—"Please attend," etc. Most Potent knocks twice five.— Senior Warden rises. Signs reversed. Most Potent knocks three times five, which is repeated by Wardens, and then by brothers with their hands, etc.

ILLUSTRIOUS KNIGHTS

ELECTED.

Opening. —Most Potent knocks ten. Grand Marshal rises. Most Potent says, "Are we all Illustrious Knights Elected?" A. We are, Most Potent. "Your place? etc. Your duty?" A. To see that the Chapter is duly guarded. "Please attend," etc. Most Potent knocks eleven. Grand Inspector rises. "Companion Inspector, what is the hour?" A. It is twelve. Most Potent knocks twelve. Companions rise. "If it is twelve, it is time to labor by the greatest of lights. " Signs given. Most Potent knocks twelve, Inspector twelve, and Companion twelve, with their hands, etc.

[Pg 150] Lecture. —Question—Are you an Illustrious Knight Elected? Answer. My name will inform you.

Q. What is that name? A. Payrawsh Bawheer, or Illustrious Knight elected.

Q. How were you admitted? A. I was hoodwinked and conducted by the Master of Ceremonies to the door of the Chapter, where he gave twelve distinct knocks.

Q. To what did they allude? A. To the twelve tribes of Israel.

Q. How were they answered? A. By twelve from within.

Q. What was then said to you? A. "Who comes there?"

Q. Your answer? A. A Master Elected of Fifteen wishes to receive the degree of Illustrious Knight.

Q. What was then said to you? A. I was asked by what further right, etc., and I was told to wait until the Most Potent was informed of my request, and his answer returned.

Q. What was that answer? A. Let him be introduced in due form.

Q. What then followed? A. I was conducted to the west, and the Most Potent inquired what I wanted.

Q. Your answer? A. To receive the degree of Illustrious Knight, as a reward for my zeal and labor.

Q. What did the Most Potent say to you then? A. My brother, you cannot receive this degree until you have given us satisfactory proof that you have not been an accomplice in the death of our Grand Master, Hiram Abiff; to assure us of this, we require you to participate in a symbolic offering, of a portion of the heart of our Respectable Master, Hiram Abiff, which we have preserved since his assassination. You are to swallow the portion we present to you. Every faithful Mason may receive it without injury, but it cannot remain in the body of one who is perjured. Are you disposed to submit to this trial?

Q. What was your answer? A. I am.

Q. What followed? A. The Most Potent directed the Master of Ceremonies to cause me to advance to the altar, by twelve upright regular steps, where the Most Potent, with the trowel, presented to me the symbolic offering which I swallowed, and was thus addressed by the Most Potent: "This mystic oblation, which, like you, we have received forms a tie so strong that nothing can oppress it; woe to him who attempts to disunite us. I then received the obligation of this degree.

Q. Repeat that obligation. A. (Same as Perfect Master.) Under penalty of having my hands nailed to my breast. So help, etc.

Q. What was then communicated to you? A. The Most Potent removed the bandage, and gave me the sign. (Cross hands on breast) it alludes to penalty.

Q. Give me the token? A. (Token of Intimate Secretary, with left hand on brother's heart.)

Q. Give me the pass-word? A. Emun.

Q. What does that word signify? A. Truth.

Q. Give me the mysterious word? A. Joha (pronounced Yo-hay).

Q. What followed? A. I was invested with the apron, gloves and jewels of this degree, and was told the device on my sash and apron, and [Pg 151] also the color of the latter, was an emblem of a heart inflamed with gratitude for the honors and rewards conferred on me, and the sword of that justice which overtook and punished the assassins, and was designed to admonish me that perjury and treason will never escape the sword of justice, and I was directed to go and salute the Inspector, and return to the east for further instruction.

Second Section. —Of what was the symbolic offering presented to you at your initiation composed? A. Of flour, milk, wine and oil.

Q. What did they represent? A. Flour represents goodness, the milk, gentleness, the wine, strength or fortitude, and the oil, light and wisdom, qualities which distinguished Hiram Abiff, and should distinguish every illustrious Knight.

Q. How were the Illustrious Knights employed at the erection of the temple? A. They had command over the twelve tribes, and by their strict attention, promoted peace and harmony, and animated the laborers with cheerfulness.

Q. What was the intention of Solomon in instituting this degree? A. To reward the zeal, etc., and also by their preferment to make more.

Closing. —Most Potent knocks ten (Grand Marshal rises). "The last as well as the first care of a Chapter of Illustrious Knights?" A. To see that the Chapter is duly guarded. "Attend to your duty, and inform the Sentinel," etc. Most Potent knocks eleven (Senior Warden rises). "Brother Inspector, what is the hour?" A. Low six. Most Potent knocks twelve (brethren rise). "Brother Inspector, give notice," etc. Signs. Most Potent knocks twelve, Inspector twelve, brethren twelve, with their hands, and Most Potent declares the Chapter duly closed.

GRAND MASTER ARCHITECTS.

Opening. —Most Potent knocks one (Grand Marshal rises). "Are we all," etc. Your place? etc. Your duty? A. To see that the Chapter is duly guarded. "Attend," etc. Most Potent knocks two.—Warden rises. Most Potent says, "What is the hour?" A. A star indicates the first instant, the first hour, and the first day, in which the Grand Architect commenced the creation of the universe. Most Potent knocks one and two.—Companions rise. Most Potent says, "Companions, it is the first instant, the first hour, the first day, the first year, when Solomon commenced the temple; the first day, the first hour, the first instant for opening this Chapter. It is time to commence our labors. Give notice," etc. Signs. Most Potent knocks one and two, Senior Warden one and two, Companions one and two, and Most Potent declares Chapter open, etc.

Lecture. —Question—Are you a Grand Master Architect? Answer—I know the use of every mathematical instrument.

Q. What are they? A. A square, a single compass, a compass with four points, a rule, a line, a compass of perfection, a quadrant, a level and plumb.

Q. Where were you received? A. In a white place, painted with flames.

[Pg 152] Q. What does that signify? A. That purity of heart and that zeal which should characterize every Grand Master Architect.

Q. How were you admitted? A. I was conducted by the Master of Ceremonies to the door of the Chapter, where he gave one and two distinct knocks.

Q. How were those knocks answered? A. One and two from within.

Q. What followed? A. I was asked, "Who comes there?"

Q. Your answer? A. An Illustrious Knight who wishes to receive the degree of Grand Architect.

Q. What then followed? A. I was conducted by the Master of Ceremonies to the west, and thus addressed: "It has become necessary to form a school of Architecture for the instruction of the brethren employed in the temple, as none but skilful Architects can bring the same to perfection. In order to prevent some brethren from receiving the honors and rewards due only to brethren of talents, we have deemed it expedient to prove and test all those who present themselves as candidates for this degree. We, therefore, require you to make the tour of the temple, for the purpose of examining the work, and to produce a plan drawn with exactness which you must present for inspection, that we may judge whether you are entitled to this degree."

Q. What followed? A. I was conducted through the anti-chamber and 'round the Lodge, when the Master of Ceremonies again stationed me in the west, and where I drew a plan according to my direction. When the same was finished, the Master of Ceremonies informed the Most Potent that I had obeyed his directions. Most Potent inquired, "My brother, what are the fruits of your travels?"

Q. Your answer? A. "Most Potent, I have brought a plan of the works of the temple, which I am ready to present for inspection."

Q. What followed? A. I was directed to approach the east, and present the plan to the Most Potent, which I accordingly did, and the Most Potent examined the same, and then passed it on to the other companions, who, after examining, returned it with expressions of approbation, and then the Most Potent addressed me thus: "It is with pleasure we witness the skill you have manifested in fulfilling the conditions prescribed to you, but we require further proof before you can be admitted among us. We again require you to travel."

Q. What followed? A. I was conducted once 'round the Lodge, to the north, where I stopped to view the north star, and was told, that as the north star was a guide to mariners, so ought virtue to be a guide to every Grand Master Architect, and was again conducted to the west, and directed to approach the east by one and two steps, which brought me to the altar, when the Most Potent inquired, "What have you learned in your travels?"

Q. Your answer? A. That virtue as well as talents should be possessed by every one who is admitted to this degree.

Q. What followed? A. I received the obligation of a Grand Master Architect.

Q. Repeat the obligation? A. (Same as Perfect Master.) Under the penalty of having my left hand cut in twain. So help, etc.

[Pg 153] Q. What then followed? A. I was then addressed by the Most Potent.

Q. What then followed? A. The Most Potent gave me the signs, words, and tokens of this degree.

Q. Give me the sign? A. (Make the motion of writing in the left hand), also alluding to penalty.

Q. Give me the token? A. (Interlace the last finger of the right hand, so as to form a square, and place the left hand on each other's right shoulder.)

Q. Give me the pass-word? A. Rab-kuam.

Q. What does it signify? A. Grand Master Architect.

Q. Give me the mysterious word? A. Jehovah (pronounced Ye-ho-wah).

Q. What was then done to you? A. The Most Potent invested me with the jewel, apron and gloves of this degree, and thus addressed me: "I have elevated," etc.

Q. What then followed? A. I was directed to salute the Senior Warden, as a Grand Architect, and return to the east for further instruction.

Q. Give me the history? A. Solomon established this degree for the purpose, etc.

Q. What do the seven small rays 'round the north star signify? A. Seven liberal arts and sciences.

Closing. —Most Potent knocks one. (Grand Marshal rises.) Most Potent says, "The last as well as the first care," etc. Most Potent knocks two. Senior Warden rises. Most Potent says, "What is the hour?" Ans. The last instant, the last hour, the last day, in which the Grand Architect completed the creation of the universe. Most Potent knocks one and two.—Companions rise. Most Potent says, "It is the last instant, etc.; it is the last hour, the last day, the last year, in which Solomon completed the temple, the last instant for closing this Chapter. Give notice," etc. Signs. Most Potent knocks one and two, Senior Warden one and two, and Companions one and two, with their hands.

KNIGHTS OF THE NINTH ARCH.

Opening. —Most Potent knocks seven. (Grand Marshal rises.) Most Potent says, "Are we all Knights of the Ninth Arch?" Ans. We are, Most Potent.—Q. Your place? etc., etc. Most Potent Knocks eight. Junior Warden rises. Q. What is the hour? A. The rising of the sun. Most Potent knocks three times three.—Companions rise. Most Potent says, "If it is the rising of the sun, it is time to commence our labors. Give notice," etc. Signs of former degrees. Then two kings kneel at the pedestal, as in the first sign, and raise each other by the token. Companions do the same. Most Potent knocks three times three, Senior Warden same, Junior Warden same, and Companions same, and Most Potent says, "I declare this Chapter open."

Lecture. —Question—Are you a Knight of the Ninth Arch? Answer—I have penetrated the bowels of the earth, through nine arches, and have seen the brilliant triangle.

Q. In what place were you admitted? A. In the audience chamber of King Solomon.

[Pg 154] Q. How did you gain admittance there? A. In company with some Intendants of the Building, Illustrious Knights, and Grand Master Architects. I was conducted by the Master of Ceremonies to the door of the audience chamber, where he gave three times three distinct knocks.

Q. To what did they allude? A. To the nine arches which led from the palace of Solomon to the secret vault, and the nine arches of the temple of Enoch.

Q.—How were they answered? A. By three times three from within.

Q.—What followed? A. I was asked, "Who comes there?"

Q.—Your answer? A. Several I. of B.'s, I. K.'s, and Grand Master Architects solicit the honor of being admitted into the secret vault under the Sanctum Sanctorum.

Q. What was then said to you? A. I was told to wait until the Most Potent had been informed of my request, and his answer returned.

Q. What was his answer? A. My brethren, your request cannot now be granted.

Q. What followed? A. We were conducted back to the anti-chamber, when the nine masters entered and thus addressed us: "My brethren, our Most Potent Master requests Grand Master Architects, Joabert, Stokin, and Gibulum to attend in the audience chamber," whereupon we were introduced into the presence of Solomon, who thus addressed us: "My brethren, you know that in digging for a foundation for the temple, we found the ruins of an ancient edifice. Among the ruins, we have already discovered much treasure which has been deposited in the secret vault. Are you willing to make further researches among the ancient ruins, and report to us your discoveries?"

Q. What was your answer. A. We are.

Q. What followed? A. We were conducted to the ruins, and commenced our labors. Among the rubbish we discovered a large iron ring, fixed in a cubic stone, which we raised with much difficulty. Upon examining the same, we discovered an inscription, of the meaning of which we were ignorant. Beneath the stone, a deep and dismal cavern appeared.

Q. Did you enter that cavern? A. I did.

Q. In what manner? A. A rope was fastened 'round my body, and descending, I found myself in an arched vault, in the floor of which was a secret opening, through which I also descended, and in like manner through a third; being in third vault, I found there was an opening for descending still further, but being afraid of pursuing my search, I gave a signal and was hoisted by my two companions. I then recounted to them what I had seen, and proposed to them to descend by turns, which they refused; upon this I determined to descend again, and told them that through every arch I passed, I would gently shake the rope. In this manner I descended from arch to arch, until I was lowered into the sixth arch, when, finding there was still another opening, my heart failed me, and giving the signal, I was again pulled up. I acquainted my two companions with the particulars of my second descent, and now earnestly urged that one of them should go down, as I was very much fatigued; but, terrified at my relation, they both refused. I then received fresh [Pg 155] courage, went down a third time, taking a lighted flambeau in my hand. When I had descended into the ninth arch, a parcel of stone and mortar suddenly fell in and extinguished my light, and I immediately saw a triangular plate of gold, richly adorned with precious stones, the brilliancy of which struck me with admiration and astonishment. Again I gave the signal, and was assisted in reascending. Having related to my two companions the scene which I had witnessed, they expressed a desire to witness the same; they also concluded to go down together, by means of a ladder of ropes, which they did, and shortly after returned with the golden plate, upon which we saw certain characters, of the meaning of which we were then ignorant.

Q. What followed? A. We repaired to the apartment of King Solomon, the King of Tyre, with him, and said, "Most Potent, we obeyed your commands and present you with the fruits of our labors, and solicit the honor of being made acquainted with the inscription on this cubic stone and this golden triangle." Upon beholding it, the two Kings raised their hands, and exclaimed "Gibulum ishtov." The Kings then examined the sacred characters with attention, and Solomon thus addressed us: "My brethren, your request cannot now be granted. God has bestowed upon you a particular favor, in permitting you to discover the most precious jewel of masonry. The promise which God made to some of the ancient patriarchs, that in fulness of time his name should be discovered, is now accomplished. As a reward for your zeal, constancy, and fidelity, I should now constitute you Knights of the Ninth Arch, and I promise you an explanation of the mysterious characters on the golden plate, when it is fixed in the place designed for it, and I will then confer on you the most sublime and mysterious degree of Perfection."

Q. What followed? A. The Most Potent directed the Master of Ceremonies to conduct us to the south-west, and from thence to approach the altar, by three times three steps, and there to take upon ourselves the obligation of this degree.

Q. Repeat that obligation? A. (Same as Perfect Master.) I further promise never to be concerned in the initiation of any brother in this degree, unless he manifests a charitable disposition for Masonry, and a zeal for the brethren, and also obtains permission, under the hands and seal of the first regular officers of a Lodge of Perfection. I further promise that I will not debauch any female related to a companion of this degree, either by blood or marriage, knowing her to be such, under penalty of being crushed under the ruins of a subterraneous temple. So help, etc.

Q. What followed? A. The Most Potent gave me the signs, token and words of this degree.

Q. Give me the sign? A. (Made by kneeling on the left knee, the right hand on the back, the left raised above the head, the palm upward, the body leaning forward, alluding to the penalty.)

Q. Give me the token? A. (Being in the last mentioned position token is made by raising each other from the same, by interlacing the fingers of the left hand.)

Q. How many pass-words are there? A. One for each arch.

[Pg 156] Q. Give them to me? A. 1st, Jov; 2d, Jeho; 3d, Juha; 4th, Havah; 5th, Elgibbor; 6th, Adonai; 7th, Joken; 8th, Eloah; 9th, Elzeboath.

Q. Give me the grand word? A. Gibulum ishtov.

Q. What does that signify? A. Gibulum is a good man.

Q. What was then done to you? A. I was invested with the jewel, apron and gloves of this degree, and directed to salute the Senior Warden as a Knight of the Ninth Arch, and return to the east for further instruction.

Second Section. —Question—Give me the history and charge of this degree? Ans. My worthy brother, it is my intention, at this time, to give you a clearer account of certain historical traditions, etc. (to the words "favored with a mystical vision"), when the Almighty thus designed to speak to him, as thou art desirous to know my name, attend, and it shall be revealed unto thee. Upon this, a mountain seemed to rise to the heavens, and Enoch was transferred to the top thereof, where he beheld a triangular plate of gold most brilliantly enlightened, and upon which were some characters which he received a strict injunction never to pronounce. Presently he seemed to be lowered perpendicularly into the bowels of the earth through nine arches, in the ninth or deepest of which he saw the same brilliant plate which was shown to him in the mountain. In digging for a foundation they discovered an ancient edifice, among which they found a considerable quantity of treasure, such as vases of gold and silver, urns, marble, jasper, and agate columns, and precious stones. All these treasures were collected and carried to Solomon, who upon deliberation concluded that they were the ruins of some ancient temple, erected before the flood, and possibly to the service of Idolatry. He, therefore, determined to build the temple in another place, lest it should be polluted. Solomon caused a cavern to be constructed under the temple, to which he gave the name of secret vault. He erected in this vault a large pillar of white marble, to support the Sanctum Sanctorum, and which, by inspiration, he called the pillar of beauty, from the beauty of the ark which it sustained. There was a long, narrow descent through nine arches from the palace of Solomon to this vault. To this place he was accustomed to retire with Hiram of Tyre, and Hiram Abiff, when he had occasion to enter upon important business. There were none else, then living, qualified to enter this vault. One of their number being removed, disordered their business for a time. As the two kings were on one occasion consulting on business of the craft, application was made to them by several I's of B., I. K. 's and Grand Master Architects, soliciting the honor of being admitted to the secret vault, to whom Solomon replied, "My brethren, your request cannot now be granted." Some days afterwards Solomon sent for the three Grand Master Architects, Gibulum, Joabert and Stokin, and directed them to go and search among the ancient ruins, in hopes of discovering more treasure. They departed, and one of them, viz. , Gibulum, in working with a pickaxe among the rubbish, discovered a large iron ring fixed in a cubic stone. On removing this stone, a cavern was discovered. Gibulum offered to descend. A rope being fastened 'round his body, and [Pg 157] in this manner he descended thrice, and discovered the golden triangle of Enoch, as was represented in the ceremony of your initiation. They then carried the stone and triangle to King Solomon, when the same circumstances occurred, which took place when you presented the same to us. The two Kings then informed the three Knights that they were ignorant of the true pronunciation of the mysterious word until that time, and that this word being handed down through a succession of ages, had been much corrupted. The two Kings, accompanied by the three Knights, descended with the sacred treasure into the secret vault. They encrusted the golden plate upon the pedestal of the pillar of beauty, and the brilliancy of the plate was sufficient to enlighten the place. The secret vault was afterwards called the sacred vault. Whenever the Lodge of Perfection was holden, nine Knights of the Ninth Arch tiled the nine arches which led to the sacred vault; the most ancient stood in the arch next to the anti-chamber of the vault, and so on in regular progression, the youngest taking his station in the first arch, which was near the apartment of Solomon. We were suffered to pass without giving the pass-words of the different arches. There were living at that time several ancient masters, who, excited by jealousy at the honors conferred upon the twenty-five brethren, deputed some of their number to wait upon Solomon, and request that they might participate in those honors. The King answered that the twenty-five masters were justly entitled to the honors conferred on them, for their zeal and fidelity. Go, said he, in peace, you may one day be rewarded according to your merits. Upon this, one of the deputies with an unbecoming warmth, observed to his companions, "What occasion have we for a higher degree? We know the word has been changed, we can travel as masters, and receive pay as such." Solomon mildly replied, "Those whom I have advanced to the degree of perfection, have wrought in the ancient ruins, and though the undertaking was difficult and dangerous, they penetrated the bowels of the earth, and brought thence treasures to enrich and adorn the Temple of God. Go in peace, wait with patience, and aspire to perfection by good works." The deputies returned and reported their reception to the masters. These masters, vexed at the refusal, unanimously determined to go to the ancient ruins, and search under ground, with a view of arrogating the merit necessary for the accomplishment of their desires. They departed the next morning, and raising the cubic stone descended into the cavern with a ladder of ropes, by the light of torches, where no sooner had the last descended, than the nine arches fell in upon them. Solomon hearing of this accident, sent Gibulum, Joabert and Stokin to inform themselves more particularly of the matter. They departed at break of day, and upon their arrival at the place, could discover no remains of the arches, nor could they learn that one single one of all those who had descended escaped the destruction. They examined the place with diligence, but found nothing except a few pieces of marble, on which were inscribed certain hieroglyphics; these they carried to Solomon, and related what they had seen. King Solomon examining these hieroglyphics, discovered that these pieces of marble were part of one of the pillars of Enoch. Solomon ordered these pieces of marble to be carefully put together and deposited in the sacred vault.

[Pg 158] Q. What followed? A. The Most Potent gave me the mysterious characters of this degree, which were engraved on the triangle of Enoch.

Closing. —Most Potent knocks seven (Grand Marshal rising), "the last as well as the first care," etc. Most Potent knocks eight, and Junior Warden rises. "Brother Junior Warden, what is the hour?" A. "The setting of the sun." Most Potent knocks three times three, and companions all rise. "Brother Junior

Warden, give notice," etc. Signs.

Most Potent knocks three times three, Junior Warden three times three, and Companions three times three, with their hands, and Most Potent declares Chapter closed.

GRAND ELECT, PERFECT, AND SUBLIME MASON.

Opening. —Most Perfect knocks three (Grand Marshal rises), "Are we all," etc. Most Perfect knocks five, and Junior Warden rises. Most Perfect says, "Brother Junior Warden, what is the hour?" Ans. "High twelve."

Q. What do you understand by high twelve? A. That the sun has gained its meridian height, and darts its rays with greatest force on this Lodge. Most Perfect says, "It is then time that we should profit by its light." Most Perfect knocks seven, and Senior Warden rises, and Most Perfect says, "Venerable Brother Senior Warden, what brings you here?" A. My love of Masonry, my obligation, and a desire for perfection.

Q. What are the proper qualities for acquiring it? A. Frequent innocence and benevolence.

Q. How are you to conduct in this place? A. With the most profound respect.

Q. Why is it that men of all conditions assembled in this place are called brethren, and are all equal? A. Because the ineffable name puts us in mind that there is one being superior to us all.

Q. Why is respect paid to the triangle? A. Because it contains the name of the Grand Architect of the universe. Most Perfect knocks nine, and brethren all rise. Most Perfect says, "Brother Senior Warden, give notice that I am going to open a Lodge of Perfect Grand Elect and Sublime Masons, by the mysterious number 3, 5, 7 and 9. Senior Warden obeys. Signs of former degrees given, then the Most Perfect knocks three, and all the brethren give the first sign of this degree. Most Perfect knocks three, and then third sign. Most Perfect knocks three, five, seven and nine, Senior Warden the same, Junior Warden the same, and then all the brethren with their hands, & Most Perfect declares Lodge open.

Note. —Behind the Master is the burning bush, in which is a transparent triangle, with five Hebrew letters signifying "God" placed therein. In the west is the pillar of beauty. The pedestal appearing to be broken is a part of the pillar of Enoch, the pieces of which were found among the ruins, and carefully put together. The Lodge is adorned with vases of gold and silver, urns, etc., which were found among the ruins. The lights are thus arranged: three in the west, behind the Junior Warden; five in the East, behind the Senior Warden; seven in the south, and nine behind the Master. The brethren are seated in a triangular form around the altar.

[Pg 159] Lecture. —Question— What are you? Ans. I am three times three, the Perfect's number of eighty-one, according to our mysterious numbers.

Q. Explain that? A. I am a Perfect Grand Elect and Sublime Mason; my trials are finished, and it is now time I should reap the fruits of my labor.

Q. Where were you made a Grand Elect Mason? A. In a place not enlightened by the sun nor moon.

Q. Where was that place situated? A. Under the Sanctum Sanctorum.

Q. How did you gain admission? A. By the nine pass-words of Knights of the Ninth Arch, which brought me to the door of the ante-chamber leading to the sacred vaults, where I gave three distinct knocks.

Q. How were they answered? A. By three from within.

Q. What was said to you? A. Who comes there?

Q. Your answer? A. A Knight of the Ninth Arch, who wishes to be admitted into the sacred vault.

Q. What was then said to you? A. I was directed to give the pass; when I did I was permitted to pass to the second door of the ante-chamber, where I gave three and five knocks, which were answered by three and five and seven from within, and the pass-word demanded as before, which I gave, and was permitted to pass to the door of the sacred vault, where I gave three, five and seven and nine distinct knocks. (Note. —These knocks are answered from within by the Junior and Senior Wardens, and Most Perfect; and Most Perfect says, "Brother Junior Warden, see who knocks there in the manner of a Perfect Grand Elect and Sublime Mason.")

Q. To what do these knocks allude? A. The three knocks signify the age of the Entered Apprentice, and the number of the Grand Marshal Architects who penetrated the bowels of the earth. The five allude to the age of the Fellow Craft and the number of the Grand Elect Perfect and Sublime Masters who placed the sacred treasure upon the pedestal of beauty.

Q. What are their names? A. Solomon, Hiram, King of Tyre, Gibulum, Joabert, and Stokin. The seven allude to the age of the Master Mason, and to Enoch who was the seventh from Adam. The nine represent the age of the Perfect Grand Elect and Sublime Mason, and the nine guards of the arches.

Q. How were these knocks answered? A. By three, five, seven and nine from within.

Q. What followed? A. I was asked, "Who comes there?"

Q. Your answer? A. A Knight of the Ninth Arch, who is desirous of being admitted into the sacred vault and arriving at perfection.

Q. What followed? A. The pass was demanded, which I gave and was ordered to wait until the Most Perfect in the East had been informed of my request and his answer returned.

Q. What was his answer? A. Let him be introduced in ancient form.

Q. What was that form? A. I was conducted to the west and placed between the Wardens, and having made the sign of admiration, was thus interrogated by the Most Perfect: "My Brother, what is your desire? A. To be made a Perfect Grand Elect and Sublime Mason."

[Pg 160] Q. What followed? A. The Most Perfect said, "Before I can initiate you, you must satisfy us that you are well skilled in Masonry, otherwise you must be sent back until you are better qualified," whereupon I was thus examined:

Q. Are you a Mason? A. My brethren all know me as such.

Q. Give me the sign, token and word? A. (Given.)

Q. Are you a Fellow Craft? A. I have seen the letter G and know the pass.

Q. Give me the sign, token and word? A. (Given.)

Q. Are you a Master Mason? A. I have seen the sprig of cassia, and know what it means.

Q. Give me the sign, token and words? A. (Given.)

Q. Are you a Secret Master? A. I have passed from the square to the compass opened to seven degrees.

Q. Give me the sign, token and words? A. (Given.)

Q. Are you a Perfect Master? A. I have seen the tomb of our respectable Master, Hiram Abiff, and have, in company with my brethren, shed tears at the same.

Q. Give me the sign, token and words? A. (Given.)

Q. Are you an Intimate Secretary? A. My curiosity is satisfied, but it nearly cost me my life.

Q. Give me the sign, token and words? A. (Given.)

Q. Are you a Provost and Judge? A. I am, and render justice to all men, without distinction.

Q. Give me the sign, token and words? A. (Given.)

Q. Are you an Intendant of the Buildings? A. I have made the five steps of exactness, I penetrated the inmost part of the temple, and have seen the great light in which were three mysterious characters, J. J. J.

Q. Give me the sign, token and words? A. (Given.)

Q. Are you an Elected Knight? A. One cavern received me, one lamp gave me light, and one fountain refreshed me.

Q. Give me the sign, token and words? A. (Given.)

Q. Are you a Master Elected of Fifteen? A. My zeal and works have procured me that honor.

Q. Give me, etc.? Are you an Illustrious Knight? A. My name will inform you.

Q. Give me, etc. Are you a Grand Master Architect? A. I know the use of the mathematical instruments.

Q. Give me, etc. Are you a Knight of the Ninth Arch? A. I have penetrated through the bowels of the earth, through nine arches, and have seen the brilliant triangle.

Q. Give me, etc. What then followed? A. The Most Perfect inquired of the brethren whether they consented that I should be exalted to the sublime and mysterious degree of Perfection, whereupon one of the brethren rose and said, "I have objections to this candidate." The Most Perfect inquired what these objections were, to which this brother answered, "I will communicate them if the candidate retires." I was then ordered to retire, which I did.

Q. What then followed? A. Shortly after, the Master of Ceremonies [Pg 161] conducted me again into the Lodge, and placing me in the west, I was asked the following questions, viz. :—1st, Have you never wilfully revealed any of the secrets of Masonry? 2d, Have you always been charitable towards your brethren? 3d, Have you never defrauded a brother? 4th, Are you in the habit of using the name of God profanely? 5th, Does your conscience accuse you of having committed any offence against your brethren, which ought to debar you from receiving this degree? Be sincere, and answer me. Which questions being answered, the Most Perfect said, "Brethren, do you consent that this candidate be admitted among us? If you do, raise your right hands." Which being done, I was directed to approach the altar, by three, five, seven and nine steps, which I did, and took upon me the obligation of a Perfect Grand Elect and Sublime Mason.

Q. Repeat that obligation? A. (Same as Perfect Master.) I further promise that I will aid all my worthy brethren in distress and sickness, as far, etc., with my counsel as well as my purse. I further promise, etc. that I will not be concerned in conferring this degree upon any Mason whose character and knowledge I disapprove, nor unless he has been elected and installed as an officer in some regular Lodge, Chapter, Encampment, or Council. I further promise that I will never fully pronounce more than once in my life the mysterious word of this degree, under penalty of having my body cut in twain. So help, etc. Amen, Amen, Amen.

Q. What followed? A. While I was still in a kneeling posture, the Most Most Perfect said, "Let us pray," which was done, and the Master of Ceremonies then presented the hod and trowel to the Most Perfect, who said, "My brother, I shall now proceed to anoint you with the holy oil wherewith Aaron, David, and the wise Solomon were anointed." And then anointing my head, lips and heart, at the same time said, "Behold how good and pleasant," etc., and then placing his hand upon me, said, "I impress you," etc.

Q. What followed? A. The Most Perfect presented me with the bread and wine, and rising, said, "Eat of this bread," etc. When this part of the ceremony was ended the brethren made a libation according to ancient usage.

Q. What followed? A. The Most Perfect raised me and said, "That which I shall now communicate to you, will make you accomplished in Masonry." He then gave me three signs, three tokens, the three pass-words, and the three grand words of this degree.

Q. Give me the signs? [First sign made like Master Mason's, with hands clenched.]

Q. To what does this sign allude? A. To the penalty of the obligation. [Second sign: bring your right hand upright, the palm outwards to guard your left cheek, your left hand supporting your elbow, then guard your right cheek with left hand, etc.]

Q. To what does that sign allude? A. To the manner in which Moses guarded his eyes from the light of the burning bush, from which the Almighty revealed to him his true name. [Third sign is that of surprise: [Pg 162] raise both hands as high as the shoulders, and step back with the right foot.]

Q. To what does this sign allude? A. To the attitude of Solomon and Hiram, when the sacred treasure was first produced.

Q. Give me the first token? [First token same as Intimate Secretary, giving the words Berith, Neder, Shelemoth]

Q. What do those signify? A. Alliance, Promise and Protection.

Q. To what do they allude? A. To the alliance of Moses and Aaron, of Solomon and Hiram, King of Tyre. The promise made by the Almighty to the ancient patriarchs that the true pronunciation of his name should be revealed to their posterity, and the perfection attained when this promise was fulfilled.

Q. Give me the second token? [Pass from Master's grip, and seize his right arm above the elbow, and place your left hand on his right shoulder.]

Q. Give me the third token? [With your left hand seize your brother's right elbow, and with your right hand, his right shoulder.]

Q. Give me the three pass-words? A. First, Master Mason's; second, El-hanon; third, Fellow Craft's, repeated thrice.

Q. Give me the three grand words? A. First, Gibulum; second, Eh-yeh-asher-eh-yeh.

Q. What does that word signify? A. I am what I am. Third, El-hod-dihu kaw-lu.

Q. What does that word signify? A. God be praised, we have finished it.

Q. What followed? A. The Most Perfect caused me to pronounce the mysterious word of this degree.

Q. Pronounce it? A. I cannot but once in my life.

Q. How will you then give it? A. * * * * [A Hebrew pronunciation of God.]

Q. What followed? A. The Most Perfect thus addressed me: "You are already acquainted with the fact, that the true pronunciation of the name of God was revealed to Enoch, and that he engraved the letters composing that name on a triangular plate of gold. The name was represented by the four Hebrew consonants, Jod, He, Vau, and He. The vowel sounds of this language being represented by points placed above the consonants, and being frequently omitted in writing, the consonants composing the mysterious word, at different ages, received different pronunciations. Hence, though the method of writing this word remained uniform, its pronunciation underwent many changes. These changes constitute what are termed the different ages of Masonry. These are 3, 5, 7 and 9. These are the three ages of Masonry, and are thus estimated:

After the death of Enoch, the ineffable name was pronounced by

3 {	Methuselah, Lamech, and Noah,	} Juha (Yu-haw.)	
7 { { [163]	Reu, Serug, Nahor, Terah, Abraham, Isaac, Judah,	} Jova (Yo-waw).	{
5 { {	Shem, Arphaxed, Salah, Eber, and Peleg,	} Jeva (Ye-waw).	{ {
9 { {	Hezron, Ram,	} (Yay-wo) Je-vo.	{ {
	Aminadab, Nasshou,	} Jevah (Ye-way).	
	Salmon, Boaz, Obed,	} Johe (Yo-hay).	
	Jesse, David,	} Jehovah (Ye-ho-waw).	

The true pronunciation of the name was revealed to Enoch, Jacob, and Moses, and on that account are not named in this enumeration. The perfect number is thus formed:—The number of corrupted words is 9. The ages of Masonry, 3, 5, 7, 9—24, multiplied by 3, the number gotten who discovered Tunsune (noticed in the degree of the Knight of the Ninth Arch), gives the product 72; to this add 9, the number of corrupted words, the amount is 81. The mysterious words which you received in the preceding degrees, are all so many corruptions of the true name (of God) which was engraved on the triangle of Enoch. In this engraving the vowel points are so arranged as to give the pronunciation which you have just received (Yow-ho). This word, when thus pronounced, is called the ineffable word, which cannot be altered as other words are, and the degrees which you have received, are called, on this account, INEFFABLE DEGREES. This word you will recollect was not found until after the death of Hiram Abiff, consequently the word engraved by him on the ark is not the true name of God."

Q. What then followed? A. The Most Perfect gave me the secret characters of this degree, and then invested me with the jewels, apron, and girdle of this degree, and I was again addressed:—"I now with the greatest pleasure salute you," etc.

Closing. —Most Perfect knocks three (Grand Marshal rises), "The last," etc., etc. Most Perfect knocks five, and Junior Warden rises. "Brother Junior Warden, what is the hour?" Most Perfect knocks seven, and Senior Warden rises. Most Perfect says, "Venerable Brother Senior Warden, how should the Grand Elect, Perfect and Sublime Mason part?" A. "They should part in peace, love, and unity." Most Perfect knocks nine, all brethren rise. Signs. Most Perfect knocks three, five, seven and nine, Junior Warden the same, Senior Warden the same, and brethren the same, with their hands, etc.

[Pg 164]

The Philosophical Lodge; or, the Key of Masonry: being the Degree of Knights Adepts of the Eagle or Sun.

This Council must be illuminated by one single light, and is enlightened by one divine light: because there is one single light that shines among men, who have the happiness of going from the darkness of ignorance and of the vulgar prejudices, to follow the only light that leads to the celestial truth. The light that is in our Lodge, is composed of a glass globe filled with water, and a light placed behind it, which renders the light more clear. The glass of reflection, the globe, when it is lighted, is placed in the south.

Robe and Sceptre. —The Grand Master or Thrice Puissant, is named "Father Adam," who is placed in the East, vested in a robe of pale yellow, like the morning. He has his hat on, and in his right hand a sceptre, on the top of which is a globe of gold. The handle or extremity of the sceptre is gilt. The reason that Father Adam carries the globe above the sceptre in this Council is, because he was constituted Sovereign Master of the world, and created Sovereign Father of all men. He carries a Sun suspended by a chain of gold around his neck; and on the reverse of this jewel of gold is a globe. When this degree is given, no jewel or apron is worn.

There is only one Warden, who sits opposite Father Adam in the west, and is called Brother Truth. He is entitled to the same ornaments as Father Adam; and the order that belongs to this degree is a broad white watered ribbon worn as a collar, with an eye of gold embroidered thereon, above the gold chain and jewel of the sun. The number of other officers is seven, and are called by the name of the cherubim, as follows: Zaphriel, Zabriel, Camiel, Uriel, Michael, Zaphael, and Gabriel. These ought to be decorated in the same manner as the Thrice Puissant Father Adam. If there are more than that number of the Knights of the Sun, they go by the name of Sylphs, and are the preparers of the Council, and assistants in all the ceremonies or operations of the Lodge. They are entitled to the same jewel, but have a ribbon of a fiery color tied to the third button-hole of their coat.

To Open the Grand Council. —Father Adam says:—"Brother Truth, what time is it on earth?" Brother Truth: "Mighty Father, it is midnight among the profane, or cowans, but the sun is in its meridian in this Lodge." Father Adam: "My dear children, profit by the favor of this austere luminary, at present showing its light to us, which will conduct us in the path of virtue, and to follow that law which is eternally to be engraved on our hearts, and the only law by which we cannot fail to come to the knowledge of pure truth." He then makes a sign, by putting his right hand on his left breast; on which all the brethren put up the first finger of the right hand above their heads, the other fingers clenched, showing by that, that there is but one God, who is the beginning of all truth; then Father Adam says, "This Lodge is opened."

Form of Reception. —After the Council is opened, the candidate is introduced into an ante-chamber, where there are a number of Sylphs, each with a bellows, blowing a large pot of fire, which the candidate [Pg 165] sees, but they take no notice of him. After he is left in that situation two or three minutes, the most ancient of the Sylphs goes to the candidate and covers his face with black crape. He must be without a sword, and is told that he must find the door of the Sanctuary, and when found, to knock on it six times with an open hand. After he finds the door and knocks, Brother Truth goes to the door, and having opened it a little, asks the candidate the following questions, which he answers by the help of the Sylphs. "Q. What do you desire? A. I desire to go out of darkness to see the true light, and to know the true light in all its purity. Q. What do you desire more? A. To divest myself of original sin, and destroy the juvenile prejudices of error, which all men are liable to, namely, the desire of all worldly attachments and pride." On which Brother Truth comes to Father Adam, and relates what the candidate has told him; when Father Adam gives orders to introduce the candidate to the true happiness. Then Brother Truth opens the door, and takes the candidate by the hand, and conducts him to the middle of the Lodge or Sanctuary, which is also covered by a black cloth, when Father Adam addresses him thus: "My son, seeing by your labor in the royal art, you are now come to the desire of knowledge of the pure and holy truth, we shall lay it open to you without any disguise or covering. But, before we do this, consult your heart, and see in this moment if you feel yourself disposed to obey her (namely truth) in all things which she commands. If you are disposed, I am sure she is ready in your heart, and you must feel an emotion that was unknown to you before. This being the case, you must hope that she will not be long to manifest herself to you. But have a care not to defile the sanctuary by a spirit of curiosity; and take care not to increase the number of the vulgar and profane, that have for so long a time ill-treated her, until Truth was obliged to depart the earth, and now can hardly trace any of her footsteps. But she always appears in her greatest glory, without disguise, to the true, good, and honest Free Masons; that is to say, to the zealous extirpators of superstition and lies. I hope, my dear brother, you will be one of her intimate favorites. The proofs that you have given, assure me of everything I have to expect of your zeal; for as nothing now can be more a secret among us, I shall order brother Truth, that he will instruct you what you are to do in order to come to true happiness." After this discourse of Father Adam, the candidate is unveiled and shown the form of the Lodge or Council, without explaining any part thereof. Brother Truth then proceeds thus: "My dear brother, by my mouth, holy truth speaketh to you, but before she can manifest herself to you, she requires of you proofs in which she is satisfied in your entrance into the Masonic order. She has appeared to you in many things which you could not have apprehended or comprehended without her assistance; but now you have the happiness to arrive at the brilliant day, nothing can be a secret to you. Learn, then, the moral use that is made of the three first parts of the furniture, which you knew after you was received an Entered Apprentice Mason, viz.: Bible, Compass and Square. By the Bible you are to understand that it is the only law you ought to follow. It is that which Adam [Pg 166] received at his creation, and which the Almighty engraved in his heart. This law is called natural law, and shows positively that there is but one God, and to adore him only without any subdivision or interpolation. The Compass gives you the faculty of judging for yourself, that whatever God has created, is well, and he is the sovereign author of every thing. Existing in himself, nothing is either good or evil; because we understand by this expression, an action done which is excellent in itself, is relative, and submits to the human understanding, or judgment, to know the value and price of such action; and that God, with whom every thing is possible, communicates nothing of his will, but such as his great goodness pleases; and every thing in the universe is governed as he has decreed it, with justice, being able to compare it with the attributes of the Divinity. I equally say, that in himself there is no evil; because he has made every thing with exactness, and that every thing exists according to his will; consequently, as it ought to be. This distance between good and evil with the Divinity, cannot be more justly and clearly compared than by a circle formed with a compass. From the points being reunited there is formed an entire circumference; and when any point in particular equally approaches or equally separates from its point, it is only a faint resemblance of the distance between good and evil, which we compare by the points of a compass forming a circle, which circle when completed is God.

Square. —By the Square we discover that God, who has made every thing equal, in the same manner that you are not able to dig a body in a quarry complete, or perfect; thus, the wish of the Eternal in creating the world by a liberal act of his own, well foresaw every matter that could possibly happen in consequence thereof; that is to say, that every thing therein contained at the same time of the creation was good.

Level. —You have also seen a level, a plumb, and a rough stone. By the level you are to learn to be upright and sincere, and not to suffer yourself to be drawn away by the multitude of the blind and ignorant people; to be always firm and steady to sustain the right of the natural law, and the pure and real knowledge of that truth which it teacheth.

Perpendicular and Rough Stone. —By these you ought to understand that the perpendicular man is polished by reason, and put censure away by the excellence of our Master.

Tressle-board. —You have seen the tressle-board, to draw plans on. This represents the man whose whole occupation is the art of thinking, and who employs his reason in that which is just and reasonable.

Cubic Stone. —You have seen the cubic stone, the moral of which, and the sense you ought to draw from it, is, to rule your actions, that they might be equally brought to the sovereign good.

Pillars. —The two pillars teacheth you that all Masons ought to attach themselves firmly to become an ornament to the order, as well as to its support; as the pillars of Hercules formerly determined the end of the ancient world.

Blazing Star. —You have seen the blazing star, the moral sense of which is, "a true Mason perfecting himself in the way of truth," that he [Pg 167] may become like a blazing star which shineth equally during the thickest darkness; and it is useful to those that it shineth upon, and who are ready and desirous of profiting by its light.

The first instructions have conducted you to the knowledge of Hiram Abiff, and the inquiries that were made in finding him out. You have been informed of the words, signs and tokens which were substituted for those we feared would have been surprised, but of which they afterwards learnt that the treacherous villains had not been able to receive any knowledge of; and this ought to be an example and salutary advice to you, to be always on your guard, and well persuaded that it is difficult to escape the snares that ignorance, joined to conceited opinion, lay every day against us, and thereby to overcome us; and the most virtuous men are liable to fall, because their candor renders them unsuspecting. But, in this case, you ought to be firm as our Respectable Father Hiram, who chose rather to be massacred than to give up what he had obtained.

This will teach you that as soon as truth shall be fixed in your heart, you ought never to consider the resolution you should take; you must live and die to sustain the light, by which we acquire the sovereign good. We must never expose ourselves to the conversation of cowans, and must be circumspect even with those with whom we are the most intimate; and not deliver up ourselves to any, excepting those whose character and behavior have proved them brothers, who are worthy to come and appear in the sacred sanctuary where holy Truth delivers her oracles.

You have passed the Secret and Perfect Master; you have been decorated with an ivory key, a symbol of your distinction; you have received the pronunciation of the ineffable name of the Great Architect of the universe, and have been placed at the first balustrade of the sanctuary; you have had rank among the Levites, after which you knew the word "Zizon," which signifies "a balustrade of the Levites;" where all those are placed, as well as yourself, to expect the knowledge of the most sublime mysteries.

Coffin and Rope. —In the degree of Perfect Master they have shown you a grave, a coffin, and a "withe rope," to raise and deposit the body in a sepulchre, made in the form of a pyramid, in the top of which was a triangle, within which was the sacred name of the Eternal, and on the pavement were the two columns of Jachin and Boaz laid across.

Ivory Key. —By the "ivory key" you are to understand that you cannot open your heart with safety, but at proper times. By the corpse and grave is represented the state of man, before he had known the happiness of our order.

Rope. —The rope to which the coffin is tied, in order to raise it, is the symbol of raising one, as you have been raised from the grave of ignorance to the celestial place where truth resides.

Pyramid. —The pyramid represents the true Mason who raises himself by degrees, till he reaches heaven, to adore the sacred and unalterable name of the Eternal Supreme.

[Pg 168] Intimate Secretary. —This new degree leads you near to Solomon and honor; and after you redoubled your zeal, you gained new honors and favors, having nearly lost your life by curiosity; which attachment to Masonry gave you the good qualities of your heart, and which obtained your pardon and let you to the "Intendant of the Buildings," where you saw a "blazing star," a large candlestick with seven branches, with altars, vases, and purification, and a great brazen sea.

Blazing Star. —By the expression of PURIFICATION you are to understand that you are to be cleansed from impiety and prejudice before you can acquire more of the sublime knowledge in passing the other degrees, to be able to support the brilliant light of reason, enlightened by truth, of which the blazing star is the figure.

Candlestick with Seven Branches. —By the candlestick with seven branches you are to remember the mysterious number of the seven Masters who were named to succeed one; and from that time it was resolved that seven Knights of Masonry, united together, were able to initiate into Masonry, and show them the seven gifts of the Eternal, which we shall give you a perfect knowledge of, when you have been purified in the Brazen Sea.

Brazen Sea. —You have passed from the Secret and Perfect Master to the Intimate Secretary, Provost and Judge, and Intendant of the Buildings. In these degrees they have shown you an ebony box, a key suspended, a balance, and an inflamed urn.

Ebony Box. —The ebony box shows you with what scrupulous attention you are to keep the secrets that have been confided to you, and which you are to reserve in the closet of your heart, of which the box is an emblem. And were you to reflect on the black color of said box, it would teach you to cover your secrets with a thick veil, in such a manner that the profane cowans cannot possibly have any knowledge thereof.

Key. —The key demonstrates that you have already obtained a key to our knowledge, and part of our mysteries; and if you behave with equity, fervor, and zeal to your brothers, you will arrive shortly to the knowledge and meaning of our society, and this indicates the reason of the balance.

Inflamed Urn. —By the inflamed urn you are to understand, that as far as you come to the knowledge of the Royal and Sublime Art, you must, by your behavior, leave behind you, in the minds of your brethren and the vulgar, a high idea of your virtue, equal to the perfume of the burning urn.

Two Kings. —In the degree of Intimate Secretary, you have seen and heard two kings who were entering into their new alliance and reciprocal promise, and of the perfection of their grand enterprise. They spoke of the death of Hiram Abiff, our Excellent Master. You saw guards, as a man who was overseen, very near of being put to death for his curiosity of peeping. You also heard of the prospect of a place called the vault, to deposit the precious treasure of Masonry, when the time should be fulfilled, and you afterwards became a brother. The conversation of the two kings is the figure of the coincidence of our laws and the natural [Pg 169] law, which forms a perfect agreement with what is expedient, and promises to those who shall have the happiness to be connected to you in the same manner and perfect alliance that they will afterwards come to the centre of true knowledge.

Tears. —The tears and regret of the two kings are the emblem of the regret you ought to have when you perceive a brother depart from the road of virtue.

The Man Peeping. —By the man you saw peeping, and who was discovered and seized, and conducted to death, is an emblem of those who come to be initiated into our sacred mysteries through a motive of curiosity; and, if so indiscreet as to divulge their obligations, we are bound to take vengeance on the treason by the destruction of the traitor. Let us pray the Eternal to preserve our order from such an evil you have hereof seen an example, in that degree to which you came, by your zeal, fervor and constancy. In that degree you have remarked, that from all the favorites that were at that time in the apartment of Solomon, only nine were elected to avenge the death of Hiram Abiff; this makes good, that a great many are often called, but few chosen. To explain this enigma, a great many of the profane have the happiness to divest themselves of that name, to see and obtain the entrance in our sanctuary; but very few are constant, zealous and fervent, to merit the happiness of coming to the height and knowledge of the sublime truth.

Requisitions To Make a Good Mason. —If you ask me what are the requisite qualities that a Mason must be possessed of, to come to the centre of truth, I answer you, that you must crush the head of the serpent of ignorance. You must shake off the yoke of infant prejudice concerning the mysteries of the reigning religion, which worship has been imaginary, and only founded on the spirit of pride, which envies to command and be distinguished, and to be at the head of the vulgar; in affecting an exterior purity, which characterizes a false piety, joined to a desire of acquiring that which is not its own, and is always the subject of this exterior pride, and unalterable source of many disorders, which being joined to gluttonness, is the daughter of hypocrisy, and employs every matter to satisfy carnal desires, and raises to these predominant passions, altars, upon which she maintains, without ceasing, the light of iniquity, and sacrifices continually offerings to luxury, voluptuousness, hatred, envy, and perjury. Behold, my dear brother, what you must fight against and destroy before you can come to the knowledge of the true good and sovereign happiness! Behold this monster which you must conquer—a serpent which we detest as an idol, that is adored by the idiot and vulgar under the name of religion.

Solomon, King Hiram, and St. John the Baptist. —In the degrees of Elected of Fifteen, Illustrious Knights, Grand Master Architects, and Knights of the Ninth Arch, you have seen many things which are only a repetition of what you have already examined. You will always find in those degrees initial letters enclosed in different triangles, or Deltas. You have also seen the planet Mercury, the chamber called "Gabaon," or the "Third Heaven;" the "winding staircase," the "Ark of Alliance," the "tomb of Hiram Abiff," facing the ark and the urn—the precious [Pg 170] treasure found by the assiduous travels—the three zealous brethren Masons—the punishment of the haughty Master Mason, in being buried under the ancient ruins of Enoch's temple—and finally, you have seen the figures of Solomon, and Hiram, King of Tyre, and St. John the Baptist.

3. I. I. I.—By the 3. I. I. I. you know the three sacred names of the Eternal and "Mount Gabaon" (Third Heaven) which you came to by seven degrees that compose the winding staircase.

The seven stars represent the seven principal and different degrees to which you must come to attain the height of glory represented by the mount, where they formerly sacrificed to the Most High! When you arrive to that, you are to subdue your passions, in not doing anything that is not prescribed in our laws.

By the planet Mercury, you are taught continually to mistrust, shun, and run away from those who, by a false practice, maintain commerce with people of a vicious life, who seem to despise the most sacred mysteries—that is, to depart from those who by the vulgar fear, or a bad understanding, are ready to deny the solemn obligations that they have contracted among us.—When you come to the foot of our arch you are to apprehend that you come to the "Sanctum Sanctorum." You are not to return; but rather to persist in sustaining the glory of our order, and the truth of our laws, principles, and mysteries, in like manner as our Respectable Father Hiram Abiff, who deserved to have been buried there for his constancy and fidelity. We have also another example in the firmness of "Galaad," the son of "Sophonia," chief of the Levites, under Surnam, the High Priest, as mentioned in the history of perfection. Learn in this moment, my dear brother, what you are to understand by the figures of Solomon, Hiram, King of Tyre, and St. John the Baptist. The two first exert you, by their zeal in the royal art, to follow the sublime road of which Solomon was the institutor, and Hiram of Tyre, the "supporter;" a title legitimately due to that king, who not only protected the order, but contributed with all his might to the construction of the temple (furnishing stone from Tyre, and the cedars of Lebanus) which Solomon built to the honor of the Almighty.

The third, or St. John the Baptist, teaches you to preach marvellous to this order, which is as much as to say, you are to make secret missions among men, which you believe to be in a state of entering the road of truth, that they may be able one day to see her virtues and visage uncovered.

Hiram Abiff was the symbol of truth on earth. Jubelum Akirop was accused by the serpent of ignorance, which to this day raises altars in the hearts of the profane and fearful. This profaneness, backened by a fanatic zeal, becomes an instrument to the religious power, which struck the first stroke in the heart of our dear Father, Hiram Abiff; which is as much as to say, undermined the foundation of the celestial temple, which the Eternal himself had ordered to be raised to the sublime truth and his glory.

The first age of the world has been witness to what I have advanced. The simple, natural law rendered to our first fathers the most [Pg 171] uninterrupted happiness. They were in those times more virtuous; but as soon as the "monster of pride" started up in the air and disclosed herself to those unhappy mortals, she promised to them every seat of happiness, and seduced them by her soft and bewitching speeches, viz.: That "they must render to the Eternal Creator of all things an adoration with more testimony, and more extensive, than they had hitherto done," etc. This Hydra with a hundred heads, at that time misled, and continues to this day to mislead men who are so weak as to submit to her empire; and it will subsist, until the moment that the true elected shall appear and destroy her entirely.

The degree of Sublime Elected, that you have passed, gives you the knowledge of those things which conducts you to the true and solid good. The grand circle represents the immensity of the Eternal Supreme, who has neither beginning nor end.

The triangle, or Delta, is the mysterious figure of the Eternal. The three letters which you see, signify as follows:—G, at the top of the triangle, "the grand cause of the Masons": the S, at the left hand, the "submission to the same order": and the U, at the right hand, the "union that ought to reign among the brethren: which, altogether make but one body, or equal figure in all its parts." This is the triangle called "equilateral." The great letter G, placed in the centre of the triangle, signifies "Great Architect of the Universe," who is God; and in this ineffable name is found all the divine attributes. This letter being placed in the centre of the triangle, is for us to understand that every true Mason must have it profoundly in his heart.

There is another triangle, on which is engraved S. B. and N., of which you have had an explanation in a preceding degree. This triangle designs the connection of the brethren in virtue. The solemn promise they have made to love each other; to help, succor, and keep inviolably secret, their mysteries of the perfection proposed, in all their enterprises. It is said in that degree, that "You have entered the Third Heaven, that means you have entered the place where pure truth resides, since she abandoned the earth to monsters who persecuted her."

The end of the degree of Perfection is a preparation to come more clearly to the knowledge of true happiness, in becoming a true Mason, enlightened by the celestial luminary of truth, in renouncing, voluntarily, all adorations but those that are made to one God, the Creator of heaven and earth, great, good, and merciful. End of Brother Truth's harangue.

Father Adam then says to the candidate, "My dear son, what you have heard from the mouth of Truth is an abridgment of all the consequences of all the degrees you have gone through, in order to come to the knowledge of the holy truth, contracted in your last engagements. Do you persist in your demand of coming to the holy brother, and is that what you desire, with a clear heart?—answer me." The candidate [Pg 172] answers, "I persist." Then Father Adam says, "Brother Truth, as the candidate persists, approach with him to the sanctuary, in order that he may take a solemn obligation to follow our laws, principles, and morals, and to attach himself to us forever." Then the candidate falls on his knees, and Father Adam takes his hands between his own, and the candidate repeats the following obligation three times:

Obligation. —I, A. B., promise, in the face of God, and between the hands of my Sovereign, and in presence of all the brethren now present, never to take arms against my country, directly or indirectly, in any conspiracy against the Government thereof. I promise never to reveal any of the degrees of the Knight of the Sun, which is now on the point of being intrusted to me, to any person or persons whatsoever, without being duly qualified to receive the same; and never to give my consent to any one to be admitted into our mysteries, only after the most scrupulous circumspection, and full knowledge of his life and conversation; and who has given at all times full proof of his zeal and fervent attachment for the order, and a submission at all times to the tribunal of the Sovereign Princes of the Royal Secret. I promise never to confer the degree of the Knights of the Sun without having a permission in writing from the Grand Council of Princes of the Royal Secret, or from the Grand Inspector or his deputy, known by their titles and authority. I promise also and swear, that I will not assist any, through my means, to form or raise a Lodge of the Sublime Orders, in this country, "without proper authority." I promise and swear to redouble my zeal for all my brethren, Knights, and Princes, that are present or absent; and if I fail in this my obligation, I consent for all my brethren, when they are convinced of my infidelity, to seize me, and thrust my tongue through with a red-hot iron; to pluck out both my eyes, and to deprive me of smelling and hearing; to cut off both my hands, and to expose me in that condition in the field, to be devoured by the voracious animals; and if none can be found, I wish the lightning of heaven might execute on me the same vengeance. O God, maintain me in right and equity. Amen. Amen. Amen.

After the obligation is three times repeated, Father Adam raises the candidate, and gives him one kiss on his forehead, being the seat of the soul. He then decorates him with the collar and jewel of the order, and gives him the following sign, token and word:— Sign : Place the right hand flat upon the heart, the thumb forming a square. The answer, raise the hand, and with the index point to heaven. This is to show that there is but one God, the source of all truth. Token : Take in your hands those of your brother, and press them gently. Some Knights, in addition to this, kiss the forehead of the brother, saying "Alpha," to which he answers, "Omega." Sacred Word : "Adonai." This word is answered by "Albra," or "Abbraak," which is rendered "a king without reproach." Some contend that this word should be written "Abrah." Pass-word :—"Stibium" (antimony). By this is intended as among the Hermetic Philosophers, "the primitive matter whence all things are formed." To this pass-word some add the following: "Helios," "Mene," "Tetragrammaton."

After these are given, the candidate goes 'round and gives them to every one, which brings him back to Father Adam. He then sits down with the rest of the brethren, and then Brother Truth gives the following explanation of the Philosophical Lodge:

Sun. —The sun represents the unity of the Eternal Supreme, the only grand work of philosophy.

[Pg 173] 3. S. S. S.—The 3 S. S. S. signify the "Stiletto, Sidech, Solo," or the residence of the Sovereign Master of all things.

Three Candlesticks. —The three candlesticks show us the three degrees of fire.

Four Triangles. —The four triangles represent the four elements.

Seven Planets. —The seven planets design the seven colors that appear in their original state, from whence we have so many different artificial ones.

Seven Cherubims. —The seven cherubims represent the seven metals, viz., gold, silver, copper, iron, lead, tin and quicksilver.

Conception in the Moon. —The conception, or woman, rising in the moon, demonstrates the purity that matter subsists of, in order to remain in its pure state unmixed with any other body, from which must come a new king, and a revolution or fulness of time filled with glory whose name is Albra.

Holy Spirit. —The Holy Spirit, under the symbol of a dove, is the image of the Universal Spirit, that gives light to all in the three states of nature; and on the animal, vegetable and mineral.

Entrance of the Temple. —The entrance of the temple is represented to you by a body, because the grand work of nature is complete as gold, potable and fixed.

Globe. —The globe represents the matter in the primeval state; that is to say, complete.

Caduceus. —The caduceus represents the double mercury that you must extract from the matter; that is to say, the mercury fixed, and from thence is extracted gold and silver.

Stibium. —The word stibium signifies the antimony, from whence, by the philosophical fire, is taken an alkali which we empty in our grand work. End of the philosophical explanation. Then Father Adam explains the

MORAL LODGE.

Sun. —The sun represents the divinity of the Eternal; for as there is but one Sun to light and invigorate the earth, so there is but one God, to whom we ought to pay our greatest adoration.

3 S. S. S.—The 3 S. S. S. are initials of the words Scienta, Sapientia, Sanctitas, and teach you that science, adorned with wisdom, creates a holy man.

Three Candlesticks. —The three candlesticks are the image of the life of man, considered in youth, manhood, and old age, and happy are those that have been enlightened in these ages, by the light of truth.

Four Triangles. —The four triangles show us the four principal duties that create our tranquil life, viz.: Fraternal love among men in general, and particularly among brethren, and in the same degree with us. Secondly. In not having anything but for the use and advantage of a brother. Thirdly. Doubting of every matter that cannot be demonstrated to you clearly, by which an attempt might be made to insinuate mysteries in matters of religion, and hereby lead you away from the holy truth. Fourthly. Never do anything to another that you would not [Pg 174] have done unto you. The last precept, well understood and followed on all occasions, is the true happiness of philosophy.

Seven Planets. —The seven planets represent the seven principal passions of man.

Seven Cherubims. —The seven cherubims are the images of the delights of life: namely, by seeing, hearing, tasting, smelling, feeling, tranquility, and health.

Conception. —The conception in the moon shows the purity of matter, and that nothing can be impure to the eyes of the Supreme.

Holy Spirit. —The Spirit is the figure of our soul, which is only the breath of the Eternal, and which cannot be soiled by the works of the body.

Temple. —The temple represents our body, which we are obliged to preserve by our natural feelings.

Figure of a Man. —The figure is in the entrance of the temple, which bears a lamb in his arms, and teaches us to be attentive to our wants, as a shepherd takes care of his sheep; to be charitable, and never let slip the present opportunity of doing good, to labor honestly, and to live in this day as if it were our last.

Columns of Jachin and Boaz. —The columns of J. and B. are the symbols of the strength of our souls in bearing equally misfortunes, as well as success in life.

Seven Steps of the Temple. —The seven steps of the temple are the figures of the seven degrees which we must pass before we arrive to the knowledge of the true God.

Globe. —The globe represents the world which we inhabit.

Lux ex Tenebris. —The device of "Lux ex tenebris" teacheth, that when man is enlightened by reason, he is able to penetrate the darkness and obscurity which ignorance and superstition spread abroad.

River. —The river across the globe represents the utility of the passions that are necessary to man in the course of his life, as water is requisite to the earth in order to replenish the plants thereof.

Cross Surrounded. —The cross surrounded by two serpents signifies that we must watch the vulgar prejudices, to be very prudent in giving any of our knowledge and secrets in matters, especially in religion. End of the moral explanation.

Lecture. —Question—Are you a Knight of the Sun? Answer—I have mounted the seven principal steps of Masonry; I have penetrated into the bowels of the earth, and among the ancient ruins of Enoch found the most grand and precious treasures of the Masons. I have seen, contemplated, and admired the great, mysterious, and formidable name engraved on the triangle; I have broken the pillar of beauty, and thrown down the two columns that supported it.

Q. Pray tell me what is that mysterious and formidable name? A. I cannot unfold the sacred characters in this manner, but substitute in its place the grand word of [represented by the Hebrew consonants Jod, He, Vau, He.]

Q. What do you understand by throwing down the columns that sustained the pillar of beauty. A. Two reasons.— First. When the temple [Pg 175] was destroyed by Nebuzaradan, general of the army of Nebuchadnezzar, I was one that helped to defend the Delta on which was engraved the ineffable name; and I broke down the columns of beauty, in order that it should not be profaned by the infidels. Second. As I have deserved, by my travel and labor, the beauty of the great "Adonai" (Lord), the mysteries of Masonry, in passing the seven principal degrees.

Q. What signifies the seven planets? A. The lights of the celestial globe and also their influence, by which every matter exists on the surface of the earth or globe.

Q. From what is the terrestrial globe formed? A. From the matter which is formed by the concord of the four elements, designed by the four triangles, that are in regard to them as the four greater planets.

Q. What are the names of the seven planets? A. Sun, Moon, Mars, Jupiter, Venus, Mercury, and Saturn.

Q. Which are the four elements? A. Air, fire, earth, and water.

Q. What influence have the seven planets on the four elements? A. Three general matters of which all bodies are composed—life, spirit, and body; otherwise, salt, sulphur and mercury.

Q. What is life or salt? A. The life given by the Eternal Supreme, or the planets, the agents of nature.

Q. What is the spirit or sulphur? A. A fixed matter, subject to several productions.

Q. What is the body or mercury? A. Matter conducted or refined to its form by the union of salt and sulphur, or the agreement of the three governors of nature.

Q. What are those three governors of nature? A. Animal, vegetable and mineral.

Q. What is animal? A. We understand in this, life—all that is divine and amiable.

Q. Which of the elements serve for his productions? A. All the four are necessary, among which, nevertheless, air and fire are predominant; and it is those that render the animal the perfection of the three governments, which man is elevated to by one-fourth of the breath of the Divine Spirit, when he receives his soul.

Q. What is the vegetable? A. All that seems attached to the earth reigns on the surface.

Q. Of what is it composed? A. Of a generative fire, formed into a body whilst it remains in the earth, and is purified by its moisture and becomes vegetable, and receives life by air and water; whereby the four elements, though different, co-operate jointly and separately.

Q. What is the mineral? A. All that is generated and secreted in the earth.

Q. What do we understand by this name? A. That which we call metals and demi-metals and minerals.

Q. What is it that composes the minerals? A. The air penetrating by the celestial influence into the earth, meets with a body, which, by its softness, fixes, congeals, and renders the mineral matter more or less perfect.

Q. Which are the perfect metals? A. Gold and silver.

[Pg 176] Q. Which are the imperfect metals? A. Brass, lead, tin, iron and quicksilver.

Q. How come we by the knowledge of these things? A. By frequent observations and the experiments made in natural philosophy, which have decided to a certainty that nature gives a perfection to all things, if she has time to complete her operations.

Q. Can art bring metal to perfection so fully as nature? A. Yes; but in order to do this, you must have an exact knowledge of nature.

Q. What will assist you to bring forth this knowledge? A. A matter brought to perfection, this has been sought for under the name of the philosopher's stone.

Q. What does the globe represent? A. An information of philosophers, for the benefit of the art in this work.

Q. What signify the words, "Lux ex tenebris?" A. That is the depth of darkness you ought to retire from, in order to gain the true light.

Q. What signifies the cross on the globe? A. The cross is the emblem of the true elected.

Q. What represent the three candlesticks? A. The three degrees of fire, which the artist must have knowledge to give, in order to procure the matters from which it proceeds.

Q. What signifies the word Stibium? A. It signifies antimony, or the first matter of all things.

Q. What signify the seven degrees? A. The different effectual degrees of Masonry which you must pass to come to the Sublime Degree of Knights of the Sun.

Q. What signify the divers attributes in those degrees? A. First. The Bible, or God's law, which we ought to follow. Second. The compass teaches us to do nothing unjust. Third. The square conducts us equal to the same end. 4th. The level demonstrates to us, all that is just and equitable. Fifth. The perpendicular, to be upright and subdue the veil of prejudice. Sixth. The tressle-board is the image of our reason, where the functions are combined to effect, compare and think. Seventh. The rough-stone is the resemblance of our vices, which we ought to reform. Eighth. The cubic stone is our passions, which we ought to surmount. Ninth. The columns signify strength in all things. Tenth. The blazing star teaches that our hearts ought to be as a clear sun, among those that are troubled with the things of this life. Eleventh. The key teaches to have a watchful eye over those who are contrary to reason. Twelfth. The box teaches to keep our secrets inviolably. Thirteenth. The urn learns us that we ought to be as delicious perfumes. Fourteenth. The brazen sea, that we ought to purify ourselves, and destroy vice. Fifteenth. The circles on the triangles demonstrate the immensity of the divinity under the symbol of truth. Sixteenth. The poniard teacheth the step of the elected, many are called, but few are chosen to the sublime knowledge of pure truth. Seventeenth. The word albra signifies a king full of glory and without blot. Eighteenth. The word Adonai signifies Sovereign Creator of all things. Nineteenth. The seven cherubims are the symbols of the delights of life, known by seeing, hearing, tasting, feeling, smelling, tranquility, and thought.

[Pg 177] Q. What represents the sun? A. It is an emblem of Divinity, which we ought to regard as the image of God. This immense body represents the infinity of God's wonderful will, as the only source of light and good. The heat of the sun produces the rule of the seasons, recruits nature, takes darkness from the winter, in order that the deliciousness of spring might succeed. End of the physical lecture.

GENERAL LECTURE IN THIS DEGREE.

Question—From whence came you? Answer—From the centre of the earth.

Q. How have you come from thence? A. By reflection, and the study of nature.

Q. Who has taught you this? A. Men in general who are blind, and lead others in their blindness.

Q. What do you understand by this blindness? A. I do not understand it to be privy to their mysteries; but I understand under the name of blindness, those who cease to be ardent, after they have been privy to the light of the spirit of reason.

Q. Who are those? A. Those who, through the prejudices of superstition and fanaticism, render their services to ignorance.

Q. What do you understand by fanaticism? A. The zeal of all particular sects which are spread over the earth, who commit crimes by making offerings to fraud and falsehood.

Q. And do you desire to rise from this darkness? A. My desire is to come to the celestial truth, and to travel by the light of the sun.

Q. What represents that body? A. It is the figure of an only God, to whom we ought to pay our adoration. The sun being the emblem of God, we ought to regard it as the image of the Divinity; for that immense body represents wonderfully the infinity of God. He invigorates and produces the seasons, and replenishes nature, by taking the horrors from winter, and produces the delights of spring.

Q. What does the triangle, with the sun in the centre, represent? A. It represents the immensity of the Supreme.

Q. What signifies the three S. S. S. ? A. Sanctitas, Scientia, and Syrentia, which signify the science accompanied with wisdom, and make men holy.

Q. What signifies the three candlesticks? A. It represents the course of life, considered in youth, manhood, and old age.

Q. Has it any other meaning? A. Yes, the triple light that shines among us, in order to take men out of darkness and ignorance into which they are plunged, and to bring them to virtue, truth, and happiness, a symbol of our perfection.

Q. What signifies the four triangles that are in the great circles? A. They are the emblems of the four principal views of the life of tranquility, etc. First. Fraternal love to all mankind in general, more particularly for our brethren, who are more attached to us, and who with honor have seen the wretchedness of the vulgar. Second. To be cautious among us of things, and not to demonstrate them clearly to any who are [Pg 178] not proper to receive them; and to be likewise cautious in giving credit to any matter, however artfully it may be disguised, without a self-conviction in the heart. Third. To cast from us every matter which we perceive we may ever repent of doing, taking care of this moral precept, "To do to every one of your fellow creatures no more than you would choose to be done to." Fourth. We ought always to confide in our Creator's bounty, and to pray without ceasing, that all our necessities might be relieved as it seems best to him for our advantage; to wait for his blessings patiently in this life; to be persuaded of his sublime decrees, that whatever might fall, contrary to our wishes, will be attended with good consequences; to take his chastisements patiently, and be assured that the end of everything has been done by him for the best, and will certainly lead us to eternal happiness hereafter.

Q. Explain the signification of the seven planets which are enclosed in a triangle, that forms the rays of the exterior circles, and are enclosed in the grand triangle. A. The seven planets, according to philosophy, represent the seven principal passions of the life of man; those passions are very useful when they are used in moderation, for which the Almighty gave them to us, but grow fatal and destroy the body when let loose: and, therefore, it is our particular duty to subdue them.

Q. Explain the seven passions to us. A. 1st. The propagation of species. 2d. Ambition of acquiring riches. 3d. Ambition to acquire glory in the arts and sciences among men in general. 4th. Superiority in civil life. 5th. Joys and pleasures of society. 6th. Amusements and gaieties of life. 7th. Religion.

Q. Which is the greatest sin of all that man can commit, and render him odious to God and man? A. Suicide and homicide.

Q. What signifies the seven cherubims whose names are written in the circle called the "First Heaven?" A. They represent the corporeal delights of this life, which the Eternal gave to man when he created him, and are, seeing, hearing, smelling, tasting, feeling, tranquility, and thought.

Q. What signifies the figure in the moon, which we regard as the figure or image of conception? A. The purity of nature, which procures the holiness of the body; and that there is nothing imperfect in the eyes of the Supreme.

Q. What signifies the figure of the columns? A. They are the emblems of our souls, which is the breath of life proceeding from the All Puissant, and ought not to be soiled by the works of the body, but to be firm as columns.

Q. What does the figure in the porch, which carries a lamb in his arms represent? Ans.—The porch ornamented with the columns of Jachin and Boaz, and surmounted with the grand I, represents our body, over which we ought to have a particular care, in watching our conversation, and also to watch our needs, as the shepherd his flock.

Q. What signify the two letters, I and B, at the porch? A. They signify our entrance in the order of Masonry; also the firmness of the soul, which we ought to possess from hour of our initiation; these we ought to merit, before we can come to the sublime degrees of knowing holy [Pg 179] truth, and we ought to preserve them, and be firm in whatever situation we may be in, not knowing whether it may return to our good or evil in the passage of this life.

Q. What signifies the large I in the triangle on the crown of the portico? A. That large I, being the initial of the mysterious name of the Great Architect of the Universe, whose greatness we should always have in our minds, and that our labors ought to be employed to please Him; which we should always have in our view as the sure and only source of our actions.

Q. What signify the seven steps that lead to the entry of the porch? A. They mark the seven degrees in Masonry, which are the principal which we ought to arrive to, in order to come to the knowledge of holy truth.

Q. What does the terrestrial globe represent? A. The world which we inhabit, and wherein Masonry is its principal ornament.

Q. What is the explanation of the great word, Adonai? A. It is the word which God gave to Adam, for him to pray by; a word which our common father never pronounced without trembling.

Q. What signifies "Lux ex tenebris?" A. A man made clear by the light of reason, penetrating this obscurity of ignorance and superstition.

Q. What signifies the river across the globe? A. It represents the utility of our passions, which are necessary to man in the course of his life, as water is necessary to render the earth fertile; as the sun draws up the water, which being purified, falls on the earth and gives verdure.

Q. What signifies the cross, surrounded by two serpents, on the top of the globe? A. It represents to us not to repeat the vulgar prejudices; to be prudent, and to know the bottom of the heart. In matters of religion to be always prepared; not to be of the sentiments with sots, idiots, and the lovers of the mysteries of religion; to avoid such, and not in the least to hold any conversation with them.

Q. What signifies the book, with the word Bible written in it? A. As the Bible is differently interpreted by the different sects who divide the different parts of the earth: Thus the true sons of light, or children of truth, ought to doubt of everything at present, as mysterious or metaphysics: Thus all the decisions of theology and philosophy, teach not to admit that which is not demonstrated as clearly as that 2 and 2 are equal to 4; and on the whole to adore God, and him only; to love him better than yourself; and always to have a confidence on the bounties and promises of our Creator. Amen. Amen. Amen.

To Close the Council. —Question (by Father Adam): Brother Truth, what progress have men made on earth to come to true happiness? Answer (by Brother Truth): Men have always fallen on the vulgar prejudices, which are nothing but falsehood; very few have struggled, and less have knocked at the door of this holy place, to attain the full light of real truth, which we all ought to acquire.

Then says Father Adam, "My dear children, depart and go among men, endeavor to inspire them with the desire of knowing holy truth, the pure source of all perfection." Father Adam then puts his right hand on his left breast; when all the brethren raise the first finger of the right [Pg 180] hand, and then the Council of the Knights of the Sun is closed by seven knocks.

PRINCES OF JERUSALEM.

Prerogatives of the Princes. —Princes of Jerusalem have a right to inspect all Lodges or Councils of an inferior degree, and can revoke and annul all the work done in such Councils or Lodges, if the same shall be inconsistent with the regulations of Masonry.

In countries where there are no Grand Lodges, they have power to confer the blue degrees. They are the supreme judges of all transactions in the lower degrees; and no appeal can be made to the Supreme Councils of the upper degrees, until an opinion has been given by the Grand Council of Princes of Jerusalem, and the result of their opinion has been made known.

A Prince of Jerusalem who visits an inferior Lodge or Council, ought to present himself in the dress and ornaments of this degree. When his approach is announced, the presiding officer must send a Prince of Jerusalem to examine him, and if he reports in his favor, the arch of steel is to be formed, and he is conducted beneath it to his seat on the left of the presiding officer. An entry of his name and rank is made on the records, that he may henceforward receive our honors without any examination.

Five Princes are necessary to form a Grand Council.

Duties of Princes. —They are carefully to observe the rules of justice and good order, and to maintain irreproachable lives. If guilty of unmasonic conduct, they are to be punished at the discretion of the Grand Council. Expulsions are to be notified to the Grand Councils of the upper degrees, and to all inferior Masonic bodies within the district.

If a Prince solicits a vote at an election, he is to be punished with perpetual exclusion.

The annual election is to take place on the twenty third day of the Jewish month Adar. The meetings of the Councils are termed Conventions.

Apartments Used in This Degree. —There are two apartments, connected by a long, narrow passage. The western represents the court of Zerubbabel, at Jerusalem. The hangings are yellow. Over the throne is a yellow canopy. On a triangular pedestal, before the throne, are placed a naked sword, an arrow of justice, a balance, and a shield on which is an equilateral triangle, a sceptre, a chandelier of five branches, which are all lighted in the latter part of the ceremony of reception. The eastern apartment represents the cabinet of Darius. It is hung with red; the canopy is red. Before the throne is a small square pedestal, and in it a drawn sword, a sceptre, paper, pens, etc. The chief Minister of State sits near Darius.

Officers of the Grand Council. —The first officer is styled "Most Equitable Prince," and is on the throne. The Senior Warden and Junior Warden are styled "Most Enlightened;" seated in the West. The other officers and the members are styled "Valiant Princes."

Dress. —The "Most Equitable" wears a yellow robe and turban. The apron is red; on it are painted the temple, a square, a buckler, a triangle, [Pg 181] and a hand; the flap is yellow; on it a balance, and the letters D. Z. [Darius and Zerubbabel.] Gloves are red. Sash is yellow, edged with gold, embroidered by a balance, a hand, a poniard, five stars, and two crowns, it is worn from right to left.

Jewel. —A golden medal; on one side a hand holding a balance in equilibris; on the other a two-edged sword, with five stars around the point, and the letters D. Z.

Alarm. —The alarm is three and two (!!! !!).

Opening. —The "Most Equitable" strikes one, and says, "Valiant Grand Master of Ceremonies, what is the first business of a Grand Council of the Princes of Jerusalem?" Grand Master of Ceremonies. "To see that the guards are at their proper stations." M. E. "Attend to that duty, and inform," etc. G. M. C.—"It is done, Most Equitable." Most Equitable strikes two; the Junior Warden rises. M. E.—"Valiant Junior Warden, what is our next business?" J. W.—"To see that all present are Princes of Jerusalem." M. E.—"Attend to that duty." J. W.—"We are all Princes of Jerusalem." Most Equitable (striking thrice).—"Valiant Senior Warden, what is the hour?" Senior Warden.—"The rising of the sun." M. E.—"What duty remains to be done?" S. W.—"To arrange the Princes in two columns, for the proper discharge of their duties." M. E. —"Attend to that duty." S. W.—"Most

Equitable, it is done." M. E.—"Valiant Junior and Senior Wardens, inform your respective columns that I am about to open this Grand Council of Princes of Jerusalem, by three and two." (That is done.) M. E.—"Attention, Valiant Princes! (The signs are given; the Most Equitable strikes three and two; this is repeated by the Wardens.) I declare this Grand Council duly opened and in order for business."

Reception. —The candidate, being hoodwinked, is led by the Master of Ceremonies to the door—the alarm is given—the door is opened without any ceremony, and the candidate is led to the east, and thus addressed: Most Equitable.—"What is your desire?" Candidate.—"I come to prefer the complaints of the people of Israel against the Samaritans, who have refused to pay the tribute imposed on them for defraying the expense of the sacrifices offered to God in the temple." M. E. (who represents Zerubbabel).—"I have no power over the Samaritans; they are subject to King Darius, who is at Babylon; it is to him that such complaints must be preferred; but as we are all interested in this thing, I will arm you, and cause you to be accompanied by four Knights, that you may more easily surmount any difficulty which may present itself in your journey to the court of the King of Persia." The bandage is now removed from the eyes of the candidate; he is armed with a sword and buckler, and decorated as a Knight of the East. The four Knights who accompany him are armed in a similar manner. They commence their journey, and are attacked by some armed ruffians, whom they repulse. They arrive at the door of the cabinet of Darius. The candidate enters with one of the Knights, and thus addresses the King:—"Mighty King! the Samaritans refuse to pay the tribute imposed on them by Cyrus, King of Persia, for defraying the expenses of the sacrifices which are offered in the temple which we have rebuilt; the people of Israel entreat [Pg 182] that you will compel the Samaritans to perform their duty." Darius.—"Your request is just and equitable; I order that the Samaritans shall immediately pay the tribute imposed on them. My Chief Minister shall deliver to you my decree for this purpose. Go in Peace!" The candidate retires; the Chief Minister follows, and delivers the decree to him. After surmounting various obstacles, candidate is met on his return by the Knights with lighted torches, and is thus conducted with triumph into the presence of Zerubbabel, and says:—"I deliver to you the decree of Darius, King of Persia, which we have obtained after defeating our enemies, and encountering many dangers in our journey." Most Equitable reads the decree as follows:— "We, Darius, 'King of Kings!' willing to favor and protect our people at Jerusalem, after the example of our illustrious predecessor, King Cyrus, do will and ordain that the Samaritans, against whom complaints have been made, shall punctually pay the tribute money which they owe for the sacrifices of the temple—otherwise they shall receive the punishment due to their disobedience. Given at Shushan, the palace, this fourth day of the second month, in the year 3534, and of our reign the third, under the seal of our faithful Darius. [L. S.]" M. E.—"The people of Jerusalem are under the greatest obligations to you for the zeal and courage displayed by you in surmounting the obstacles which you encountered in your journey; as a reward we shall confer on you the mysteries of the degree of Prince of Jerusalem. Are you willing to take an obligation, binding you to an exact observance of our laws, and a careful concealment of our mysteries?" Candidate.—"I am." M. E.— "Kneel before the altar for that purpose."

Obligation. —I, A. B., do solemnly promise and swear, in the presence of Almighty God, the Great Architect of heaven and earth, and of these Valiant Princes of Jerusalem, that I will never reveal the mysteries of the degree of Prince of Jerusalem to any one of an inferior degree, or to any other person whatever. I promise and swear, as a Prince of Jerusalem, to do justice to my brethren, and not to rule them tyranically, but in love. I promise and swear that I will never, by word or deed, attack the honor of any Prince of Jerusalem; and that I will not assist in conferring this degree except in a lawful Grand Council of Princes of Jerusalem. All this I promise and swear, under the penalty of being stripped naked, and having my heart pierced with a poniard. So help me God. Amen! Amen! Amen!

The Most Equitable raises the candidate, and gives him the following signs, tokens, and words:— First Sign —Extend the right arm horizontally at the height of the shoulder. This is termed the sign of command. First Token .— Each places his left hand on his left hip, and the right hand on his brother's left shoulder. Second Token .—Join left hands, placing the thumb on the second joint of the little finger; with the thumb strike five times on that joint. Password. —"Tebeth." The name of the Jewish month in which the Ambassadors entered Jerusalem. Sacred Word .—"Adar." The name of the month in which thanks were given to God for the completion of the temple. In some Councils the following sign is given, viz.:—Present yourself before your brother with your sword advanced, and your left hand resting on your hip, as if to commence a [Pg 183] combat. He will answer the sign by extending his arm at the height of the shoulder, the right foot forming a square with the toe of the left. The March .—Five steps on the diagonal of the square towards the throne. Age. —The age of a Prince of Jerusalem, is 5 times 15.

Most Equitable.—"I now appoint and constitute you, with your four companions, Princes and Governors of Jerusalem, that you may render justice to all the people. I decorate you with a yellow sash, to which is attached a gold medal. The 'balance' on it is to admonish you to make equity and justice your guides. The 'hand of justice' is a mark of your authority over the people. The 'emblems' of the 'apron' with which I now invest you, have reference to the works and virtues of Masons, and to your duty in the high office with which you are invested. As Princes of

Jerusalem, you will assemble in two chambers of the temple. Be just, merciful, and wise."

Lecture .—Question—Are you a Prince of Jerusalem? Answer—I know the road to Babylon.

Q. What were you formerly? A. A Knight of the East.

Q. How did you arrive at the dignity of a Prince of Jerusalem? A. By the favor of Zerubbabel, and the courage which I manifested in many conflicts.

Q. Where did the Prince of Jerusalem travel? A. From Jerusalem to Babylon.

Q. Why? A. The Samaritans having refused to pay the tribute imposed on them for defraying the expense of the sacrifices offered to God in the temple, an embassy was dispatched to Babylon, to obtain justice of King Darius.

Q. How many Knights constituted this embassy? A. Five.

Q. Did they encounter any difficulty in their journey? A. They did. The Samaritans, against whom they were to prefer a complaint, armed themselves and attacked the ambassadors, but were defeated.

Q. What did they obtain from Darius? A. A decree ordering the Samaritans to pay the tribute, or suffer punishment.

Q. How were the ambassadors received on their return to Jerusalem? A. At some distance from the city they were met by the people, who accompanied them to the temple singing songs of joy. On reaching the temple and making their report, and presenting the decree of Darius, they were constituted Princes of Jerusalem.

Q. How were they habited as Princes of Jerusalem? A. In cloth of gold.

Q. What were their decorations? A. A yellow sash trimmed with gold from right to left; to which was attached a golden medal, on which was engraved a balance, a sword, five stars, and the letters D. Z.

Q. What is signified by the five stars on the sash? A. They are emblematic of the five Knights who journeyed from Jerusalem to Babylon.

Q. What is the age of a Prince of Jerusalem? A. Five times fifteen.

Close. —Most Equitable. "Most Enlightened Junior and Senior Wardens, announce to your respective columns that I am about to close this Grand Council by five times fifteen." Each Warden strikes five; all rise and the notice is given. M. E. "Attention, Princes of Jerusalem? (The [Pg 184] signs are given. The Most Equitable strikes five times fifteen, which is repeated by the Wardens.) Be just, merciful and wise! I declare this Grand Council duly closed. "

KNIGHTS OF THE EAST AND WEST.

Form of the Grand Council .—The Grand Council of Knights of the East and West, must be hung with red and sprinkled with gold stars. In the east of the Council Chamber must be a canopy, elevated by seven steps, supported by four lions and four eagles, and between them an angel, or seraphim, with six wings. On one side of the throne there must be a transparent painting of the sun, and, on the other side, one of the moon; below them is stretched a rainbow. In the east there must be a basin with perfume, and a basin of water, and a human skull. On the south side there must be six small canopies, and on the north side five, elevated by three steps, for the Venerable Ancients, and opposite the throne, in the west, are two canopies, elevated by five steps, for the two Venerable Wardens, who act in this Council as Grand Officers, or Wardens. A full Grand Council must be composed of twenty-four Knights. On the pedestal there must be a large Bible, with seven seals suspended therefrom.

The Venerable Master is called "Most Puissant;" the Wardens, and the twenty-one other brethren, are called "Respectable Ancients." If there are more brethren present, they are styled "Respectable Knights," and are placed north and south, behind the small canopies.

The first canopy, at the right side of the Puissant, is always vacant for the candidate. All the brethren are clothed in white, with a zone of gold 'round the waist, long white beards and golden crowns on their heads. The Knights, in their ordinary habits, wear a broad, white ribbon from the right shoulder to the left hip, with the jewel suspended thereto. They also wear a cross of the order, suspended by a black ribbon, 'round their necks. The Most Puissant has his right hand on the large Bible on the pedestal with seven seals. The draft (or carpet) of the Council, is an heptagon in a circle—over the angles are these letters, B. D. S. P. H. F. In the centre, a man clothed in a white robe, with a girdle of gold 'round his waist—his right hand extended and surrounded with seven stars—he has a long white beard, his head surrounded with a glory, and a two-edged sword in his mouth—with seven candlesticks 'round him, and over them the following letters: H. D. P. I. P. R. C.

The jewel is an heptagon of silver—at each angle, a star of gold and one of these letters B. D. S. P. H. G. S. in the centre. A lamb on a book with seven seals—on the reverse, the same letters in the angles, and in the centre, a two-edged sword between a balance.

The apron is white, lined with red, bordered with yellow, or gold; on the flap is painted a two-edged sword, surrounded with the seven holy letters—or the apron may have the plan of the draft painted on it.

To Open the Council .—The Most Puissant, with his right hand on the Bible sealed with seven seals, demands, "Venerable Knights Princes, what is your duty?" A. "To know if we are secure." Most Puissant. "See that we are so." A. "Most Puissant, we are in perfect security." [Pg 185] The Most Puissant strikes seven times, and says, "Respectable Knights Princes, the Grand Council of Knights of the East and West is open; I claim your attention to the business thereof." A. "We promise obedience to the Most Puissant's commands." They rise and salute him, when he returns the compliment, and requests them to be seated.

Reception. —The candidate must be in an antechamber, which must be hung with red, and lighted with seven lights, where he is clothed with a white robe, as an emblem of the purity of his life and manners. The Master of Ceremonies brings him barefooted to the Council Chamber door, on which he knocks seven times, which is answered by the Most Puissant, who desires the youngest Knight to go to the door, and demand who knocks. The master of Ceremonies answers, "It is a valiant brother and Most Excellent Prince of Jerusalem, who requests to be admitted to the Venerable and Most Puissant." The Knight reports the same answer to the Most Puissant, who desires the candidate to be introduced. The Most Ancient Respectable Senior Grand Warden then goes to the door, and takes the candidate by the hand, and says, "Come, my dear brother, I will show you mysteries worthy the contemplation of a sensible man. Give me the sign, token, and word of a prince of Jerusalem;" after which the candidate kneels on both knees, about six feet from the throne, when the Most Ancient Respectable Senior Grand Warden says to him, "Brother, you, no doubt, have always borne in memory the obligations of your former degrees, and that you have, as far as in the power of human nature, lived agreeably to them?" Candidate. "I have ever made it my study, and, I trust, my actions and life will prove it." Q. "Have you particularly regarded your obligations as a 'Sublime Knight of Perfection,' 'Knight of the East and Prince of Jerusalem?' Do you recollect having injured a brother in any respect whatsoever? or have you seen or known of his being injured by others, without giving him timely notice, as far as was in your power? I pray you answer me with candor." Candidate. "I have in all respects done my duty, and acted with integrity to the best of my abilities." The Most Puissant says, "You will be pleased to recollect, my brother, that the questions which have now been put to you, are absolutely necessary for us to demand, in order that the purity of our Most Respectable Council may not be sullied; and it behooves you to be particular in your recollection, as the indispensable ties which we are going to lay you under, will, in case of your default, only increase your sins, and serve to hurl you sooner to destruction, should you have deviated from your duty: answer me, my dear brother." Candidate. "I never have." The Most Puissant says, "We are happy, my brother, that your declaration coincides with our opinion, and are rejoiced to have it into our power to introduce you into our society. Increase our joy by complying with our rules, and declare if you are willing to be united to us by taking a most solemn obligation." Candidate. "I ardently wish to receive it, and to have the honor of being united to so respectable and virtuous a society." The Most Puissant orders one of the Knights to bring an ewer containing some perfume, a basin of water, and a clean white napkin to the candidate, who washes his hands. The Most Puissant repeats the six first verses of the 24th [Pg 186] Psalm. Then the candidate is brought close to the foot of the throne, where he kneels on both knees, and placing his right hand on the Bible, his left hand between the hands of the Most Puissant, in which position he takes the following

Obligation .—I, ——, do promise and solemnly swear, and declare, in the awful presence of the only One Most Holy Puissant Almighty and Most Merciful Grand Architect of heaven and earth, who created the universe and myself through his infinite goodness, and conducts it with wisdom and justice—and in the presence of the Most Excellent and upright Princes and Knights of the East and West, here present in convocation and Grand Council, on my sacred word of honor and under every tie, both moral and religious, that I never will reveal to any person whomsoever below me, or to whom the same may not belong, by being legally and lawfully initiated, the secrets of this degree which is now about to be communicated to me, under the penalty of not only being dishonored, but to consider my life as the immediate forfeiture, and that to be taken from me with all the tortures and pains to be inflicted in manner as I have consented to in my preceding degrees. I further promise and solemnly swear, that I never will fight or combat with my brother Knights, but will, at all times, when he has justice on his side, be ready to draw my sword in his defence, or against such of his enemies who seek the destruction of his person, his honor, peace, or prosperity; that I never will revile a brother, or suffer others to reflect on his character in his absence, without informing him thereof, or noticing it myself, at my option; that I will remember, on all occasions, to observe my former obligations, and be just, upright, and benevolent to all my fellow creatures, as far as in my power. I further solemnly promise and swear, that I will pay due obedience and submission to all the degrees of Masonry; and that I will do all in my power to support them in all justifiable measures for the good of the craft, and advantage thereof, agreeably to the Grand Constitutions.—All this I solemnly swear and sincerely promise, upon my sacred word of honor, under the penalty of the severe wrath of the Almighty Creator of heaven and earth, and may He have mercy on my soul, on the great and awful day of judgment, agreeably to my conformity thereto. Amen. Amen. Amen.

The Most Puissant then takes the ewer filled with perfumed ointment, and anoints his head, eyes, mouth, heart, the tip of his right ear, hand, and foot, and says, "You are now, my dear brother, received a member of our society; you will recollect to live up to the precepts of it, and also remember that those parts of your body which have the greatest power of assisting you in good or evil, have this day been made holy!" The Master of Ceremonies then places the candidate between the two Wardens, with the craft before him. The Senior Warden says to him, "Examine with deliberation and attention everything which the Most Puissant is going to show you." After a short pause, he, the Senior Warden, says—"Is there mortal here worthy to open the book with the seven seals?" All the brethren cast their eyes down and sigh. The Senior Warden, hearing their sighs, says to them, "Venerable and respectable brethren, be not afflicted; here is a victim (pointing to the candidate), whose courage will give you content." Senior Warden to the candidate, "Do you know the reason why the ancients have a long white beard?" Candidate. "I do not, but I presume you do." S. W. "They are those who came here, after passing through great tribulation, and having washed their robes in their own blood; will you purchase such robes at so great a price?" Candidate. "Yes; I am willing." The Wardens then conduct him to the basin, and bare both his arms—they place a ligature [Pg 187] on each, the same as in performing the operation of blood-letting. Each Warden being armed with a lancet, makes an incision in each of his arms, just deep enough to draw a drop of blood, which is wiped on a napkin, and shown to the brethren. The Senior Warden then says, "See, my brethren, a man who has spilled his blood to acquire a knowledge of our mysteries, and shrunk not from the trial!" Then the Most Puissant opens the first Seal of the great book, and takes from thence a bone quiver, filled with arrows, and a crown, and gives them to one of the Ancients, and says to him, "Depart and continue the conquest." He opens the second Seal, and takes out a sword, and gives it to the next aged, and says, "Go, and destroy peace among the profane and wicked brethren, that they may never appear in our Council." He opens the third Seal, and takes a balance, and gives it to the next aged, and says, "Dispense rigid justice to the profane and wicked brethren." He opens the fourth Seal, and takes out a scull, and gives it to the next aged, and says, "Go, and endeavor to convince the wicked that death is the reward of their guilt." He opens the fifth Seal, and takes out a cloth, stained with blood, and gives it to the next aged, and says, "When is the time (or, the time will arrive,) that we shall revenge and punish the profane and wicked, who have destroyed so many of their brethren by false accusations." He opens the sixth Seal, and that moment the sun is darkened and the moon stained with blood! He opens the seventh Seal, and takes out incense, which he gives to a brother; and also a vase, with seven trumpets, and gives one to each of the seven aged brethren. After this, the four old men, in the four corners, show their inflated bladders (beeves' bladders, filled with wind under their arms), representing the four winds: when the Most Puissant says "Here is seen the fulfilment of a prophecy;" (Rev. vii. 3). Strike not, nor punish the profane and wicked of our order, until I have selected the true and worthy Masons! Then the four winds raise their bladders, and one of the trumpets sound, when the two Wardens cover the candidate's arms, and take from him his apron and jewel of the last degree. The second trumpet sounds, when the Junior Warden gives the candidate the apron and jewel of this degree. The third trumpet sounds, when the Senior Warden gives him a long white beard. The fourth trumpet sounds, and the Junior Warden gives him a crown of gold. The fifth trumpet sounds, and the Senior Warden gives him a girdle of gold. The sixth trumpet sounds, and the Junior Warden gives him the sign, token and words, as follows:— Sign. —Look at your right shoulder, it will be answered by looking at the left shoulder. One says, "Abaddon," the other "Jubulum." First Token. —Place your left hand in the right hand of your brother, who will cover it with his left; both at the same time look over their right shoulder. Second Token. —Touch your brother's left shoulder with your left hand; he replies by touching your right shoulder with his right hand. Sign for entering the Lodge. —Place your right hand on the brother's forehead (i.e., the Tyler's), he will do the same. Pass-word. —"Jubulum," or, according to some, "Perignan" and "Gadaon." Sacred Word. —"Abaddon." This name will be found in Rev. ix. 11. The seventh trumpet sounds, on which they all sound together, when the Senior Warden conducts the candidate to the vacant canopy.

[Pg 188] Origin of this Degree. —When the Knights and Princes were embodied to conquer the Holy Land, they took a cross to distinguish them, as a mark of being under its banners; they also took an oath to spend the last drop of their blood to establish the true religion of the Most High God. Peace being made, they could not fulfil their vows, and, therefore, returning home to their respective countries, they resolved to do in theory what they could not do by practice, and determined never to admit, or initiate, any into their mystic ceremonies, but those who had given proofs of friendship, zeal, and discretion. They took the name of Knights of the East and West, in memory of their homes and the place where the order began; and they have ever since strictly adhered to their ancient customs and forms. In the year 1118, the first Knights, to the number of eleven, took their vows between the hands of Garimont, Patriarch and Prince of Jerusalem, from whence the custom is derived of taking the obligation in the same position.

Lecture. —Question—Are you a Knight of the East and West? A. I am.

Q. What did you see when you were received? A. Things that were marvellous.

Q. How were you received? A. By water and the effusion of blood.

Q. Explain this to me? A. A Mason should not hesitate to spill his blood for the support of Masonry.

Q. What are the ornaments of the Grand Council? A. Superb thrones, sun, more perfumed ointment, and a basin of water.

Q. What is the figure of the draft? A. An heptagon within a circle.

Q. What is the representation of it? A. A man vested in a white robe, with a golden girdle 'round his waist—'round his right hand seven stars—his head surrounded with a glory, a long, white beard—a two-edged sword across his mouth, surrounded by seven candlesticks, with these letters: H. D. P. I. P. R.

Q. What signifies the circle? A. As the circle is finished by a point, so should a Lodge be united by brotherly love and affection.

Q. What signifies the heptagon? A. Our mystic number which is enclosed in seven letters.

Q. What are the seven letters? A. B. D. W. P. H. G. S.; which signifies Beauty, Divinity, Wisdom, Power, Honor, Glory, and Strength.

Q. Give me the explanation of these words? A. Beauty to adorn; Divinity, that Masonry is of divine origin; Wisdom, a quality to invent; Power, to destroy the profane and unworthy brethren; Honor, is an indispensable quality in a Mason, that he may support himself in his engagements with respectability; Glory, that a good Mason is on an equality with the greatest prince; and Strength, is necessary to sustain us.

Q. What signifies the seven stars? A. The seven qualities which Masons should be possessed of: Friendship, Union, Submission, Discretion, Fidelity, Prudence and Temperance.

Q. Why should a Mason be possessed of these qualities? A. Friendship, is a virtue that should reign among brothers; Union, is the foundation of society; Submission, to the laws, regulations, and decrees of the Lodge, without murmuring; Discretion, that a Mason should always be on his guard, and never suffer himself to be surprised; Fidelity, in [Pg 189] observing strictly our obligations; Prudence, to conduct ourselves in such a manner that the profane, though jealous, may never be able to censure our conduct; and Temperance, to avoid all excesses that may injure either body or soul.

Q. What signifies the seven candlesticks, with their seven letters? A. seven crimes, which Masons should always avoid, viz.: Hatred, Discord, Pride, Indiscretion, Perfidy, Rashness, and Calumny.

Q. What are the reasons that Masons should particularly avoid these crimes? A. Because they are incompatible with the principles and qualities of a good Mason, who should avoid doing an injury to a brother, even should he be ill-treated by him, and to unite in himself all the qualities of a good and upright man. Discord, is contrary to the very principles of society; Pride, prevents the exercise of humanity; Indiscretion, is fatal to Masonry; Perfidy, should be execrated by every honest man; Rashness, may lead us into unpleasant and disagreeable dilemmas; and Calumny, the worst of all, should be shunned as a vice which saps the very foundation of friendship and society.

Q. What signifies the two-edged sword? A. It expresses the superiority of this degree over all others that precede it.

Q. Are there any higher degrees than this? A. Yes; there are several.

Q. What signifies the book with seven seals, which none but one can open? A. A Lodge, or Council, of Masons, which the Most Puissant alone has a right to convene and open.

Q. What is enclosed in the first seal? A. One bow, one arrow, and one crown.

Q. What in the second? A. A two-edged sword.

Q. What in the third? A. A balance.

Q. What in the fourth? A. Death's head.

Q. What in the fifth? A. A cloth stained with blood.

Q. What in the sixth? A. The power to darken the sun, and tinge the moon with blood.

Q. What in the seventh? A. Seven trumpets and perfumes.

Q. Explain these things to me? A. The bow, arrow, and crown, signifies that the orders of this respectable council should be executed with as much quickness as the arrow flies from the bow, and be received with as much submission as if it came from a crowned head, or the chief of a nation. The sword, that the Council is always armed to punish the guilty. The balance is a symbol of justice. The skull is the image of a brother who is excluded from a Lodge or Council. This idea must make all tremble when they recollect the penalties they have imposed on themselves under the most solemn obligations! The cloth stained with blood, that we should not hesitate to spill ours for the good of Masonry. The power of obscuring the sun and tinging the moon with blood, is the representation of the power of the Superior Councils—in interdicting their works, if they are irregular, until they have acknowledged their error, and submitted to the rules and regulations of the craft established by the Grand Constitutions. The seven trumpets, signify that Masonry is extended over the surface of the earth, on the wings of fame, and supports itself with honor. The perfumes denote that the life of a good [Pg 190] Mason should be, and is free from all reproach, and is perfumed by means of good report.

Q. What age are you? A. Very ancient.

Q. Who are you? A. I am a Patmian: (i.e., of Patmos.)

Q. Whence came you? A. From Patmos. End of the lecture.

To Close. —Q. What is the o'clock? Ans. There is no more time. The Most Puissant strikes seven, and says, "Venerable Knights Princes, the Council is closed." The two Wardens repeat the same, and the Council is closed.

SOVEREIGN PRINCES, MASTERS ADVITIAM, OR VENERABLE GRAND MASTERS OF ALL SYMBOLIC LODGES.

Decorations, etc. —This Lodge must be decorated with blue and yellow. The Grand Master sits on a throne elevated by nine steps, under a canopy before it is an altar, on which is a sword, bible, compass, square, mallet, etc., as in the Symbolic Lodges. Between the altar and the south is a candlestick with nine branches, which is always lighted in this Lodge. There are two Wardens in the west. The Grand Master represents Cyrus Artaxerxes (the Masonic name of Cambyses), wearing his royal ornaments, and a large blue and yellow ribbon crossing each other.

To Open. —Grand Master: "I desire to open the Lodge." He then descends to the lowest step of the throne, and when he is assured that the Lodge is tyled, he knocks one and two with his mallet. Each Warden repeats the same, which makes nine. G. M.—"Where is your Master placed?" Warden: "In the East." G. M.—"Why in the East?" W. "Because the glorious sun rises in the East to illumine the world." G. M. "As I sit in the East, I open this Lodge," which is repeated by the Wardens. Then all the brethren clap their hands one and two.

Reception. —The candidate represents Zerubbabel, who enters the Lodge by himself, without being introduced, decorated with the jewels and badges of the highest degrees he has taken. The Wardens take him by the hand, and place him in a blue elbow chair, opposite to the Grand Master, who demands from him all the words, from an Entered Apprentice upwards; and after he has satisfied the Grand Master, and is found worthy to hold a sceptre, they make him travel nine times 'round the Lodge, beginning in the South, and then by nine square steps he advances to the throne, and walks over two drawn swords, laid across. There must be a pot with burning charcoal close by the throne, that the candidate may feel the heat of the fire while taking the obligation; in doing which, he lays his right hand on the Bible, which is covered by the Grand Master's right hand, and then takes the following obligation:

Obligation. —I, A. B., do solemnly and sincerely swear and promise, under the penalties of all my former obligations, to protect the craft and my brethren with all my might, and not to acknowledge any one for a true Mason who was not made in a regularly constituted and lawful Lodge. I furthermore do swear, that I will strictly observe and obey all the statutes and regulations of the Lodge; and that I never will disclose [Pg 191] or discover the secrets of this degree, either directly or indirectly, except by virtue of a full power in writing, given me for that purpose by the Grand Inspector or his deputy, and then to such only as have been Masters of a regular Lodge. All this I swear under the penalties of being forever despised and dishonored by the Craft in general. He then kisses the Bible.

Here follow the signs, token, and word, viz.:— First Sign. —Form four squares, thus: with the fingers joined, and the thumb elevated, place your right hand on your heart (this forms two squares). Place the left hand on the lips, the thumb elevated so as to form a third square; place the heels so as to form a square with the feet. Second Sign. —Place yourself on your knees, elbows on the ground, the head inclined towards the left. Third Sign. —Cross the hands on the breast, the right over the left, fingers extended, thumbs elevated, and the feet forming a square. Token. —Take reciprocally the right elbow with the right hand, the thumb on the outside, the fingers joined, and on the inside; press the elbow thus four times, slip the hands down to the wrists, raising the three last fingers, and press the index on the wrist. Sacred Word. —"Razabassi," or "Razahaz Betzi-Yah." Pass-Words. —"Jechson," "Jubellum," "Zanabosan." Some, however, give Jehovah as the sacred word, and "Belshazzar" as the pass-word.

Lecture. —Question—Are you a Grand Master of all Symbolic Lodges? Answer.—They know me at Jerusalem to be such.

Q. How shall I know that you are a Grand Master of all Symbolic Lodges? A. By observing my zeal in rebuilding the temple.

Q. Which way did you travel? A. From the South to the East.

Q. How often? A. Nine.

Q. Why so many? A. In memory of the Grand Masters who traveled to Jerusalem.

Q. Can you give me their names? A. Their names are Esdras, Zerubbabel, Phachi, Joshua, Elial, Toyada, Homen, Nehemias, and Malchias.

Q. What are the pass-words? A. "Jechson," "Jubellum," and "Zanabosan."

Q. What object engaged your attention most, when you first entered the Lodge of Grand Masters? A. The candlestick with nine branches.

Q. Why are the nine candles therein always kept burning in this Lodge? A. To remind us that there cannot be less than nine Masters to form a Grand Master's Lodge.

Q. What were your reasons for wishing to be admitted and received in this Lodge of Grand Masters? A. That I might receive the benefit of the two lights I was unacquainted with.

Q. Have you received those lights, and in what manner? A. In receiving first the small light.

Q. Explain this? A. When I was received by steel and fire.

Q. What signifies the steel? A. To remind us of the steel by which our Most Respectable Chief, Hiram Abiff, lost his life, and which I am sworn to make use of whenever I can revenge that horrible murder of the traitors of Masonry.

[Pg 192] Q. What means the fire? A. To put us in mind that our forefathers were purified by fire.

Q. By whom were you received? A. By Cyrus.

Q. Why by Cyrus? A. Because it was he who ordered Zerubbabel to rebuild the temple.

Q. What did you promise and swear to perform when you received this degree? A. I swore that I would see the laws, statutes, and regulations strictly observed in our Lodge.

Q. What was your name before you received this degree? A. Zerubbabel.

Q. What is your name now? A. Cyrus.

Q. What means the word Animani? A. "I am that, I am;" and it is also the name of him who found the lion's den.

Q. Why is the Lodge decorated with blue and yellow? A. To remind us that the Eternal appeared to Moses on Mount Sinai, in clouds of gold and azure, when he gave to his people the laws of infinite wisdom.

Q. Where do you find the records of our order? A. In the archives of Kilwinning, in the north of Scotland.

Q. Why did you travel from the South 'round to the East? A. In allusion to the power of the Grand Architect of the universe, which extends throughout all the world.

Q. Why did you wash your hands in the taking of one or the previous degrees? A. To show my innocence.

Q. Why is the history of Hiram Abiff so much spoken of? A. To put us always in mind that he chose rather to sacrifice his life than reveal the secrets of Masonry.

Q. Why is the triangle, with the word secret on it, considered as the most precious jewel in Masonry? A. Because by its justness, equality, and proportion, it represents our redemption.

Q. By what mark was the place discovered where Hiram Abiff was buried by his assassins? A. By a sprig of cassia (say granate).

Q. For what reason do the Master Masons in the Symbolic Lodges speak of a sprig of cassia? A. Because the Sublime Grand Elected descendants of the ancient Patriarchs did not think proper to give the real name or truth of Masonry; therefore, they agreed to say that it was a sprig of cassia, because it had a strong smell.

Q. What are the reasons for the different knocks at the door to gain admittance? A. To know and be assured that they have passed the different degrees, which number we must understand.

Q. For what reasons do we keep our mysteries with such circumspection and secrecy? A. For fear there might be found amongst us some traitorous villains similar to the three Fellow Crafts who murdered our chief, Hiram Abiff.

Q. What is the reason that the Grand Masters of all Lodges are received with so much honor in the Symbolic Lodges? A. Those homages are due to their virtues as Princes of Masons, whose firmness has been shown on so many occasions, by spilling their blood in support of Masonry and the fraternity.

[Pg 193] Q. Why do we applaud with our hands? A. In that manner we express our happiness and satisfaction at having done a good action, and rendered justice.

Q. What reflections occur, when contemplating the conduct of Solomon? A. That a wise man may err, and when he is sensible of his fault, correct himself by acknowledging that fault, whereby he claims the indulgence of his brethren.

Q. Why do the Symbolic Lodges take the name of St. John of Jerusalem? A. Because in the time of the Crusades, the Perfect Masons, Knights, and Princes, communicated their mysteries to the Knights of that order; whereupon it was determined to celebrate their festival annually, on St. John's day, being under the same law.

Q. Who was the first architect that conducted the works of Solomon's temple? A. Hiram Abiff; which signifies the inspired man.

Q. Who laid the first stone? A. Solomon cut and laid the first stone, which afterwards supported the temple.

Q. Was there anything enclosed in that stone? A. Yes; some characters, which were, like the name of the Grand Architect of the Universe, only known to Solomon.

Q. What stone was it? A. An agate of a foot square.

Q. What was the form of it? A. Cubical.

Q. At what time of the day was the stone laid? A. Before sunrise.

Q. For what reason? A. To show that we must begin early and work with vigilance and assiduity.

Q. What cement did he make use of? A. A cement which was composed of the finest and purest flour, milk, oil, and wine.

Q. Is there any meaning in this composition? A. Yes; when the Grand Architect of the Universe determined to create the world, he employed his sweetness, bounty, wisdom and power.

Q. What is the reason why the number eighty-one is held in such esteem among Princes of Masons? A. Because that number explains the triple alliance which the Eternal operates by the triple triangle, which was seen at the time Solomon consecrated the temple to God; and also that Hiram Abiff was eighty-one years of age when he was murdered.

Q. Was anything else perceived at the consecration? A. A perfume which not only filled the temple, but all Jerusalem.

Q. Who destroyed the temple? A. Nebuchadnezzar.

Q. How many years after it was built? A. Four hundred and seventy years, six months, and ten days, after its foundation.

Q. Who built the second temple? A. Zerubbabel, by the grant and aid of Cyrus, King of Persia. It was finished in the reign of Darius, when he was known to be a Prince of Jerusalem. Cyrus not only gave Zerubbabel and the captive Masons their liberty, but ordered all the treasures of the old temple to be restored to them, that they might embellish the second temple, which he had ordered Zerubbabel to build.

Q. What signifies the jewel of the Right Worshipful Grand Master of all Lodges being a triangle? A. He wears it in remembrance of the [Pg 194] presents given by monarchs and the protectors of the order, in recompense for their zeal, fervor, and constancy.

Q. What way have you traveled to become a Right Worshipful Grand Master of all Lodges, and Grand Patriarch? A. By the four elements.

Q. Why by the four elements? A. To put us in mind of this world, and the troubles in which we live; to cleanse ourselves from all impurities, and thereby render ourselves worthy of perfect virtue.

Q. Where was the Lodge of Grand Masters first held? A. In the sacred vault, east of the temple.

Q. Where is that lodge held at present? A. All over the world, agreeably to the orders of Solomon, when he told us to travel and to spread over the universe, to teach Masonry to those whom we should find worthy of it, but especially to those who should receive us kindly, and who were virtuous men.

Q. What did Solomon give you to remember him at your departure? A. He rewarded the merits of all the workmen, and showed to the Chief Master the cubic stone of agate, on which was engraved, on a gold plate, the sacred name of God.

Q. How was the agate stone supported? A. On a pedestal of a triangular form, surrounded with three cross pillars, which were also surrounded by a circle of brass.

Q. What signifies the three pillars? A. Strength, wisdom and beauty.

Q. What was in the middle of the circle? A. The point of exactness, which teaches us the point of perfection.

Q. What else did Solomon give you? A. The great sign of admiration and consternation, by which I am known by a brother. He also put a ring on my finger, in remembrance of my alliance with virtue, and loaded us with kindness.

Q. Why have you a sun on the jewel of perfection? A. To show that we have received the full light, and know Masonry in its perfection.

Q. Who destroyed the second temple which was finished by the Princes of Jerusalem? A. Pompey began its destruction, and King Herodes the Great finished it.

Q. Who rebuilt it again? A. King Herodes repenting the action he had unjustly done, recalled all the Masons to Jerusalem who had fled, and directed them to rebuild the temple.

Q. Who destroyed the third temple? A. Tito, the son of the Emperor Vespasian. The Masons, who with sorrow saw the temple again destroyed, departed from Rome, after having embraced the Catholic religion, and determined never to assist in constructing another.

Q. What became of those Masons afterwards? A. They divided themselves into several companies, and went into different parts of Europe, but the greatest part of them went to Scotland, and built a town which they called Kilwinning; at this time there is a Lodge there, bearing the same name.

Q. What happened to them afterwards? A. Twenty-seven thousand of the Masons in Scotland determined to assist the Christian Princes and Knights, who were at that time at Jerusalem, in a crusade for the [Pg 195] purpose of taking the Holy Land and city from the infidels, who were then in possession of it; and they accordingly obtained leave of the Scottish monarch.

Q. What happened most remarkable to them? A. Their bravery and good conduct gained them the esteem and respect of all the Knights of St. John of Jerusalem. The general of that order, and the principal officers, took the resolution of being admitted into the secrets of Masonry, which they accordingly received; and in return they admitted them into their order.

Q. What became of those Masons afterwards? A. After the crusade they returned and spread Masonry throughout all Europe, which flourished for a long time in France and England; but the Scotch, to their great praise be it spoken, were the only people who kept up the practice of it.

Q. How came it again in vogue in France? A. A Scotch nobleman went to France and became a resident at Bordeaux, where he establishes a Lodge of Perfection, from the members of the Lodge in 1744; in which he was assisted by a French gentleman, who took great pleasure in all the Masonic degrees. This still exists in a most splendid manner.

Q. What means the fire in our Lodge? A. Submission, purification of morals, and equality among brethren.

Q. What signifies the air? A. The purity, virtue, and truth of this degree.

Q. What does the sign of the sun mean? A. It signifies that some of us are more enlightened than others in the Mysteries of Masonry; and for that reason we are often called Knights of the Sun.

Q. How many signs have you in this degree of Grand Pontiff, which is Grand Master of all Lodges? A. 1st, The sign of the earth, or Apprentice; 2d, of water—Fellow Craft; 3d, of terror—the Master; 4th, of fire; 5th, of air; 6th, of the point in view; 7th, of the sun; 8th, of astonishment; 9th, of honor; 10th, of stench, or strong smell; 11th, of admiration; 12th, of consternation. End of the Lecture.

To Close. —The Grand Master says, "My brother, enter into the cave of Silol—work with Grand Rofadam—measure your steps to the sun, and then the great black eagle will cover you with his wings, to the end of what you desire, by the help of the Most Sublime Princes Grand Commanders." He then strikes four and two, makes the sign of four squares, which is repeated by the Wardens, and the Lodge is closed.

The examination of a brother in the foregoing degree is as follows:

Q. From whence came you? A. From the sacred vault at Jerusalem.

Q. What are you come to do here? A. I am come to see and visit your works and show you mine, that we may work together and rectify our morals, and, if possible, sanctify the profane—but only by permission of a Prince Adept, or Prince of the Royal Secret (if one is present).

Q. What have you brought? A. Glory, grandeur and beauty.

Q. Why do you give the name of St. John to our Lodge? A. Formerly all the Lodges were under the name of Solomon's Lodge, as the founder of Masonry; but since the crusades we have agreed with the Knights [Pg 196] Templars, or Hospitallers, to dedicate them to St. John, as he was the support of the Christians and the new laws.

Q. What do you ask more? A. Your will and pleasure as you may find me worthy, obedient, and virtuous.

PRINCE OF THE ROYAL SECRET.

The Assembly of Princes is termed a "Consistory."

Officers. —The first officer represents Frederick II., King of Prussia; he is styled "Sovereign of Sovereigns," "Grand Prince," "Illustrious Commander in Chief." The two next officers are styled "Lieutenant Commanders." The fourth officer is the "Minister of State," who acts as the orator. The fifth officer is the "Grand Chancellor." Then the "Grand Secretary;" the "Grand Treasurer;" the "Grand Captain of the Guards;" a "Standard Bearer;" a "Grand Master Architect;" and two "Tylers."

Place of Meeting. —This is to be a building at least two stories in height, situated on elevated ground, in the open country. Three apartments on the second floor are necessary in this degree. In the first of these the guards are stationed. The second is used as a preparation room. The third is occupied by the members of the Consistory. This last apartment is hung with black, sprinkled with tears, "death's heads," "cross bones," and "skeletons." The throne is in the East, elevated by seven steps. On the throne is the chair of state, lined with black satin, flamed with red. Before the chair is a table covered with black satin, strewed with tears. On this cloth, in front, is a "death's head" and "cross bones;" over the "death's head" is the letter I; and under the "cross bones" is the letter M. On the table is placed a naked sword, a buckler, a sceptre, a balance, and a book containing the statutes of the order. In the West is placed another table covered with crimson, bordered with black, and strewed with tears; on the front of this cloth are the letters N. K. M. K. in gold.

Dress and Stations of Officers. —The "Sovereign of Sovereigns" is dressed in royal robes, and seated in the chair of state. The Lieutenant Commanders dressed like the modern princes of Europe, and seated at the table in the West; their swords are crossed on the table. The Minister of State is placed at the Sovereign's right hand. The Grand Chancellor stands on the left hand of the Sovereign. Next to the Minister of State is placed the Grand Secretary. Next to the Grand Chancellor is placed the Grand Treasurer. Below the last named officers are placed on one side the Standard Bearer, the Grand Master Architect, and the Captain of the Guards. Below these officers are placed six members dressed in red, without aprons, wearing the jewel of the order, suspended on the breast by a black ribbon.

Collar of the Order. —The collar is black, and edged with silver. On its point is embroidered in red a Teutonic cross. On the middle of the cross is a double headed eagle in silver. The collar is lined with scarlet, on which is embroidered a black Teutonic cross. Around the waist is girded a black sash, embroidered with silver. The cross is embroidered on that part of the girdle which is in front.

[Pg 197] Jewel. —The jewel is a golden Teutonic cross.

Qualifications of Candidate. —The candidate who receives this degree must be faithfully examined in the previous degree prior to admission. The Master of Ceremonies will acquaint him with the pass-word, which he is to give to the Lieutenant Commander. The Master of Ceremonies will then lead him to the Sovereign of Sovereigns.

Opening and Closing. —The Sovereign of Sovereigns says, "Sal ix." The Lieutenants reply, "Noni." They then together say, "Tengu." All give the sign. The Sovereign of Sovereigns says: Let us imitate our Grand Master Jacques De Molay, Hiram Abiff, who to the last placed all his hopes in the Great Architect of the Universe; and pronounced the following words just as he passed from this transient life into eternal bliss:—"Spes mea in Deo est" (My hope is in God).

Description of the Carpet representing the Camp. —On the carpet is drawn an "enneagen," in which is inscribed a pentagon; within this is an equilateral triangle, and in the triangle a circle. Between the heptagon and pentagon, upon the sides of the latter, are placed the standards of the five Standard Bearers, and the pavilions inscribed by the letters T. E. N. G. U. The emblems on the standard T. are the "ark of the covenant," an "olive tree," and a "lighted candlestick," on each side. The ground color of this standard is purple. On the ark is written the motto "Laus Deo." The standard E. bears a golden lion, holding in his mouth a "golden key;" wearing around his neck a golden collar, on which is engraved "515." The ground is azure; the motto "Admajorem Dei glorium." On the standard N. is an "inflamed heart," in red, with two wings, surrounded by a laurel crown. The ground is white. The flag G. bears a double-headed eagle, crowned, holding a sword in his right claw, and in his left a bloody heart. Ground is sea green. The flag U. has an ox, sable (black), on a golden ground. On the sides of the enneagen are nine tents, and on its angles nine pendants, each belonging to its appropriate tent. The pendants are distinguished by numerals, and the tents by the letters I. N. O. N. X. I. L. A. S. disposed from right to left. These tents signify the different grades of Masonry. Thus:

Tent S. is Malachi—pendant, white, spotted with red; represents Knights of the East and West, and Princes of Jerusalem. Tent A. is Zerubbabel—pendant, light green; represents Knights of the East. Tent L. is Neamiah—pendant, red; represents Grand Elect, Perfect, and Sublime Masons. Tent I. is Hobben or Johaben—pendant, black and red; represents Sublime Elect, and Elect of Fifteen. Tent X. is Peleg—pendant, black; represents Elect of Nine, or Grand Master Architect. Tent N. is Joiada—pendant, red and black in lozenges; represents Provost and Judges. Tent O. is Aholiab—pendant, red and green; represents Intendant of the Buildings and Intimate Secretary. Tent N. is Joshua—pendant, green; represents Perfect Master. Tent I. is Ezra—pendant, blue; represents Master, Fellow Craft, and Entered Apprentice.

The equilateral triangle in the middle represents the centre of the army, and shows where the Knights of Malta are to be placed who have been admitted to our mysteries, and have proved themselves faithful guardians. They are to be joined with the Knights of Kadosh. The [Pg 198] corps in the centre is to be commanded by five princes, who command jointly, or in rotation, according to their degrees, and receive their orders immediately from the Sovereign of Sovereigns. These five Princes must place their standards in the five angles of the pentagon, as above described. These Princes, who are Standard Bearers, have the following name, viz.:—

Standard. { T. ... } Names.
  Bezaleel
  E. ...
  Aholiab
  N. ...
  Mahuzen
  G. ...
  Garimont
  U. ...
  Amariah

The heptagon points out the Encampment destined for the Princes of Libanus, Jerusalem, etc.; and these are to receive their orders from the five Princes. The enneagen shows the general order of Masons of all degrees.

Instructions for the reunion of the brethren, Knights, Princes, and Commanders of the Royal Secret or Kadosh, which really signifies Holy brethren of all degrees separated .

Frederick III., King of Prussia, Grand

Master and Commander in Chief, Sovereign of Sovereigns, with an army composed of the Knights, Princes of the White and Black Eagle, including Prussian, English, and French; likewise joined by the Knights Adepts of the Sun, Princes of Libanus or the Royal Axe, the Knights of the Rose Croix or St. Andrew, Knights of the East and West, the Princes of Jerusalem, Knights of the East or Sword, the Grand Elect Perfect and Sublime Masons, the Knights of the Royal Arch (ninth Arch), Sublime Knights Elected, etc.

The hour for the departure or march of the army is the fifth after the setting of the sun; and is to be made known by the firing of five great guns in the following order (0)—(0 0 0 0)—that is, with an interval between the first and second. The first rendezvous is to be the port of Naples—from Naples to the port of Rhodes—from Rhodes to Cyprus and Malta, whence the whole naval force of all nations is to assemble. The second rendezvous is to be at Cyprus, etc. The third rendezvous is to be at Jerusalem, where they will be joined by our faithful guardians. The watchwords of every day of the week are as follows and they are not to be changed but by express order from the King of Prussia:

	Protectors of Masonry.	
Sunday,	Cyrus,	{ Answer. }
Monday,	Darius,	{ }
Tuesday,	Xerxes,	{ }
Wednes.,	Alexander,	
Thurs.,	Philadelphus,	
Friday,	Herod,	
Saturday,	Hezekiah,	

Sign. —Place the right hand on the heart; extend it forward, the palm downward; let it fall by the right side. Sacred words. —Those of the Carpet, which are to be read backward 'round the circle from right to left, thus:—One says "Salix," to which the other replies "Noni;" both then repeat (by letters) the word "Tengu." Pass words. —"Phual Kol," which signifies "separated;" "Pharas Kol," which signifies "reunited;" [Pg 199] "Nekam Makah," which signifies "to avenge;" each then letters the word "Shaddai," which signifies "Omnipotent."

Charge Addressed to the Candidate. — My dear brother:—The Saracens having taken possession of the Holy Land, those who were engaged in the Crusades not being able to expel them, agreed with Godfrey de Bouillon, the conductor and chief of the Crusaders, to veil the mysteries of religion under emblems, by which they would be able to maintain the devotion of the soldier, and protect themselves from the incursion of those who were their enemies, after the example of the Scriptures, the style of which is figurative. Those zealous brethren chose Solomon's temple for their model. This building has strong allusions to the Christian church. Since that period they (Masons) have been known by the name of Master Architect; and they have employed themselves in improving the law of that admirable Master. From hence it appears that the mysteries of the craft are the mysteries of religion. Those brethren were careful not to entrust this important secret to any whose discretion they had not proved. For this reason they invented different degrees to try those who entered among them; and only gave them symbolical secrets, without explanation, to prevent treachery, and to make themselves known only to each other. For this purpose it was resolved to use different signs, words, and tokens, in every degree, by which they would be secured against cowans and Saracens. The different degrees were fixed first to the number of seven by the example of the Grand Architect of the Universe, who built all things in six days and rested on the seventh. This is distinguished by seven points of reception in the Master's degrees. Enoch employed six days to construct the arches, and on the seventh, having deposited the secret treasure in the lowest arch, was translated to the abodes of the blessed. Solomon employed six years in constructing his temple; and celebrated its dedication on the seventh, with all the solemnity worthy of the divinity himself. This sacred edifice we choose to make the basis of figurative Masonry. In the first degree are three symbols to be applied. First, the first of the creation, which was only chaos, is figured by the candidate's coming out of the black chamber, neither naked nor clothed, deprived, etc. ; and his suffering the painful trial at his reception, etc. The candidate sees nothing before he is brought to light; and his powers of imagination relative to what he has to go through are suspended, which alludes to the figure of the creation of that vast luminous body confused among the other parts of creation before it was extracted from darkness and fixed by the Almighty fiat. Secondly, the candidate approaches the footstool of the Master, and there renounces all cowans; he promises to subdue his passions, by which means he is united to virtue, and by his regularity of life, demonstrates what he proposes. This is figured to him by the steps that he takes in approaching the altar; the symbolic meaning of which is the separation of the firmament from the earth and water on the second day of creation. (The charge proceeds by giving a figurative interpretation of the ceremonies, etc., of the first and second part of the third degree, which I pass over as uninteresting to my readers, and [Pg 200] commence with an interpretation which will be as novel to the Craft of the lower grades as to the cowans, or non-initiated.)

In the Master's degree is represented the assassination of Hiram by false brethren. This ought to put us in mind of the fate of Adam, occasioned by perverseness in his disobeying his great and awful Creator. The symbolic mystery of the death of Hiram Abiff represents to us that of the Messiah; for the three blows which were given to Hiram Abiff, at the three gates of the temple, allude to the three points of condemnation against Christ, at the High Priest's Caiphas, Herod, and Pilate. It was from the last that he was led to that most violent and excruciating death. The said three blows with the square, gauge, and gavel are symbols of the blow on the cheek, the flagellation, and the crown of thorns. The brethren assembled around the tomb of Hiram, is a representation of the disciples lamenting the death of Christ on the cross. The Master's word, which is said to be lost, since the death of Hiram Abiff, is the same that Christ pronounced on the cross, and which the Jews did not comprehend, "Eli, Eli, lama sabacthani," "my God, my God, why hast thou forsaken me! have pity on and forgive my enemies."—Instead of which words were substituted, M. B. N. (Mac-be-nac), which, in Arabian, signifies, "The son of the widow is dead." The false brethren represent Judas Iscariot, who sold Christ. The red collar worn by the Grand Elect Perfect and Sublime Masons, calls to remembrance the blood of Christ. The sprig of cassia is the figure of the cross, because of this wood was the cross made. The captivity of the Grand Elect and Sublime Masons (i.e., by the Chaldeans), shows us the persecution of the Christian religion under the Roman emperors, and its liberty under Constantine the Great. It also calls to our remembrance the persecution of the Templars, and the situation of Jacques De Molay, who, lying in irons nearly seven years, at the end of which our worthy Grand Master was burnt alive with his four companions, on the eleventh of March, 1314, creating pity and tears in the people, who saw him die with firmness and heroic constancy, sealing his innocence with his blood. My dear brother, in passing to the degree of Perfect Master, in which you shed tears at the tomb of Hiram Abiff, and in some other degrees, has not your heart been led to revenge? Has not the crime of Jubelum Akirop been represented in the most hideous light?—Would it be unjust to compare the conduct of Philip the Fair to his, and the infamous accusers of the Templars, to the two ruffians who were accomplices with Akirop? Do they not kindle in your heart an equal aversion? The different stages you have traveled, and the time you have taken in learning these historical events, no doubt, will lead you to make the proper applications; and by the degree of Master Elect and Kadosh, you are properly disposed to fulfil all your engagements, and to bear an implacable hatred to the Knights of Malta, and to avenge the death of Jacques De Molay. Your extensive acquaintance with symbolic Masonry, which you have attained by your discretion, leaves you nothing more to desire here. You see, my dear brother, how, and by whom, Masonry has come to us. You are to endeavor by every just means to regain our rights, and to remember that we are joined by a society of men, whose courage, merit, and [Pg 201] good conduct, hold out to us that rank that birth alone gave to our ancestors. You are now on the same level with them. Avoid every evil by keeping your obligations, and carefully conceal from the vulgar what you are, and wait that happy moment when we all shall be reunited under the same Sovereign in the mansions of eternal bliss. Let us imitate the example of our Grand Master, Jaques De Molay, who to the end put his hope in God, and at his last dying moments ended his life saying, "Spes mea in Deo est!"

Obligation. —I do, of my own free will and accord, in the presence of the Grand Architect of the Universe, and this consistory of Sovereign Princes of the Royal Secret, or Knights of St. Andrew, faithful guardians of the faithful treasure; most solemnly vow and swear, under all the different penalties of my former obligations, that I will never directly or indirectly reveal or make known to any person or persons whatsoever, any or the least part of this Royal degree, unless to one duly qualified in the body of a regularly constituted Consistory of the same, or to him or them whom I shall find such after strict and due trial. I furthermore vow and swear, under the above penalties, to always abide and regulate myself agreeably to the statutes and regulations now before me; and when in a Consistory to behave and demean myself as one worthy of being honored with so high a degree, that no part of my conduct may in the least reflect discredit on the Royal Consistory, or disgrace myself. So may God maintain me in equity and justice! Amen! Amen! Amen! Amen!

SOVEREIGN GRAND INSPECTOR GENERAL.

The number of Inspectors of a Kingdom or Republic is not to exceed nine. They claim jurisdiction over all the ineffable and sublime degrees, and in reality form an aristocratic body, with power to appoint their own successors, and act as "Sovereigns of Masonry."

Decorations of the Place of Meeting. —The hangings are purple, embroidered with skeletons, death's-heads, and cross-bones. Before the canopy is a transparent delta (equilateral triangle). In the middle of the room is a grand triangular pedestal, near which is seen a skeleton holding in his left hand the standard of the order, and in his right hand a poniard in the attitude of striking. Above the door, or place of entrance, is the motto of the order, "Deus meumque jus." In the East is a chandelier of five branches; in the South is one of two branches; in the West is one of three; and in the North a single one.

Officers and Titles. —The assembly is termed "Supreme Council." The first officer, "Thrice Puissant Sovereign Grand Master." He represents Frederick II. The second officer is termed "Sovereign Lieutenant Commander." Besides these there is a "Treasurer of the Holy Empire;" an "Illustrious Grand Secretary of the Holy Empire;" an "Illustrious Master of Ceremonies;" and an "Illustrious Captain of the Guards"—in all, seven officers.

Dress. —The Thrice Puissant Sovereign wears a crimson robe, bordered with white—a crown on his head, and a sword in his hand. The Lieutenant Commander wears a ducal crown.

[Pg 202] Sash. —The sash is black, edged with gold, from left to right; at the bottom a rose of red, white and green. On the part crossing the breast is a delta, with rays traversed by a poniard, and in the midst the figure "33."

Jewel. —A black double-headed eagle holding a sword. His beak, claws, and sword are of gold. [Pass-words, signs, etc., as may from time to time be agreed upon.]

[THE END.]

FOOTNOTES:

[1] A person wishing to become a Mason must get some one who is a Mason to present his petition to a Lodge, when, if there are no serious objections, it will be entered on the minutes, and a committee of two or three appointed to inquire into his character, and report to the next regular communication. The following is the form of a petition used by a candidate; but a worthy candidate will not be rejected for the want of formality in his petition.

To the Worshipful Master, Wardens, and Brethren of Lodge No. ——, of Free and Accepted Masons.

The subscriber, residing in ——, of lawful age, and by occupation a ——, begs leave to state that, unbiassed by friends, and uninfluenced by mercenary motives, he freely and voluntarily offers himself a candidate for the mysteries of Masonry, and that he is prompt to solicit this privilege by a favorable opinion conceived of the institution, a desire of knowledge, and a sincere wish of being serviceable to his fellow-creatures. Should his petition be granted, he will cheerfully conform to all the ancient established usages and customs of the Fraternity.

(Signed) A. B.

[2] In many Lodges this is put in the form of a question, thus: "Are you willing to take an obligation upon you that does not affect your politics or religion?" The promise "to conform," made before entering the Lodge, the "assurance that the oath is not to interfere with their political or religious principles" and the manner the obligation is administered, only two or three words being repeated at a time, consequently not fully understood, are among the reasons which have led many great and good men to take oaths incompatible with the laws of God and our country.

[3] Literally a rope several yards in length, but mystically three miles; so that a Master Mason must go on a brother Master Mason's errand whenever required, the distance of three miles, should he have to go barefoot and bareheaded. In the degrees of knighthood the distance is forty miles.

[4] In some Lodges the Master takes the candidate by the Master's grip and says, "Brother, you will please rise," assisting him.

[5] There is much diversity of opinion among Masons respecting this word; some insist that Giblem is the right word; others, that Gibelum is the right word; the latter word was rejected, because it was used by "Jachin and Boaz."

[6] This charge is frequently omitted when conferring the degree on a candidate, but never when really installing a Master of a Lodge.

[7] Here the brethren divest themselves of their jewels, sashes, aprons, etc.

[8] The ark, which had been carried by two brethren in the procession, is here placed on the altar.

[9] At these words the candidate is received into the procession.

[10] Here all kneel in a circle around the altar.

[11] At the words, "For He is good," the Most Excellent Master, who is High Priest of the Chapter, kneels and joins hands with the rest; they all then repeat in concert the words, "For He is good, for His mercy endureth forever" six times, each time bowing their heads low towards the floor.

[12] There is a great difference in the manner of giving the Royal Arch word in the different Chapters. Sometimes it is given at the opening, as above stated; sometimes they commence with the word God , each one pronouncing a letter of it in succession, until they have each pronounced every letter of the word, then the word Jehovah , a syllable at a time, and then the word Jahbuhlun as described. There are also Chapters in which the latter word is not known, and there are others in which the word is not given at all at opening.

[13] This clause is sometimes made a distinct point in the obligation in the following form, viz.: Furthermore, do I promise and swear, that I will vote for a companion Royal Arch Mason before any other of equal qualifications; and in some Chapters both are left out of the obligation.

[14] In some Chapters this is administered: All the secrets of a companion without exception.

[15] This is frequently represented in this manner: When the person reading comes to that part where it says, "God called to him out of the midst of the bush and said," etc., he stops reading, and a person behind the bushes calls out, "Moses, Moses." The conductor answers, "Here am I." The person behind the bush then says, "Draw not nigh hither; put off thy shoes from off thy feet; for the place whereon thou standeth is holy ground (his shoes are then slipped off). Moreover, I am the God of Abraham, the God of Isaac, and the God of Jacob." The person first reading then says, "And Moses hid his face; for he was afraid to look upon God." At these words the bandage is placed over the candidate's eyes.

[16] By this tremendous imprecation, the candidate, of his "own free will and accord," volunteers (in case of a violation) to come forth to the resurrection of damnation and receive the sentence, "Depart thou accursed into everlasting fire prepared for the devil and his angels."

[17] See the Apocryphal books, 1 Esdras, chapters iii. and iv.

[18] Diplomas of this degree, "In the name of the Holy and Undivided Trinity ," recommend the bearer as a true and faithful soldier of Jesus Christ.

HISTORICAL SKETCH OF THE KIDNAPPING OF WILLIAM MORGAN.

Captain Morgan was born in Virginia, and was a mason by trade. He commenced the business of a brewer at York, Upper Canada, in 1821, but having lost all his property by fire, he removed to New York State, and worked at his trade both in Rochester and Batavia. In the year 1826 rumors were heard that Morgan, in connection with other persons, was preparing and intended to publish a book which would reveal the secrets of Freemasonry, and an excitement of some kind existed in relation to the publication of the book. In the month of September he was seized under feigned process of the law, in the day time, in the village of Batavia, and forcibly carried to Canandaigua. Captain Morgan was at this time getting ready his book, which purported to reveal the secrets of Freemasonry. This contemplated publication excited the alarm of the fraternity, and numbers of its members were heard to say that it should be suppressed at all events. Meetings of delegates from the different Lodges in the Western counties has been held to devise means for most effectually preventing the publication. The zealous members of the fraternity were angry, excited, and alarmed, and occasionally individuals threw out dark and desperate threats. About this time an incendiary attempt was made to fire the office of Col. Miller, the publisher of the book. The gang who seized Morgan at Batavia were Masons. They took him to Canandaigua; after a mock trial he was discharged, but was immediately arrested and committed to prison on a debt. The next night, in the absence of the jailer, he was released from prison by the pretended friendship of a false and hollow-hearted brother Mason. Upon leaving the prison door he was seized in the streets of Canandaigua, and notwithstanding his cries of murder, he was thrust with ruffian violence into a carriage prepared for that purpose. At Batavia he had been torn from his home—from his wife and infant children. At Canandaigua he was falsely beguiled from the safe custody of the law, and was forcibly carried, by relays of horses, through a thickly populated country, in the space of little more than twenty-four hours, to the distance of one hundred and fifteen miles, and secured as a prisoner in the magazine of Fort Niagara. This was clearly proved on the trial of persons concerned in the outrage, and who were found guilty and [Pg 203] sentenced to various terms of imprisonment. The fate of Captain Morgan was never known, but it is supposed he was taken out into the lake, where his throat was cut, and his body sunken fifty fathoms in water. About the same time, Col. David C. Miller, the publisher of the book, was also seized, in Batavia, under the color of legal process, and taken to Le Roy. The avowed intention of Col. Miller's seizure was to take him where Morgan was—and where that was may be best gathered from the impious declaration of one of the conspirators, James Ganson, for several years a member of our Legislature—that "he was put where he would stay put until God should call for him." Miller was, however, set at liberty, as the inhabitants of Le Roy interfered with the schemes of his kidnappers. He soon after put to press the first part of the volume which is here presented to the public. Additions have been made to Captain Morgan's revelations, from time to time, until we are now able to make public all the Masonic degrees of any note or interest, entered into by modern Freemasons.

Typographical errors corrected in text:

Page 8: Futhermore replaced with Furthermore
Page 23: appetites replaced with appetites
Page 23: tessel replaced with tressel
Page 32: synonomous replaced with synonymous
Page 57: emblematicol replaced with emblematical
Page 58: "a gentlemen" replaced with "a gentleman"
Page 61: decend replaced with descend
Page 65: "never against attempt" replaced with "never again attempt"
Page 78: repution replaced with reputation
Page 85: Th replaced with To
Page 90: sanctum sanctortum replaced with sanctum sanctorium
Page 90: wood replaced with word
Page 104: Corrected one of the questions which was incorrectly ended with an exclamation mark
Page 113: Inserted the missing "A." on three of the Questions
Page 128: Mot replaced with Most
Page 128: replaced "support and bear that that cross?" with "support and bear that cross?"
Page 135: "repeated by then Warden" replaced with "repeated by the Warden"
Page 150: Inserted the missing "A." in one of the Questions
Page 158: Removed duplicate "the" from "among the the ruins"
Page 177: Replaced "A." with "Q." at beginning of paragraph
Page 183: Inserted the missing "A." in one of the Questions
Page 188-9: oberving replaced with observing

***